POPULATION CONCERNS IN INDIA

SAGE was founded in 1965 by Sara Miller McCune to support the dissemination of usable knowledge by publishing innovative and high-quality research and teaching content. Today, we publish over 900 journals, including those of more than 400 learned societies, more than 800 new books per year, and a growing range of library products including archives, data, case studies, reports, and video. SAGE remains majority-owned by our founder, and after Sara's lifetime will become owned by a charitable trust that secures our continued independence.

Los Angeles | London | New Delhi | Singapore | Washington DC | Melbourne

POPULATION CONCERNS IN INDIA
SHIFTING TRENDS, POLICIES AND PROGRAMS

KRISHNAMURTHY SRINIVASAN

Los Angeles | London | New Delhi
Singapore | Washington DC | Melbourne

First published in 2017 by

SAGE Publications India Pvt Ltd
B1/I-1 Mohan Cooperative Industrial Area
Mathura Road, New Delhi 110 044, India
www.sagepub.in

SAGE Publications Inc
2455 Teller Road
Thousand Oaks, California 91320, USA

SAGE Publications Ltd
1 Oliver's Yard, 55 City Road
London EC1Y 1SP, United Kingdom

SAGE Publications Asia-Pacific Pte Ltd
3 Church Street
#10-04 Samsung Hub
Singapore 049483

Published by Vivek Mehra for SAGE Publications India Pvt Ltd, typeset in 10/12pt Times New Roman by JMV Design Solutions, Chandigarh 31D, and printed at Saurabh Printers Pvt Ltd, Greater Noida.

Library of Congress Cataloging-in-Publication Data
Name: Srinivasan, K. (Krishnamurthy), author.
Title: Population concerns in India: shifting trends, policies and programs/ Krishnamurthy Srinivasan.
Description: Thousand Oaks: SAGE Publications India Pvt Ltd, [2017] | Includes bibliographical references and index.
Identifiers: LCCN 2017011399 | ISBN 9789386446145 (print (hb): alk. paper) | ISBN 9789386446169 (e-pub 2.0) | ISBN 9789386446152 (e-book)
Subjects: LCSH: India—Population policy—21st century. | Family planning—India—History—21st century. | India—Population—21st century.
Classification: LCCHQ766.5.I4 S75 2017 | DDC 363.90954—dc23 LC record available at https://lccn.loc.gov/2017011399

ISBN: 978-93-864-4614-5 (HB)

SAGE Team: Rajesh Dey, Guneet Kaur Gulati, Kumar Indra Mishra, and Rajinder Kaur

Dedicated to millions of sterilized couples of India who have, by their sacrifice, contributed directly and indirectly to the development of this country

Contents

List of Tables

List of Figures

Preface

My concern with the population issues in India and other countries spans over five decades—since 1959, when I joined the Pilot Health Project in Gandhigram, Tamil Nadu (then called Madras State), as a young statistician. I have maintained my interest in these issues almost continuously, sometimes proactively but most of the times professionally. I have witnessed the anxious expectation for the announcements of the 1961 census results—a population figure of 439 million—and the subsequent reaction "Oh God, this large!" The figure then spiraled upwards census after census, with the last census of 2011 giving the population size as 1,210 million without practically any concern from the Central Government. The question now appears to be: "So what? A few millions, this way or that way, do not appear to matter." India's population surge is seen as a mere statistical exercise without any increasing concern for the life and well-being of this large population.

My earlier book, *Regulating Reproduction in India's Population: Efforts, Results, and Recommendations* (SAGE Publications, 1995), focused on population issues and efforts to tackle them until 1992. Since then, especially after the International Conference on Population and Development (ICPD) in Cairo by the United Nations in 1994, the population concerns have shifted from fertility–mortality reduction programs to gender-related issues, such as gender equity, women's health, reproductive health etc. The areas of concern related to population have changed over time in the past 60 years, partly out of domestic concerns for accelerating development and partly due to international pressures. This book is a historical trace and analysis of these shifts and the reasons thereof, as I understand them, and the challenges that remain till date.

Chapter 1 traces the origins of population concerns before independence, when these concerns were dominated by fertility–mortality reduction programs, specifically family planning programs undertaken as neo-Malthusian measures to reduce population growth to prevent famines and epidemics, as recommended by scholars from within and outside India. Chapters 2 and 3 are reorganized and revised versions of Chapter 2 of my earlier book. Chapter 2 traces and reviews the family planning/welfare programs initiated in 1952, after independence over a 25 year period until 1977, including the period of national emergency during 1975–77. Chapter 3 traces the program during 1977 to 1995 which is the post emergency recoil and recovery phase of the program. Chapter 4 reviews the program during 1996 to 2015. This chapter is the first major substantive addition to the earlier book.

Over the past two decades, many changes have taken place within the country and in the international arena on population policies and programs, and population issues have been largely played down nationally and internationally. Since 1994 after the ICPD, the programs seem to be located under the aura of human rights, women's rights and women's reproductive health and population growth per se received little attention. During the past two and a half decades (1991–2016), the population of India has increased by about 444 million, from 846 to 1,290 million, the highest for any country in the world during the past quarter century, including China that has a larger population but a lower growth rate. How the population problem has been perceived and what types of policies and programs were considered most appropriate in different situations, polity and aspirations of the people in India is worth recording, and from that perspective, this is a record book.

In spite of its federally structured democratic framework, based essentially on the Westminster model, with many languages, religions and other social stratifications prevailing in the country, India has maintained its democracy more and more vibrantly with every election, and is becoming a model of relative peace and ordered development for many developing countries of the world that are in great turmoil. The elections of 2014 that changed the government at the center with an absolute majority, with over 600 million people voting to remove the earlier party in power, leading to a smooth and peaceful transition of power at the center, were a big surprise for the world. In contrast, in all the neighboring large countries, such a change has taken place with enormous violence and political upheavals. How India has handled or mishandled the population issue is a major area of interest for its political, policy-related and developmental implications, and is something that deserves to be recorded for posterity.

The role of culture is a powerful factor in the day-to-day life of all Indians, binding them together, and hence, it has definitely an impact on fertility, marriage, gender issues and child care. The influence of culture on natural fertility—defined as fertility in the absence of any deliberate control—is discussed in Chapter 5.

The topic of nuptiality and the stability of the institution of marriage are discussed in Chapter 6, and it is brought out that the continuing system of arranged marriages within the religion and caste structure has contributed to this stability. Chapter 7 presents a broad picture on the levels and trends in the various demographic parameters at the state level in India, and identifies the major challenges they pose for the policymakers and program personnel. Chapter 8 provides a comparison of India as a country in the international context with large developed and developing countries on the selected parameters of demography and development with a view to identify the areas where we have gone very wrong. Chapter 9 describes the wobbling policies and program strategies in the population scene at the international level by the United Nations and major donor agencies. Chapter 10, as an epilogue, attempts to bring out a summary of the major population issues that remain to date and some suggestions on how to proceed in the future.

Making a general statement or expressing an opinion on India is a risky endeavor since it is likely to attract immediate criticism and differing points of view. This difficulty arises because of the enormous heterogeneity of the population in language, religion, ethnicity, cultural values, traditional norms and socioeconomic conditions. India's large population base of over 1,290 million by mid-2016 (growing at the rate of 1.2 percent per year) creates images of severe Malthusian checks looming large in the near future. In many European nations, such population pressures and extensive poverty were alleviated in the eighteenth century, largely through mass migration of the people, mostly belonging to the lower socioeconomic strata, to other continents—America and Australia—and the growing need for resources were met through conquests and colonization of other countries. Such an option is not available for India, or for that matter any other country, in the modern times.

The material presented here was mostly prepared in the past two years during my tenure as a National Fellow at the Indian Council for Social Science Research (ICSSR) and my affiliation with the Madras Institute of Development Studies (MIDS) at Chennai. I wish to place on record my sincere thanks to my daughter Dr Padmavathi Srinivasan who motivated me to write this book, kept the pressure to continue and edited the chapters. My sincere apologies and thanks to my wife Bharathi who had to put up with long hours of separation from me day after day when I was wedded to the computer, writing this book. My special thanks to Mr M. Senthil Selvan, Research Assistant, who has tirelessly compiled the needed data for this volume from different sources, tabulated them, assisted me in the preparation of the preliminary draft and seeing through the text and tables at various stages of editing. I thank ICSSR for giving me a fellowship as a National Fellow and MIDS, Chennai, with which I was associated as a Fellow for the past two years. The errors of omission and commission found in this volume are, however, wholly mine.

K. Srinivasan
Chennai (June 2017)

1

Origins of Family Planning Program: Population Concerns in British India

The explicit concern over India's rapid rise in population originated in the third decade of the last century. Until 1920, India's population had been growing very slowly owing to the heavy toll from famines, epidemics and invasions and colonization. According to census data, the population of India within its present geographical boundaries actually declined between 1911 and 1921, from 252.1 to 251.3 million, because of the high mortality inflicted by the worldwide influenza pandemic of 1918–19. About 5 percent of the country's population—some 13 million— died in that epidemic (Davis 1951). The population has increased slowly and steadily since 1921, largely because of sanitation measures undertaken by the provincial governments. For the first time since the initiation of a systematic population census in 1881, India's population increased slightly more than 10 percent (or 27.7 million) within a decade, with the 1931 census enumerating a population of 279.0 million (Registrar General of India 1951: Paper 1). Concerns over this rapid rise in population arose from four quarters: intellectuals, social reformers (especially those interested in improving the status of women), the Congress party (the leading political party that spearheaded the movement for political independence) and the government.

During the first two decades of the century, a steady stream of Indian intellectuals and civil servants visited England for higher education and training for posts in the Indian Civil Services. During their stay in England, they were exposed to Malthusian theories and to the establishment of Neo-Malthusian Leagues in England and elsewhere in Europe. As a result, they became aware of the positive checks likely to operate on a population increasing beyond its means of subsistence. In the Western world, India was routinely cited as an example of a population likely to be subjected to such positive checks—wars, famines and epidemics—because of the extreme poverty prevailing in the country and the high levels of fertility that many European nations had experienced earlier.

England's famous 1878 Bradlaugh–Besant trial, during which the ethics of public advocacy and sale of artificial methods of birth control were debated extensively in the court, made people aware of the various methods of birth control. The Indians who visited England became keenly committed to the idea of birth control as a means of regulating population growth and formed the Madras Neo-Malthusian League in July 1929. Some prominent public personalities joined the League in Madras. They published a propaganda journal of high merit, *The Madras Birth Control Bulletin* (Himes 1961: 123). They had periodic discussions on the population problems and measures that could be taken to control fertility, including the propagation of various artificial methods of family planning. Paying tribute to the work of this League, the Census Commissioner Hutton (1932: 1) wrote:

> A definite movement towards artificial birth control appears to be taking place, perhaps less hampered by misplaced prudery than in some countries which claim to be more civilized; thus not only is artificial control publicly advocated by a number of medical writers, but Madras can boast of a Neo-Malthusian League, with two Maharajahs, three High Court judges and four or five men very prominent in public life as its sponsors.

The need for promoting modern methods of contraception among married couples, the beginning of a trend of getting married at a later age and an optimistic note on the spread of the use of contraceptives in the population in Madras Province in the future was perceived by Yeats, the Census Superintendent of Madras Province. In the 1931 census report for the province, he observed:

> [Until recently] artificial modes of keeping down the population have not been consciously adopted [on any considerable scale] …but there is a tendency for men certainly to marry later, and the beginnings of a like tendency in the other sex will probably appear ere long. The effects of this should be seen ultimately in a lower birth rate and a slower increase in

population. Birth control, though advocated by among others a Judge of the High Court, and extensively advertised in the press, and not unknown in higher social circles, cannot be said to have as yet taken any marked place in the social system. When it will, however, is merely deferred, and ten years should show a marked growth in its popularity. Books on the subject are to be found in any bookstall or publisher's list and...It is unlikely that they can fail to exert some influence.... Contraception of a crude kind has been observed among Goudans of Salem apparently in order to prevent the undue growth of families, and consequent fragmentation of holdings and weakening of the joint family system and influence. The portent is of great interest. (Yeats 1931: 46)

Neo-Malthusian Leagues were started in other cities of India as well, especially Poona and Bombay (now Pune and Mumbai, respectively). Madras (now Chennai) and Bombay seem to be the first two Indian cities where concerns over rapid population growth gained momentum. Real action on the birth-control front seems to have started in Bombay, not as a means of regulating the population's fertility but as a method of liberating women from perpetual pregnancy and childbearing, preventing unwanted births and reducing the hazards to the life and health of many poor pregnant women who were often willing to expose themselves to primitive and dangerous methods of induced abortion to avoid having more children.

Professor R. D. Karve, a lecturer of mathematics in a Bombay college, undertook a lifelong mission to improve the status of women and advocated widow remarriage and the practice of artificial methods of family planning. He lived the life of a saint and was totally devoted to his cause. In 1921, he published books, written in English, on birth control and venereal diseases, and in 1927, he started a Marathi magazine, *Samaj Swasthya* (social hygiene), which was published regularly until his death in 1953. In 1921, he started a contraceptive center in Girgaum (or Girgaon) in the heart of Bombay. Improvement in the status of women in Maharashtra is largely attributed to the pioneering efforts of Professor Karve.

Unfortunately, the birth-control program initiated in Bombay and Madras did not spread very rapidly because of Mahatma Gandhi's strong moral opposition to the use of artificial methods of birth control. Gandhi, the most influential leader of the Congress party and the Indian freedom movement, conceded that India's population growth had to be contained by reducing the number of children each couple had, but he stoutly denounced the artificial methods of birth control. He argued that sexual abstinence was the only ethical means for birth control. He wrote periodically on birth control in his magazines *Young India* and *Navajivan* (new life):

> The society that has already become enervated through a variety of causes will become still further enervated by the adoption of artificial methods. Those men, therefore, who are lightheartedly advocating artificial methods cannot do better than study the subject afresh, state their injurious activity and popularize brahmacharya (celibacy) both for the married and the unmarried. That is the only noble and straight method of birth control. (Gandhi 1925, cited in Prabhu 1959: 5)

Gandhi's views on sex and its use were clear and dogmatic: absolute continence for the unmarried and intercourse only for procreation for the married. Since he believed and taught that sexual intercourse for pleasure alone was wrong, he was vehement in his condemnation of any artificial birth control. Contraception was considered immoral and damaging for individuals and for the nation. He wrote:

> Sex urge is a fine and noble thing. There is nothing to be ashamed of in it, but it is meant only for the act of creation. Any other use of it is a sin against God and humanity. Contraceptives of a kind there were before and there will be hereafter, but the use of them was formerly regarded as sinful. It was reserved for our generation to glorify vice by calling it virtue. (Gandhi 1936, cited in Prabhu 1959: 31)

The well-known personalities in England and the United States of America, who were passionately advocating family planning and birth control as a means of liberating women from childbearing and improving their status as individuals in society, approached Gandhi for his support on birth-control methods. Two eminent pioneers of the family planning movement, Edith How-Martyn from England and Margaret Sanger from the United States of America, had discussions and correspondence with Gandhi on this matter. However, to Mrs How-Martyn, Gandhi wrote:

> The creation of a new life is nearest the divine, I agree. All I want to say is that one should approach the act in a divine way.... Man unfortunately forgets he is nearest the divine, hankers after the brute instinct in himself and becomes less than the brute.... Man must choose either of the two courses, the upward or the downward; but as he has the brute in him, he will more easily choose the downward course than the upward, especially when the downward course is presented to him in a beautiful garb of virtue and that is what Marie Slopes and others are doing. (Gandhi 1936, cited in Prabhu 1959: 20–29)

With Margaret Sanger, he was equally emphatic. When she cited cases of women suffering because of frequent pregnancies imposed on them, he answered:

> I agree that there are hard cases. Else, birth-control enthusiasts would have no case. But I would say, 'Go and devise remedies by all means, but the remedies should be other than the ones you advise.' I carry on correspondence with many of these peoples and they describe their ailments to me. I simply say that if I were to present them with this method of birth control they would lead far worse lives. (Gandhi 1936, cited in Prabhu 1959: 20–29)

In spite of the opposition put forward by Gandhi for the use of artificial birth-control methods, the women's movement in India and various voluntary organizations continued to propagandize and support the use of artificial methods of family planning. At their 1935 annual meeting in Trivandrum, the All India Women's Conference, constituted to improve the status of women in society, focused on birth control and invited How-Martyn and Margaret Sanger. A number of opposing views were expressed, but after a considerable debate, the conference adopted a resolution approving birth control for health and welfare reasons. How-Martyn and Sanger took this opportunity to meet with Gandhi to discuss the use of artificial methods of family planning. Despite their efforts to convert him to their side, Gandhi stood firm in his conviction and rejected the use of artificial methods of family planning.

During the period of British rule in India, there was no official policy regarding population growth. Although some thoughtful British administrators clearly saw the necessity of introducing birth control in India, in general, they were not in favor of the birth-control movement that had started making its presence felt in England in the mid-nineteenth century. They measured the success of their rule in India in terms of the magnitude of net addition to India's population. British rule in India could be justified only if the population of India was increasing substantially. A good illustration of the prevalence of this kind of thinking among British government authorities can be seen in the reply of Sir Richard Temple, Governor of Bombay, when presented with a request "to use his high character and transcendent ability to restrain, in some measures at all events, the inordinate aptitude of the people to increase population" (Hutton 1932: 31). Sir Richard replied indignantly that he would do everything in his power for the increase and nothing for the diminution of Her Majesty's subjects. Some of the reasons for the British apathy towards the escalating population in India and the problems arising from it are as follows:

1. The British rulers had adopted a policy of noninterference, in principle, in Indian social matters and, as far as possible, did not take any measure that could be considered an intrusion not just in traditions, customs, values and beliefs but also economic and health problems of their subjects in the colonies.

2. Large populations in the colonies worked to the economic advantage of the British. The colonial rulers were not interested in educated and well-nourished indigenous populations but in large mass of impoverished and desperate human capital that could be exploited fully in labor-intensive manufacturing and agrarian sectors, the end products of which were channeled to the homeland. By the same token, England did not have to bear the direct burden nor make any resource investment to support the bourgeoning population.

3. The issue of birth control was itself largely controversial in the British homeland.

However, even when the opposition to birth control started diluting in England and other Western countries, medical doctors in India still maintained a low profile about promoting it. In a textbook for British probationers of the Indian Civil Services, Sir John Megaw, former Director of the Indian Medical Service, wrote:

> Such a problem as that of overpopulation would have to be handled with discretion, but there can be no objection to the treatment of the subject on strictly biological lines. The advocacy of any special method of population control is quite unnecessary; all that is needed is a presentation of the underlying principles. These ticklish questions can best be dealt with by Indians who usually discuss them far more freely than is possible for Europeans, restrained as they are by the fear of giving offence. (Megaw 1936: 22)

However, largely because of the intellectual foundations laid by Neo-Malthusian Leagues in various parts of the country and Karve's convincing argument for birth control, chiefly to protect the health and lives of women, the government of the princely state of Mysore, under the enlightened leadership of Maharaja Krishnaraja Wadiyar IV, officially sanctioned the opening of four family planning clinics in 1930. Only two clinics were started immediately: one at Vanivilas Hospital in Bangalore and the other at Cheluvamba Hospital in Mysore. They were the first family planning clinics in the world to be started under government auspices.

The efforts of the pioneers who wanted to propagandize family planning activities in India came to a standstill in 1939 with the beginning of World War II. The shift in national priorities as a result of the imminent problems arising from the war created a lull in birth-control activities during 1939–45. The end of the war, however, brought renewed interest in family planning and revalorized efforts to promote its use.

After the death of Mahatma Gandhi in January 1948, the moralistic opposition to artificial methods of family planning declined. In 1949, the Family Planning Association of India (originally called the Family Planning Committee) was formed. Its members included pioneers such as Professor Karve, Dr A. P. Pillay, Lady Dhanvanthi Rama Rau, Mrs Vembu and Mrs A. B. Wadia, who had been active in family planning programs before the war and had evinced a keen interest during the All India Women's Conference held earlier in 1935.

Founding the Family Planning Association of India in Bombay in 1949 triggered a new epoch in the family planning movement, not only in India but also in many other countries. The International Planned Parenthood Federation, which coordinates voluntary activities in family planning worldwide, also began in Bombay in 1952. At the suggestion of Margaret Sanger, the International Committee on Family Planning organized the Third International Conference of the International Planned Parenthood Federation with the family planning associations in India, the United Kingdom, the United States of America, Sweden, Holland, Hong Kong, Singapore and West Germany as the founding members and with Margaret Sanger and Lady Dhanvanthi Rama Rau as joint presidents. Launching this international movement in Bombay was a milestone in the history of family planning activities, not only in India but for many other countries, because it gave a new impetus to voluntary family planning movements.

In the decade 1931–40, the Indian population soared from 279.0 million to 318.7 million: a 14 percent spurt in ten years, the highest ever achieved in India until that time. The majority of people continued to live under precariously poor conditions and standards of living continued to deteriorate. A severe drought towards the end of 1942 created a serious food shortage in several parts of the country in 1943, culminating in a large-scale famine, followed by outbreaks of epidemics in Bengal. The 1943 famine was the most devastating in modern history; an astronomical four million people were estimated to have died in this one famine alone. Historians suggest that the huge loss of lives, as high as this, could have been prevented if it had not been for the deliberate callousness and apathy of the British administration (Mukerjee 1959).

The Bengal Famine of 1943–44 was not unique. Famines had been occurring on a frequent basis in the Indian subcontinent (India, Pakistan and Bangladesh). However, the famines seemed to have been particularly devastating in the late eighteenth and nineteenth centuries under the British Raj. Droughts, combined with often deliberate policy failures on the part of the British government, had periodically led to major Indian famines with tremendous loss of lives. It has been estimated that famines in India resulted in more than 60 million deaths over the course of the eighteenth, nineteenth and early twentieth centuries. The famine of 1866 was a severe and terrible event in the history of Odisha in which about a third of the population died. This famine left an estimated 1,553 orphans (Samal 1990) whose guardians were to receive an amount of ₹3 per month until the age of 17 and 16 for boys and girls respectively. Similar famines followed in the western Ganges region, Rajasthan, Central India (1868–70), Bengal and Eastern India (1873–74), Deccan (1876–78) and again in the Ganges region, Madras, Hyderabad, Mysore and Bombay (1876–78). The famine of 1876–78, also known as the Great Famine of 1876–78, caused a large migration of agricultural laborers and artisans from Southern India to British tropical colonies, where they worked as indentured laborers on plantations. The large death toll—about 10.3 million—offset the usual population growth in Bombay and Madras Presidencies between the first and second censuses of British India in 1871 and 1881, respectively (see Table 1.1).

A lot of researches by economists and other social scientists have been carried out on the causes underlying the Bengal Famine—whether it was a problem of short supply, distribution, hoarding and price fixation or a combination of these. Actually, there was no real shortage of food production in Bengal during 1942–43, but the famine occurred mainly because of deliberate apathy from the British rulers and the redirection of food stock from India to England to feed the British population during wartime food shortage (Mukerjee 2010). There is an infamous quote attributed to Winston Churchill, who was the Prime Minister of Britain at that time, which sums up the attitude held by the British rulers towards the plight of their colonies. When informed by then Viceroy and Governor General of India, Archibald Wavell, about the severity of the famine in Bengal and enormous death toll (Ghose 1982), Churchill's response

Table 1.1:
Famines in India during British rule

Year	Name of Famine	British Territory	Indian Kingdoms/ Princely States	Mortality
1769–70	The Great Bengal famine	Bihar, Northern and Central Bengal		10 million (about one-third of the then population of Bengal). Disputed as excessive.
1782–83	Madras Famine	Madras city and surrounding areas	Kingdom of Mysore	Severe famine. Large areas were depopulated.
1783–84	The Chalisa famine		Delhi, Western Oudh, Eastern Punjab region, Rajputana and Kashmir	Up to 11 million people may have died during the years 1782–84.
1791–92	The Doji Bara famine or the Skull Famine		Hyderabad, Southern Maratha country, Deccan, Gujarat and Marwar	One of the most severe famines known. People died in such numbers that they could not be cremated or buried. It is thought that 11 million people may have died during the years 1788–94.
1837–38	The Agra famine of 1837–38	Central Doab and trans-Jumna districts of the North-Western Provinces (later Agra Province), including Delhi and Hissar		800,000
1860–61	The Upper Doab famine of 1860–61	Upper Doab of Agra; Delhi and Hissar divisions of the Punjab	Eastern Rajputana	2 million
1865–67	The Orissa famine of 1866	Orissa (also 1867) and Bihar; Bellary and Ganjam districts of Madras		1 million (814,469 in Orissa, 135,676 in Bihar and 10,898 in Ganjam).
1868–70	The Rajputana famine of 1869	Ajmer, Western Agra, Eastern Punjab	Rajputana	1.5 million (mostly in the princely states of Rajputana).

(Table 1.1 continued)

(Table 1.1 continued)

Year	Name of Famine	British Territory	Indian Kingdoms/ Princely States	Mortality
1873–74	The Bihar famine of 1873–74	Bihar		An extensive relief effort was organized by the Bengal government. There were little to none significant mortalities during the famine.
1876–78	The Great famine of 1876–78 (also Southern India famine of 1876–78)	Madras and Bombay	Mysore and Hyderabad	5.5 million in British territory. Mortality unknown for princely states. Total famine mortality estimates vary from 6.1 to 10.3 million.
1888–89		Ganjam, Orissa and North Bihar		150,000 deaths in Ganjam. Deaths were due to starvation as famine relief was not provided in time.
1896–97	The Indian famine of 1896–97	Madras, Bombay Deccan, Bengal, United Provinces, Central Provinces	Northern and eastern Rajputana, parts of Central India and Hyderabad	5 million in British territory.
1899–1900	The Indian famine of 1899–1900	Bombay, Central Provinces, Berar, Ajmer	Hyderabad, Rajputana, Central India, Baroda, Kathiawar, Cutch,	1 million (in British territories). Mortality unknown for princely states.
1905–06		Bombay	Bundelkhand	235,062 in Bombay (of which 28,369 attributed to Cholera). Mortality unknown for Bundelkhand.
1943–44	The Bengal famine of 1943	Bengal		1.5 million from starvation; 3.5 million including deaths from epidemics.

Sources: Imperial Gazetteer of India vol. III (1907); McAlpin, Michelle B. (1983).
Note: The total number of deaths estimated from above famines is 55 to 60 millions.

was to ask peevishly, "[If that was indeed the case] Why Gandhi hasn't died yet?"

The economist Amartya Sen points out,

[H]ow urgently and how actively the government will act will also depend on the nature of the politics of the country and the forces that operate on the government to act without delay. Depending on the nature of the political structure, it is often possible for an inactive or uncaring government to get away with implicit manslaughter, if not murder. (Sen 1977)

So in a democratic country with elected leaders being held accountable for the welfare of the people in their respective constituencies, such large famines are unlikely to happen. "No famine has ever taken place in the history of the world in a functioning democracy," Sen wrote in *Democracy as Freedom* (Sen 1999). This, he explained, is because democratic governments "have to win elections and face public criticism, and have a strong incentive to undertake measures to avert famines and other catastrophes." From this perspective, it would seem that England has to bear for ages to come to terms with the moral burden of deliberately allowing so many of the citizens in their colonies to die like flies under natural and man-made calamities occurring during their occupation.

The proposition that fully functioning democracies do not experience famines and loss of lives from famines has been advanced in a host of books and articles, and has shaped the thinking of a generation of policymakers, scholars and relief workers who deal with famines. It has also helped promote democracy as a major political ideology. The fact that India, after independence, has never witnessed a disaster on the scale of the Bengal Famine of 1943 is to be credited to popular democracy whereby the elected leaders are accountable for avoiding such calamities.

Even after independence, a famine on a much smaller scale did occur in Bihar in December 1966, but deaths were few. There were also frequent droughts in Maharashtra in 1970–73 and suicides by farmers but without the large-scale fatality witnessed during the colonial occupation. It was due to the successful famine prevention contingencies implemented by the state and central governments. In a democratic society where the governments at the state and the central levels are elected by and become accountable to the people, such famines are very unlikely to happen.

Undoubtedly, the famines during British India were severe enough to have a substantial impact on the long-term population growth of the country in the nineteenth and early twentieth centuries. Knowing that the shift of power was definitely going to occur in July 1944, directly after World War I, the Indian Government appointed the Bengal Famine Inquiry Commission under the chairmanship of John Woodhead, Governor of Bengal, and included as one of its members R. A. Gopalaswamy, an Indian civil servant who later became the first Census Commissioner and Registrar General of independent India. The entire commission investigations, findings and the final reports were prepared under the directives and leadership of the British, who were still ruling the country, and as such placed minimal responsibilities on the governance and handling of the crisis on occupying force and absolved them of deliberately, or otherwise, creating, exacerbating or mismanaging the crisis to the extent that it would result in such an enormous fatality rate. However, though the report might have been biased and partial, the recommendations continued to strongly influence and shape the economic and population policies of India for decades after independence.

Several references to the potential dangers to the economy, arising out of rapid population growth outstripping food production, and the consequences, especially for population living in abject poverty, malnourished and deprived of the basic essentials of life, are made in the minutes in the final report.

> During normal years the consumption increases, and carry-over is possible only when the production is much above the requirements. Such occasions have become rare since population increases has outstripped food supply... There has been no increase in food production and a steep rise in population. (Government of India 1945: 184)

The commission recommended very strongly that a population control program should become an integral part of any governmental development policy. It also emphasized the need to collect, compile and analyze population-related data necessary for developmental assistance to different areas, especially compulsory registration of births and deaths. The 1945 recommendations paved the way for the Government of India to launch an official program of family planning as a part of its developmental strategy immediately after the attainment of independence in 1947.

The second major study that helped encourage a population policy was the report of the Health Survey and Development Committee (also called Bhore Committee), constituted by the Government of India in 1943 (under the chairmanship of Sir Joseph Bhore). This committee's

1946 report identified India's major health problems and recommended various measures to improve public health, environmental sanitation, nutrition and prevention of communicable diseases. It also suggested the organizational structure most appropriate for implementing these programs. This report devoted an entire chapter to population, strongly recommending the adoption of a national family planning program as an essential public health program. The specific recommendations contained in the reports of the Bengal Famine Inquiry Commission and the Bhore Committee were instrumental in the family planning program becoming a constituent part of India's developmental strategy, starting with the First Five-Year Plan in 1951.

On the political side, there appears to have been ambivalence with regard to the position of the Congress party on the use of artificial methods of family planning. While many Congress party leaders strongly felt the need to curtail the rapidly rising population growth via artificial methods of family planning, there were a few (following the viewpoint of Mahatma Gandhi) holding a strong moral opposition to these methods. These divisive views and ambivalence persisted for a few years following Gandhi's death. In 1938, the Indian National Congress under the chairmanship of Subhas Chandra Bose advocated a definite restriction on population growth. The National Planning Commission, appointed by the Congress and placed under the chairmanship of the would-be Prime Minister Jawaharlal Nehru, prepared a national development plan that included a section on population. It recommended a restriction on numbers, as indicated in this guarded statement:

While measures for the improvement of the quality of the population and limiting excessive population pressure are necessary, the basic solution of the present disparity between population and standard of living lies in the economic progress of the country on a comprehensive and planned basis. (Report of the All India Congress Committee 1938, quoted in Raina 1988: 28)

Though there was no strong support coming forth for the advocates of artificial methods of family planning in India, the National Planning Commission recommended their use. These included methods of self-control, mainly in the hope of reducing the undesirable effects of injurious methods of birth controls, specifically induced abortion. The commission supported raising the age at marriage, discouraging polygamy and introducing a birth-control program, including sterilization of persons with serious genetically transmittable diseases such as epilepsy and insanity. Thus, while the attitude of the Congress party was not so positive in its support for family planning, the attitudes of the government, voluntary organizations and the intellectuals were becoming more and more favorable towards launching a national program of family planning. After the death of Mahatma Gandhi, the opposition of the Congress party workers towards artificial methods of family planning weakened, though not eliminated. Many of Gandhi's followers, who were in favor of artificial methods but were hesitant to oppose Gandhi's strong sentiments in the matter, now came forward to support a family planning program and the distribution of artificial means of birth control.

The strong recommendations for population control contained in the reports of the Bengal Famine Enquiry Commissions and the Bhore Committee, submitted in 1945 and 1946, the sustained initiatives taken by the Family Planning Association of India to start a national program of family planning in India to protect the health of mothers and children, and the intellectual support for fertility regulation given through Neo-Malthusian Leagues in the country were the factors that facilitated a national program of family planning to be sponsored by the Government of independent India as a part of its developmental strategy. Thus was born the first national program of family planning—the first of its kind to be started anywhere in the developing world.

Despite the successful launch of a formal population control program in the country, after the initial, rather uncertain, start, there is still an undercurrent of quiet hostility towards artificial methods of family planning among the Gandhians in India, especially those from the older generations who have had the opportunity to meet and work with Gandhi. The view that using artificial family planning methods, especially on a regular basis, is immoral and unethical continues to pervade the psyche of a considerable section of Indian society. The hesitancy on the part of many couples seems to be more in the repetitive use of artificial methods for the spacing of children rather than towards the adoption of a one-time permanent method, such as sterilization, once the desired family size is reached.

2

Population Policies and Programs since Independence until 1977: Birth of the Official Birth-Control Program

Planning in India

India attained independence from the sovereignty of Great Britain on August 15, 1947, after more than 100 years of political struggle. The means adopted in the struggle for independence were essentially nonviolent methods of noncooperation with the rulers, organized under the leadership of Mahatma Gandhi since 1920.

The achievement of independence in 1947 was accompanied by the painful partition of India into two nations, India and Pakistan. Pakistan, consisting of East and West Pakistan, two widely separated, geographically and linguistically distinct parts, was constituted as an Islamic state, while India remained secular. During the few months before and after the partition, the country witnessed considerable streams of migrants crossing the borders—a good number of Muslims moving from India to Pakistan, and Hindus and Sikhs migrating from Pakistan to India. For various linguistic, cultural and political factors, East Pakistan chose to become an independent nation and Bangladesh was born in 1971.

After the independence, India chose to follow the political philosophy of democratic socialism as a federation of states and union territories (centrally administered regions). The Constitution, adopted in 1950, delineates the powers of the central and state governments and guarantees certain basic fundamental rights to every citizen of the country. The states were formed on the basis of the languages spoken in the area and on the recommendations of the States Reorganization Commission, a body set up under the Constitution of India in 1950, and implemented in 1956. The States Reorganization Act 1956 was a major reform of the boundaries of India's states and territories, organizing them along linguistic lines.

Although additional changes to India's state boundaries have been made since 1956, the States Reorganization Act of 1956 remains the single most extensive change in state boundaries since the independence in 1947. The Act came into effect at the same time as the Constitution (Seventh Amendment) Act, 1956, which (among other things) restructured the constitutional framework for India's existing states and the requirements to pass the States Reorganization Act, 1956, under the provisions of Articles 3 and 4 of the constitution.

Initially there were 14 large states and 6 union territories, the latter being small geographical units under the control of the central government. These states were first formed on linguistic basis and later on, on political and other considerations. As of date, there are 29 states, and 7 union territories, including the National Capital Region of Delhi. The latest addition to the list of states is Telangana, formed by the bifurcation of Andhra Pradesh in 2014. For administrative purposes, the states and union territories are further divided into districts. A district forms the basic administrative unit for the implementation of the policies and programs of the central and state governments. In 2011, there were 640 districts and a district had an average population of 1.8 million, varying widely from state to state. Since 1991, four new states have been carved out from the larger states—Uttarakhand from erstwhile Uttar Pradesh, Jharkhand from Bihar, Chhattisgarh from Madhya Pradesh, all the three formed in 2000, and the fourth, Telangana, from Andhra Pradesh in 2014. Some union territories were also upgraded as states. According to the census of 2011, there were 28 states and 6 union territories in the country, administratively divided into 640 districts. With the formation of new state of Telangana in 2014, there were, in 2015, 30 states and 6 union territories.* Even after 2011, 36 new districts have been formed

---

* Though "Delhi" as the National Capital Territory is officially and politically considered as still a Union Territory (1991 Amendment to the Constitution), for demographic purposes it is considered as a "State" by the Census Commissioner and the Registrar

and, at present, there are 676 districts in total—a significant increase from 640 in 2011 census and 593 in 2001. Since the rate of formation of the new districts is almost the same as the population, the average population size of a district remains constant at 1.8 million. Maps showing the population size at the time of the 2011 census and the density per sq. km are given in Figure 2.1 and Figure 2.2, respectively. Figure 2.1, which shows the districts by population size, reveals that there are 231 districts with a population of over 2 million, according to the 2011 census, and they are mostly in the states of Andhra Pradesh, Maharashtra, West Bengal, Punjab, Bihar and Uttar Pradesh.

Figure 2.2, which gives the population density at the district level in India, reveals an interesting pattern. High-density districts, with over 723 persons per sq. km, are in the coastal areas of Kerala, Tamil Nadu, Andhra Pradesh, West Bengal, Maharashtra and the northern districts of Bihar and Uttar Pradesh, bordering Nepal and Bangladesh. The density is quite low in the central part of the country and there appears to be a continuous internal migration to the coastal areas and to the state capitals. There is also a group of high-density districts in the northern districts of Bihar and Uttar Pradesh that is to be investigated further.

After independence, India initiated a process of development to raise living standards and to open new opportunities for a richer, more varied life. The country is committed to some basic goals, namely, modernization, growth with social justice, self-reliance, and the path chosen to realize these objectives is one of democratic planning. The Planning Commission was set up in 1949, and the First Five-Year Plan covered the years 1951–56. Eleven such five-year plans have been completed so far, with a three-year gap—or plan holiday—between the Third and the Fourth Plan and annual plans after the Seventh Plan. Since April 2012, the Twelfth Five-Year Plan has been in effect covering the period April 2012 to March 2017. With the coming to power of the new BJP-led government at the center the process of 5-year planning for development, that has been long been in vogue in the country since 1951, has been given a goodbye and the Planning Commission has been replaced by The National Institution for Transforming India, also called NITI Aayog, and formed by a resolution of the Union Cabinet on January 1, 2015. NITI Aayog

General of India. With the inclusion of Delhi in the category of states, there are now 30 states and 6 union territories. (The Constitution, Sixty-ninth Amendment Act, 1991) Ref http://indiacode.nic.in/coiweb/amend/amend69.htm

Figure 2.1:
Population size by districts of India in 2011

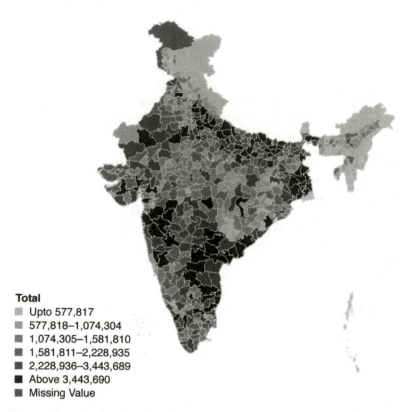

Total
- Upto 577,817
- 577,818–1,074,304
- 1,074,305–1,581,810
- 1,581,811–2,228,935
- 2,228,936–3,443,689
- Above 3,443,690
- Missing Value

Source: Created using DevInfo India tool provided by Census of India, http://www.
devinfo.org/indiacensuspca/libraries/aspx/home.aspx
Note: Figure is not scaled.

plans for development within each Ministry without a uniform time specification as five year plans.

A notable characteristic of India's democratic planning is the coexistence of the private and public sectors, which is supposed to function as parts of a unified system. To attain the larger social goals, it was imperative for the public sector to take the initiative in such vital areas as transport, communication, power generation, education, health and social welfare.

Figure 2.2:
India's district population density in census 2011

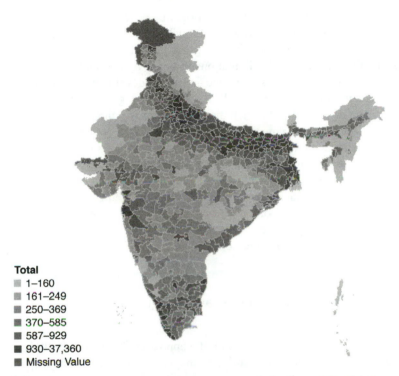

Total
- 1–160
- 161–249
- 250–369
- 370–585
- 587–929
- 930–37,360
- Missing Value

Source: Created using DevInfo India tool provided by Census of India, http://www.
devinfo.org/indiacensuspca/libraries/aspx/home.aspx
Note: Figure is not to scale.

The various social and economic institutions in India, such as the caste system and the zamindari system (land ownership), are legacies of the past, some in existence for over 1,000 years. To achieve the goals of economic and social development for India, many of the elements of such institutions had to be transformed. These changes have to be brought about not by force or compulsion but through democratic planning, which emphasizes individual freedom and initiative, not allowing coercion of any type.

The constraints imposed by this political philosophy, chosen by India for its development and the complexities arising out of the heterogeneity and diversity of the population, pose a big challenge to the process of development in India, especially in the field of social change. For example, while a country like China with one-party communist rule can impose on its people a stringent family size norm of one child per couple, and achieve considerable success without much popular revolt, India has not realized even the moderate fertility goals postulated in any of its first seven five-year plans. The limitations imposed by the political philosophy, within which various economic and social developmental programs operate, must be kept in mind when evaluating programs such as family planning or public health in India and comparing their achievements with those of other countries. A brief review of population policies, program strategies and their effects on the population, as they developed over successive five-year plans, is provided in the following sections. The objective of the review is to have a critical assessment of the strengths and weaknesses of the Indian Family Planning programs as judged from a hindsight of contemporary experiences. Greater emphasis has been placed on the major trends and shifts in the program strategies as they occurred over time and the reasons thereof.

Official Population Policies and Programs

In April 1950, the Government of India appointed the Population Policy Committee under the chairmanship of the minister of planning and, upon the committee's recommendation, a family planning cell was created in the office of the Directorate General of Health Services. The First Five-Year Plan document, presented to parliament in December 1952, referred to a program for "family limitation and population control." It sought to reduce the birth rate "to the extent necessary to stabilize the population at a level consistent with the requirements of the national economy." This was the genesis of the first official national family planning program in the world and a brief review of the population policy component in the first and successive five-year plans to follow.

The First Five-Year Plan (1951–56)

The First Five-Year Plan formulated that the program for family limitation and population control should:

1. Present a clear picture of the factors contributing to the rapid population increase in India;
2. Discover suitable techniques of family planning and devise methods by which knowledge of these techniques could be widely disseminated and
3. Give advice on family planning as an integral part of the service of government hospitals and public agencies.

The goal stated was "the reduction of the birth rate to the extent necessary to stabilize the population at a level consistent with the requirements of the national economy" (First Five-Year Plan, Planning Commission 1951, quoted in Raina 1988: 6).

A sum of ₹6.5 million (or US$ 1.44 million at the exchange rate of 1 US$ – ₹4.5) was allocated by the central government to the Ministry of Health for a family planning program which included a plethora of activities: Providing contraceptive advice; experimenting in the field with different family planning methods to determine their suitability, acceptability and effectiveness in different sectors of the population; developing suitable ways to educate the people on family planning methods; collecting information on reproductive patterns, attitudes and motivations affecting family size; studying the interrelationships among economic, social and population changes; and researching the physiological and medical aspects of human fertility control. The budget allotted to the program was in no way consistent with outputs expected from the program. This gross inconsistency with budget inputs and expected outputs were continued from plan to plan. The belief that "there was already some intrinsic demand for family planning services and that supply would induce demand" prompted the government to open family planning clinics as service centers during this period. "The people were expected to go on their own to these clinics to demand and receive family planning services" (Plan document, First Five-Year Plan, quoted in Raina 1988: 5). The methods recommended were the use of the diaphragm and jelly, vaginal foam tablets and condoms. Sterilization services, especially vasectomies, were provided in some states. No numerical goals were set for the crude birth rate (CBR) or for the population growth rate. The Central Family Planning Board was constituted as an apex advisory body at the national level (Raina 1988: 6).

and urban hospitals and family welfare training centers. Based on field experiments conducted at Gandhigram in Tamil Nadu, the change in strategy involved using interested and influential village leaders in promoting the small family norm and carrying the message of family planning to couples (Raina 1988). The objectives of this extension–education approach, which continues to be a pervasive methodology in the Indian family planning program over range of the period, were as follows:

- Creating a group norm of a small family size in every community by educating and involving opinion leaders.
- Providing information on available contraceptive methods to every eligible couple.
- Furnishing contraceptive services in a socially and psychologically acceptable manner.

The family planning program was made an integral part of the public health departments in all the states. Unlike the clinic approach, wherein family planning personnel waited for eligible couples to come to their clinics for advice and supplies, the extension–education approach relied on peripheral health workers, particularly auxiliary nurses midwives (ANMs) and family planning health assistants (FPHAs), for the crucial task of identifying, informing and motivating eligible couples. It is observable from a hindsight that these peripheral health workers, who were neither well paid nor well qualified, were charged with the stupendous task of motivation of couples for the small family norm, but the strategy helped to spread the message of family planning to every village in the country.

The "cafeteria approach" to methods of family planning was officially adopted. The choice was left to the acceptor, but there was an official emphasis on sterilization. Responsibility of distributing simple contraceptives and giving general advice on family planning was given largely to voluntary organizations, paramedical personnel and extension educators trained in family planning. Detailed plans concerning the production of contraceptives by the government and private firms were drawn up. The assistance of voluntary organizations, labor unions and other organizations was sought on as large a scale as possible. The system of giving compensation money to acceptors of sterilization and incentives to the motivator who influenced a couple to accept the terminal method of family planning was introduced in most of the states during this plan period.

The symbol of an inverted red triangle, representing the message of family planning, was introduced. It continues to be the family planning logo in the country.

The Third Five-Year Plan is unique because, for the first time, a demographic goal was set in 1962: a CBR of 25 by 1972, a goal judged in retrospect as overly ambitious. The goal was more of an expression of a desire and a preference for a digit ending with "5," an Indian tradition, than based on feasibility and inputs in the program. This habit of fixing unrealistic demographic goals continued plan after plan, in spite of the fact that the goals set in the earlier plan were not realized and unrealizable. This malaise of the Planning Commission is not only applicable to family planning program but also to various other development programs. The demographic goals set and the strategies adopted in various plan periods is given in Table 2.1.

The family planning program was viewed not simply as a social welfare measure for improving women's health and status, or in helping

Table 2.1:
Desired demographic for the Indian family planning program during the period 1962 to 2012

Year of Statement	Specified Goal	Target Year for Achieving Goal
1962	CBR, 25	1972
1966	CBR, 25	As promptly as possible
1968	CBR, 23	1978–79
1969	CBR, 32	1974–75
(start of the Fourth Five-Year Plan)	CBR, 25	1979–81
1974	CBR, 30	1979
(start of the Fifth Five-Year Plan)	CBR, 25	1984
April 1976	CBR, 30	1978–79
(First Plan Period)	CBR, 25	1983–84
April 1977	CBR, 30	1978–79
(Second Plan Period)	CBR, 25	1983–84
January 1978	CBR, 30	1982–83
(Central Council of Health)		

(Table 2.1 continued)

widely from state to state, depending on the availability of adequately skilled personnel, training facilities, organizational capabilities and general socioeconomic conditions of the area.

4. The program advocated a cafeteria approach, but in practice, emphasis was mainly on sterilization, particularly vasectomy. The intrauterine device (IUD) was introduced into the program in 1965 but without adequate informational and educational programs or suitable facilities for training personnel involved in the program, without proper case selection and techniques of insertion and without follow-up care.

Because of the lack of good services and inadequate follow-up care, IUD fell into disrepute. In addition, a good number of medical specialists campaigned against IUD, so it was practically withdrawn from the program after two years of unsuccessful attempts to encourage it as a routine family planning device in India. Viewed in retrospect, this was an unfortunate and strategic mistake since a family planning method that could have been extremely useful for spacing purposes and accepted by younger couples was brought into disrepute. Later experiences with IUD's in China, Korea and Thailand proved that this method of family planning was equally, if not more, effective in reducing fertility levels. The program had to rely heavily on sterilization, particularly vasectomy, and slightly higher incentives were given to all those concerned with sterilization—the acceptor, the doctor and the motivator. In 1966, the target for CBR was refixed at 25, to be realized by 1975–76, but it was again revised in 1968 stipulating a CBR of 23 by 1978–79. The expenditure during the three-year plan holiday on family planning was ₹704.6 million, almost three times more than the five years of the Third Plan.

The Fourth Five-Year Plan (1969–74)

In the Fourth Five-Year Plan, family planning was included among programs given the highest priority. A numerical target was set for reducing CBR from 39, estimated at the beginning of the plan, to 32 in five years and to 25 per thousand by 1979. To achieve this goal, a target of the number of sterilizations to be conducted in the population was specified. For reaching this target, a concrete program was devised for expanding family planning service facilities and motivational educational aspects through the mass media. A sum of ₹3,150 million was budgeted for the program; however, the actual expenditure was ₹2,844.3 million. The infrastructure was considerably expanded during this period. The number of conventional contraceptive (CC) users doubled, from 1.5 million in 1969–70 to 3 million by 1974–75, and the number of sterilization acceptors rose from 1.4 (of which 75 percent were vasectomies) to 3.1 million in 1972–73 but plummeted to 0.9 million in 1973–74, with a small rise to 1.4 million in 1974–75. As a result of the program, an estimated 28 million couples were protected by 1973–74, and an estimated 12 million births were averted during the plan period.

During this plan period, the program to popularize oral contraceptives expanded considerably. Again, due to lack of preparatory educational, motivational and training programs, the pill did not gain the popular acceptance it deserved. A system for free condom distribution (the depot holders system) was introduced. Surgical equipment was provided in rural and urban family welfare centers for vasectomies— once again, the major plank in the strategy to meet the time-bound targets mentioned in the Fourth Plan documents. Plans were made to popularize sterilization and achieve the targets. Increased emphasis was put on the camp approach, whereby sterilizations were carried out in villages, at suitable locations for conducting surgery, and rural facilities were strengthened to meet the additional needs of this camp approach. The incentive payment was also raised. The famous Ernakulam camp in Kerala state, in which over 65,000 vasectomies were done in two weeks, was organized during this plan and became a model for other such camps. Population Council, New York, published a special issue in their journal studies in family planning on Ernakulam camp, making it appear as if it was a model camp.

Toward the end of this plan period, the mass-camp approach was replaced by the mini-camp approach—not more than 25 men could be sterilized in any one camp. This changeover was necessary since numerous postoperative complaints were received from men operated on in large camps. The program suffered a setback in 1973–74 when the number of sterilizations declined by 2.2 million from the number recorded in the previous year.

Increased emphasis was placed to postpartum programs in major hospitals, urban family welfare training centers and selected PHCs. In 1971, the Indian Parliament passed a law liberalizing induced abortions under the Medical Termination of Pregnancies Act, which became effective in April 1972, making it possible for pregnant women to have legal abortions almost on demand.

powers to the central government headed by the prime minister. A state of emergency was officially issued by the President Fakhruddin Ali Ahmed under Article 352(1) of the Constitution for "internal disturbance," and the emergency was in effect from June 25, 1975 until its withdrawal on March 21, 1977. The order bestowed upon the prime minister the authority to rule by diktat, allowing elections to be suspended and civil liberties to be curtailed. Sanjay Gandhi, the second son of Indira Gandhi, who after a few years died in a plane crash, called all the shots of policies and programs. For much of the Emergency, most of Gandhi's political opponents were imprisoned and the press was censored. Several other atrocities were reported from the time, including a forced mass-sterilization campaign especially spearheaded by Sanjay Gandhi. The Emergency is, even now after 40 years, considered one of the darkest periods of India's independent history.

An aggressive family planning program was launched as an integral element of the Emergency under the mistaken assumption, partly supported by many international donor agencies, that rapid curtailment of the population through reduction of fertility to an average family size of two would accelerate economic development with a hindsight. It is found that during the same time, in the mid-seventies, China was launching a one-child policy and, under the communist authoritarian rule, it was able to continue undeterred with the policy and reduce the birth rate to half within a period of 10 years. On the other hand, with its democratic framework well in place, India could not continue with its aggressive family planning program of two child norms even for two years.

The First Official "National Population Policy and Family Planning Program" Passed by Parliament

The aggressive family planning drive, as it was called, started immediately after the Emergency in June 1975 as a part of the five-point program of Sanjay Gandhi, focusing on vasectomy, of men with three or more children and wife in the reproductive period 15–44. Vasectomies were held in many government offices, schools, large railway stations, etc. The vasectomy booths set up in the Churchgate and VT stations in Mumbai became notorious because of its ruthless nature: they gathered the young male passengers getting down the electric trains and made them pass through the vasectomy booths and sterilized them, unless they have card for already been sterilized. Probably, Indira Gandhi and Sanjay Gandhi were aware of the one-child policy that was planned to be launched in China and thought a similar policy to limit the Indian couples with two children through sterilization would work. While the method promoted for achieving the one-child policy in China was IUD, which is reversible, this was not the case with sterilization adopted in India. From June 1975 to March 1976, almost 6.5 million sterilizations were done, the largest ever done in any country in the world even over a five-year period. While objections among the rival political parties in power at the state level were building up, Sanjay Gandhi thought it necessary to change an act of Parliament on this matter and override or push the states to such an aggressive program. A National Population Policy (NPP), the first of its kind to be proposed in Indian Parliament, was passed by a majority vote in April 1976 (Appendix A).

The eighteen points of NPP 1976 that have been reproduced in Appendix A aimed at making a "frontal attack on the problems of population." This was implemented in a misplaced and wrongly directed way. It made people its enemy. Mainly, to underline the fault, the underlying motivation to have such a strong phase of policies was the slow phase of economic development experienced in the country since independence, and high population growth played the role of a villain that had to be controlled at any cost. The agony and frustrations of the political leadership in the continuing slow economic development of the country are evident in the above paragraphs. However to blame this lack of development mainly on the shoulders of high population growth rates was a mistake. Many of the thoughts expressed therein are still valid, after four decades in India, though the earlier blames on population growth have eroded.

Innovative political and fiscal incentives were offered to the state governments to implement the family planning program very seriously. Representation to parliament from each state would be frozen at the 1971 census levels, up to the year 2001, making it politically unattractive for any state to increase its relative population size in the hope of securing political strength at the center. There was a scheme for community incentives to villages and towns achieving high levels of contraceptive protection.

More than any other measure, concerted efforts to improve the program's organizational efficiency by insisting on performance targets from the vast army of family planning personnel and the coordinated

Call for Elections in 1977 and Return to Democracy: An Estimate of the Vulnerability to Authoritarianism

Mrs Indira Gandhi thought, because of her large-scale insulation from the reactions of the people from her policies, that she was a very popular leader and people loved her in spite of the various court verdicts against her and called for general elections in February 1977. That was the beginning of the end of her power and the Emergency. The February 1977 elections brought a major defeat to the party in power at the center and in most of the states. One of the key election issues was government's imposition of a coercive family planning program. With the change of political parties at the center, the program became a victim of political controversies and almost completely collapsed during 1977–78. Before we go into the post-Emergency reaction to family planning programs, the data on vasectomies done during the two-year period, from 1975 to 1977 (covering the 21 month emergency), compared with the performance in the earlier two years, 1973–75, gives a measure of the virulence with which the states pursued the central diktat, overriding the demands of the people (index of vulnerability to authoritarianism; IVA). It can be considered a measure of the vulnerability or susceptibility at the state level of a dictatorial rule from the center and an IVA. Table 2.3 presents such data on the index values. This can be considered an index of coercion during the Emergency. It is interesting to see from the table that the large Hindi speaking states of the north—Uttar Pradesh, Bihar, Rajasthan and Delhi—had recorded the maximum proportionate rise in vasectomy during the emergency period 1975–77 compared to the two-year pre-Emergency period 1973–75. This validates the general impression that the Emergency had relatively less impact in south India. The southern states have recorded relatively lower rise. As a political reaction to the policy of June 1976, the minister of health and family planning announced a new statement of policy on the Family Welfare Program (Appendix B) in April 1977; the term "family planning" was changed to "family welfare." The new government, however, reiterated its total commitment to the Family Welfare Program and bringing the birth rate down to 25 per thousand by 1984, as stipulated in the 1976 policy.

The policy statements of 1976 and 1977 shared a number of common elements, although they came from different party lines. Both the policies emphasized on raising the age at marriage, expanding facilities for women's education, introducing population education programs in

Table 2.3:
Sterilization around emergency period

S. No.	State/UT	Vasectomy Acceptors				Tubectomy Acceptors			IUD Acceptors				Sterilization		
		1976-77	1975-76	1974-75	1973-74 (Sterilizations)	1976-77	1975-76	1974-75	1976-77	1975-76	1974-75	1973-74	1973-75	1975-77	IVA
1	Arunachal Pradesh	272	0	0	11	48	0	0	2,627	0	0	12	11	320	2,909.09
2	Delhi	112,695	6,671	0	8,968	25,822	15,839	0	726	18,202	0	7,752	8,968	161,027	1,795.57
3	Himachal Pradesh	80,384	0	0	5,988	20,356	0	0	8,373	0	0	1,982	5,988	100,740	1,682.36
4	Bihar	568,361	113,191	22,492	29,782	118,623	52,346	9,902	21,557	30,739	13,866	17,407	62,176	852,521	1,371.14
5	West Bengal	731,079	112,180	16,530	27,545	151,512	94,244	39,887	27,686	22,859	13,639	7,472	83,962	1,089,015	1,297.03
6	Madhya Pradesh	904,809	47,264	0	44,545	97,372	64,899	42,965	21,724	41,814	35,866	37,268	87,510	1,114,344	1,273.39
7	Uttar Pradesh	690,041	54,010	22,583	28,583	148,030	74,719	28,139	160,237	165,312	107,203	80,018	79,305	966,800	1,219.09
8	Ministry of Railway	69,313	15,812	0	11,554	17,438	11,595	0	547,521	4,593	0	3,101	11,554	114,158	988.039
9	Rajasthan	323,484	53,285	20,676	25,970	41,276	32,972	17,395	11,812	22,764	16,705	16,152	64,041	451,017	704.263
10	Assam	205,423	128,403	32,066	20,822	20,738	19,142	7,321	12,153	16,978	5,457	2,765	60,209	373,706	620.681
11	Tripura	12,493	3,805	684	2,642	228	354	162	278	419	118	180	3,488	16,881	483.974

(Table 2.3 continued)

(Table 2.3 continued)

S. No.	State/UT	Vasectomy Acceptors				Tubectomy Acceptors			IUD Acceptors			Sterilization			
		1976–77	1975–76	1974–75	1973–74 (Sterilizations)	1976–77	1975–76	1974–75	1976–77	1975–76	1974–75	1973–74	1973–75	1975–77	IVA
12	Andaman Nicobar Islands	764	96	58	181	612	146	105	260,114	196	67	94	344	1618	470.349
13	Karnataka	225,776	20,997	4,335	66,967	204,293	99,674	57,355	30,392	27,581	13,671	10,942	128,657	550,740	428.068
14	Lakshadweep	143	59	23	33	4	0	0	222	15	0	3	56	206	367.857
15	Odisha	158,911	68,319	47,281	55,252	164,073	56,721	21,690	19,066	23,976	20,176	28,341	124,223	448,024	360.661
16	Haryana	186,154	35,012	44,103	17,063	36,584	22,930	18,009	85,683	56,652	46,880	21,460	79,175	280,680	354.506
17	Andhra Pradesh	571,662	36,873	22,665	142,778	188,613	128,290	108,894	14,264	17,762	13,271	30,042	274,337	925,438	337.336
18	Punjab	67,472	10,617	6,686	21,290	72,433	42,466	29,774	38,063	38,711	29,637	21,715	57,750	192,988	334.178
19	Tamil Nadu	380,208	178,662	13,0261	110,095	186,829	32,972	67,499	32,505	26,790	26,209	23,360	307,855	778,671	252.934
20	Gujarat	206,070	79,999	87,342	59,997	111,043	73,024	67,415	28,175	23,113	24,155	17,332	214,754	470,136	218.918
21	Maharashtra	518,781	0	91,279	192,050	343,699	0	146,881	15,195	0	13,774	11,467	430,210	862,480	200.479
22	Goa	1,161	270	276	2,042	4,410	2,516	1,931	10	1,047	330	258	4,249	8,357	196.682
23	Dadra & Nagar Haveli	628	202	206	257	68	39	27	11,421	6	0	9	490	937	191.224
24	Mizoram	49	40	28	193	630	865	628	4,956	409	219	104	849	1,584	186.572
25	Chandigarh	1,156	188	117	1,091	1,434	795	933	22	2,848	2,140	1,182	2,141	3,573	166.885

No.	State/Category												
26	Ministry of Defence	0	7,505	0	9,938	0	6,938	0	4,715	0	3,952	9,938	14,843	149.356
27	Meghalaya	0	1,011	302	758		1,076	628	863	510	493	1,688	2,087	123.637
28	Puducherry	0	2,144	1,143	1,152	0	2,544	1,641	1,394	771	712	3,936	4,688	119.106
29	Jammu & Kashmir		5,581	3,003	4,056	0	3,921	2,202	5,055	4,216	3,102	9,261	9,502	102.602
30	Kerala	0		18,466	50,389			43,685	28,302	22,221	21,703	112,540	0	0
31	Manipur	0	0	0	450	0	0	181		1,660	1,214	631	0	0
32	Above All	6,017,289	1,076,867	572,605	0	1,956,168	962,616	715,249	583,115	412,761	0	1,287,854	10,012,940	777.49
33	All India	1,076,867	572,605	349,190	942,402	962,616	715,249	451,290	412,761	308,150	371,594	1,742,882	3,327,337	190.91

Source: Family planning year book 1976–77, 1975–76, and 1974–75.

schools, involving all government departments plus voluntary youth and women's organizations in the program, linking the percentage of the central government's assistance to the states to their performance in family planning, conducting research in reproductive biology, making use of all media, and seeking people's participation in the program.

The 1977 policy made some notable departures from the government's previous approach to achieving the targets. While the earlier policy considered it impractical to wait for education and economic development to bring about lower fertility and sought a direct assault on population problems, the 1977 policy chose to achieve the same goal through a program of education and motivation. The 1976 policy allowed state governments, if they felt the necessity, to enact legislation for compulsory sterilization, while the 1977 policy was totally against the compulsory sterilization legislation of any kind. It stated, "Compulsion in the area of family welfare must be ruled out for all times to come. Our approach is educational and wholly voluntary."

Further, while the 1976 policy depended mainly on sterilization for achieving the target, the new policy (1977) emphasized on the methods of family planning with the belief that

> By and large the people of India are conscious of the importance of responsible parenthood; given the necessary information and adequate services they will accept a small family norm. We will promote all methods with equal emphasis and it will be left to every family to decide what method of contraception it will like to adopt.

The minimum age at marriage of 18 for girls and 21 for boys, recommended in the 1976 population policy, was enacted into a law by the new government in October 1978. However, the implementation of this law even after 15 years of its enactment remains weak and many marriages continue to take place for girls below the age of 18. Because of the lack of political will and support for the program, the lack of organizational efficiency and the rapid decline of morale and interest among family planning workers, the program slumped and less than one million sterilizations (one-eighth of the number performed in the previous year) were done in 1977–78; however, the expenditure incurred that year remained the same. During the provisional Sixth Plan period 1978–79 and 1979–80, program expenditure was ₹2,260.5 million; almost equal the amount spent in the previous two years, mostly on salaries. Nevertheless, the average annual performance in the three years 1977–80 was dismal despite heavy expenditures. The change of government in January 1980 marked another turning point in the program and helped to restore it, with the emphasis continuing on its voluntary nature.

The significant experiences with the family planning program during 1976–78 revealed that, in the democratic Indian setting, compulsion in family planning had to be ruled out. Unlike communist China, which could enforce a one-child family policy and motivate people to accept it without expressing options or alternatives in desired family size, in India the implementation of a compulsory two- or three-child norm had been very difficult, if not impossible. The defeat of the government in 1977 was partly attributable to the form of persuasion introduced in family planning in some states during 1976. The 1977 policy was welcomed as a type of liberation for the expression of individual attitudes and opinions on family size and freedom of choice of contraceptive methods to be used by couples.

From a retrospective analysis of developments during this period, it seems that India made a sacrifice in terms of delayed demographic transition, and possibly socioeconomic development, to safeguard its people's democratic rights. It is doubtful whether a compulsory family planning program can ever be implemented in India within the present political structure or that centrally specified demographic goals can be imposed on the states. The bad publicity led the new Janata party government to change the name of the program. Furthermore, every government since 1977 has stressed that family planning is an entirely voluntary program.

3

Post-Emergency Recovery of the Program (1977–95): Recoil and Recovery

The Sixth Five-Year Plan (1980–85)

As discussed in the previous chapter, the family planning program almost totally collapsed after the Emergency was lifted, and the ruling Congress party was routed out of power in the general elections in 1977, the forceful sterilization of many men, especially in the North Indian states, being the major factor in the defeat of the party. When the recovery took place, rather slowly, it was women of the country who came in numbers to accept sterilizations for controlling their family size. A working group on population policy was set up by the Planning Commission in 1979 to formulate long-term policy goals and program targets for the family welfare program. This group (of which the author was a member) recommended the adoption of a long-term demographic goal of reaching the net reproduction rate (NRR) of one by the year 1996 for the country as a whole, and by the year 2001 in all the states. The change in focus from CBR to NRR as the demographic goal and from a short-time to long-time targets arose out of a realization—from historical and more recent demographic experiences within India and outside—that low birth rates have never been achieved without substantial reductions in death rates, especially in infant mortality. As per the report of the working group, the fertility rates of a population are an integral part of the levels of development of the society and low fertility rates can be sustained only in the context of a certain level of development. There is practically no historical evidence of crude birth rates of below 20 per thousand sustained in a population which is economically and socially backward.

The working group felt that a stage had come in the demographic transition of India where its future fertility goals should be linked with some developmental variables, if these goals were to be realized and sustained.

One of the universally agreed goals of development is the reduction in the levels of mortality of the population, particularly infant mortality, leading to a higher expectation of life. Increased span of life is a universally accepted index of development. Fertility goals can be linked to mortality levels through the index of NRR. The expert committees on population projections have assumed a steady increase in the expectation of life of the population of India, from its present levels to about 64 years for both males and females by the year 2001. It appears that the nation should have a long-term demographic goal, specified in terms of NRR of unity. This level has to be reached if the population has eventually to attain a stationary condition.

> We feel that this NRR should be achieved in the minimum amount of time, not later than the turn of the century. The NRR of unity, or one, implies that for a given set of conditions of mortality and fertility, on an average, a woman will be replaced by just one daughter, and the two-child family will be the normal pattern in the society by the year 2001 (Planning Commission 1980: 16–17).

Under these conditions, it was calculated that by the turn of the century, India's CBR would be 21, crude death rate (CDR) 9, infant mortality rate (IMR) 60, life expectancy at birth 64 years, and that 60 percent of couples in the reproductive age would be effectively protected by contraception. Fixing long-term goals in terms of NRR of one has a number of advantages that are as follows:

1. An NRR of one has the inherent substantive validity of linking fertility decline to mortality decline—a necessity to reach stable low levels of fertility.
2. While systematic changes in NRR cause smooth changes in the age distribution of a population, constant reduction in CBR may cause uneven changes or jerks in its age structure.

3. Achieving an NRR of one and maintaining the same level would ultimately lead to zero population growth (ZPG), which may be the ultimate long-term demographic goal of every country.

4. The goal of an NRR of unity requires that organized programs for mortality reduction be undertaken as necessary adjuncts of fertility reduction programs.

5. An additional advantage of fixing long-term demographic goals of an NRR of one is that this macro-level concept is equivalent to the micro-level family size norm, the expected family size, or the average number of living daughters a couple has when they cross the reproductive period—an NRR of one essentially advocates a two-child family norm.

The time by which an NRR of one is to be achieved can be adjusted according to the plans and resources of a country, but it seems to be a significant intermediate goal to realize before achieving the ultimate goal of ZPG. Methods of estimating family planning targets to achieve a given trend of NRR values are illustrated for different states of India in the work of Srinivasan, Roy and Gogale (1980).

The experience with target setting in terms of CBRs to be achieved over five or ten years, as formulated in the earlier five-year plans, indicates that targets were never achieved and goals had to be revised time and again on the basis of actual performance (see Table 3.1).

Until 1980, fertility goals were not linked to mortality goals, and often efforts in fulfilling family planning targets were at the cost of

Table 3.1:
Governmental expenditure on family planning programs: India (1951–91)

		Expenditure in Rupees		
Five-Year Plan	*Period*	*Total (millions)*	*Per Capita*	*Per Sterilization Equivalent*
First	1951–56	1.45	0	NA
Second	1956–61	2,156	0Q5	NA
Third	1961–66	248.6	34	NA
Annual	1966–67	134.26	27	110.41
	1967–68	26,523	52	126.97
	1968–69	305.15	59	162.49
Fourth	1969–70	361.84	0.68	218.11

Five-Year Plan	Period	Expenditure in Rupees		
		Total (millions)	Per Capita	Per Sterilization Equivalent
	1970–71	489.04	0.9	306.03
	1971–72	61,756	1.11	248.91
	1972–73	797.48	141	236.43
	1973–74	578.46	1	469.15
Fifth	1974–75	620.48	1.05	378.8
	1975–76	806.14	133	262.75
	1976–77	1,729.82	2.79	199.68
	1977–78	93,337	1.48	751.51
Annual	1978–79	1,075.45	1.66	576.65
	1979–80	1,185.11	1.79	547.39
Sixth	1980–81	1,408.98	1.79	56,837
	1981–82	1,930.20	2.1	58,455
	1982–83	2,883.20	2.79	614.89
	1983–84	3,829.84	531	666.06
	1984–85	4,240.66	530	763.4
Seventh	1985–86	4,796.80	637	719.89
	1986–87	5,688.50	7.4	801.21
	1987–88	5,841.70	7.7	828.72
	1988–89	6,718.40	8.41	926.17
	1989–90	8,006.60	959	1,129.35
	1990–91	8,498.90	10.04	1,205.45

Source: Ministry of Health and Family Welfare, Department of Family Welfare (1992).
Note: NA = not available.

fulfilling the targets of the MCH program or other public health programs, since the same personnel were involved at the peripheral level as well. From the view of linking fertility and mortality goals and achieving a smooth transition in the age structure, as an intermediate step to reaching ZPG and for ease in popularizing a given family size, it seems advantageous to focus long-term fertility goals on an NRR of unity and planning programs of fertility and mortality reduction simultaneously.

In countries like India, where mortality is still relatively high (though declining), involving health personnel in the family planning program and evaluating their performance mainly on family planning acceptance targets is bound to slow down the progress on the public health front and eventually in the family planning program. Emphasizing the family planning program solely as a means of fertility reduction has some justification only in areas or countries where the life expectancy is high (probably over 60 years) and infant mortality is relatively low. For example, adopting a one-child family norm in China is partly validated on the grounds that China had by 1978 already realized substantial reductions in mortality, particularly infant mortality, so a couple could be assured a better chance of the child surviving to reach adulthood. Ensuring child survival seems to be a very important reason for a couple to adopt a limited family size norm of two or three children. Linking mortality to fertility goals, and specifying targets in terms of NRR, is a fundamental conceptual departure in the setting of demographic goals adopted in the Sixth Five-Year Plan.

A policy perspective emerges from an analysis of a changing age pattern of marital fertility recently observed in India as in many other developing countries. It has been observed that fertility declines since the 1970s (discussed in detail in subsequent chapters) are mainly because of declines in the marital fertility of women aged 30 and above. These declines suggest that in the earlier stages of program development, family planning methods have been used predominantly to limit family size rather than to space children. The data also reveal that marital fertility rates of women under age 30 had actually increased in the last two decades in a number of Indian states, indicating an increase in the natural fertility of younger couples and the absence of any increase in spacing children. The tendency among Indian couples thus far seems to be to have the desired number of children, following customs and traditions as far as possible, and then to stop childbearing permanently via sterilization. Sterilization perfects into this cultural framework, but it had its own negative effect.

For many years, public health specialists and family planning and medical personnel have advocated child spacing to promote the health of mothers and children, but the idea does not appear to have taken root, nor is it likely to in the near future without appropriate planning and program strategy. Even spacing methods, such as pill and IUD, seem to be used by married women essentially for limitation purposes. While cultural values and traditional norms seem to accommodate use of modern methods, especially sterilization, to limit family size, they do not seem to encourage or universally accommodate the use of spacing methods.

Surprisingly, the recent trends in family planning acceptance even in Western countries reveal that the proportion of eligible couples adopting permanent methods such as vasectomy or tubectomy has increased substantially in the past decade. These findings suggest that the emphasis placed thus far in India on sterilization has been consistent with global trends, and that the country should substantially increase and improve sterilization facilities, if possible, reversible sterilization procedures. Seemingly, the strategic deficiency is the lack of intensive and well-orchestrated information–education–communication programs on spacing methods and extending the availability of spacing methods with back-stopping facilities for induced abortion. Induced abortion seems to be gaining popularity among those who have used a nonpermanent method and failed. Also noteworthy is a global trend towards methods of contraception among women who may dictate family size and fertility levels in the future. Considering the aforementioned factors, the Sixth Plan document envisaged the long-term and short-term goals that are mentioned as follows.

Long-term Goals

1. Reducing the average family size from 4.2 children in 1979 to 2.3 by 2001.
2. Reducing the birth rate per thousand from 33 in 1978 to 21 by 2001.
3. Reducing the death rate per thousand from about 14 in 1978 to 9, and the IMR from 129 to 60 or less by 2001.
4. Protecting 60 percent of eligible couples by modern family planning methods by 2000 instead of about 22 percent in 1978.

Short-term Goals

If the above-mentioned long-term goals were to be achieved during the Sixth Five-Year Plan (1980–85), the estimated number of sterilizations would have been 22 million, the number of IUDs to be inserted would have been 22 million and the number of users of CCs (condoms, oral contraceptives and other conventional methods) would have increased annually to reach an estimated 11 million in the period of 1984–85.

Achieving these targets was expected to ensure an increase in the effective couple protection rate to 36.6 percent by 1985. In addition to these targets for the family planning program, there were specific targets for general and MCH services to ensure the reduction of general health and infant mortality and to work towards the desired long-term goals.

The program strategy adopted to reach the goals included the involvement of a large number of community health workers (CHWs; later redesignated village health guides [VHGs]) to promote people's participation. For each village or group of hamlets (covering a total population of 1,000), one CHW was selected based on his qualifications, interest in health and family planning activities in the village and leadership qualities. CHWs received three months of training and a kit of simple medicines and contraceptive devices (condoms and pills). They were supervised and guided by program personnel. CHWs were paid a nominal monthly honorarium and were considered community leaders, providing liaison between the official health workers and the community. This system, implemented in most of the Indian states, revealed that the active involvement of community leaders promoted the people's health and the practice of family planning. Unfortunately, not all the CHWs were interested in health and family planning, nor were many of them influential in their communities.

Evaluation of the Sixth Five-Year Plan, in terms of actual performance versus the targets, revealed that against a target of 24 million sterilizations, only about 17 million had been carried out; against a target of 7.9 million IUD insertions, about 7 million had been done; and against a target of 11 million CC users during 1984–85, only about 9.3 million had been enrolled in the program during the year. Program achievement in relation to targets had been quite high during this five-year plan.

The Seventh Five-Year Plan document (1985), reviewing critically the performance of the program during the Sixth Plan, came to the following conclusions:

1. Achievements fell short of the target, particularly in sterilization. IUD insertions and CC users reached a high level, around 80 percent and above.
2. The effective couple protection rate achieved by March 1985 was about 32 percent, an increase of 10 percentage points in 5 years, though still below the Sixth Plan target of 36.6 percent.
3. While, in the first two years of the Sixth Five-Year Plan, couple protection grew only by about 0.5 percent and 1 percent respectively,

couple protection accelerated to about 2.5 percent each year in the last three years of the plan.

Thus, there seems to have been a resurgence of the tempo of the program since 1980. The performance analysis by states reveals that national averages are substantially lower because of the relatively poor performance in Uttar Pradesh, Bihar and Rajasthan. These three northern states, which account for 31 percent of the Indian population, had in 1985 couple protection rates under 20 percent—Uttar Pradesh 16.7 percent, Bihar 16.8 percent and Rajasthan 19.3 percent—against the national average of 32 percent. Madhya Pradesh and West Bengal—the two other large northern states, together accounting for 16 percent of India's population— had couple protection rates of 29 percent. Special efforts for raising the couple protection rate appeared necessary in these five states.

During the Sixth Plan, an allocation of ₹10,780 million was made in the sector of family welfare; the actual expenditure was estimated at ₹14,480 million (or US$ 1,200 million at the exchange rate of 1 US$ = ₹12 in 1985). The Sixth Plan increased the per capita expenditure on the family planning to its highest since the implementation of the program as an official development policy.

The Seventh Five-Year Plan (1986–91)

The Seventh Five-Year Plan document, covering 1985 to 1990, endorsed the long-term demographic policy of reaching an NRR of one by the year 2000. However, in the context of the actual performance during the Sixth Plan, the cautious expectation was that this goal could be realized only during the years 2006–11. The goal of achieving the replacement level of fertility would be postponed by another 10 years. In terms of specific family planning goals, the following targets were stipulated to be realized by 1990:

1. An effective couple protection rate of 42 percent
2. CBR of 29.1
3. CDR of 10.4
4. IMR of 90 per 1,000 live births
5. Universal immunization of children
6. Antenatal care for 75 percent of all pregnant women

To reach these targets, particularly 42 percent couple protection, the Seventh Plan stipulated 31 million sterilizations, 21.25 million IUD insertions and 14.5 million users of CCs by the end of 1989–90. Special schemes for improving program efficiency and effectiveness in five states—Uttar Pradesh, Bihar, Rajasthan, Madhya Pradesh and West Bengal—were also formulated. The interesting and welcome fact is that most of the goals set for the Seventh Five-Year Plan, to be realized by 1990, seem to have been achieved (see Table 3.1).

To achieve the long-term demographic goals, launching the special educational programs through the mass media to enlighten people on the benefits of late marriages was proposed. Methods of social enforcement of the minimum age at marriage were also suggested.

Incentives for attracting younger couples with fewer than two children to accept spacing methods were also proposed. Intersectoral coordination and cooperation and the involvement of voluntary agencies in the program were implemented on a larger scale in the field of health and family welfare. Community participation was proposed to be achieved through nongovernmental organizations (NGOs), informal community leaders, satisfied acceptors, political leaders and other social workers.

Special programs to reduce infant mortality to 90 children per thousand births per year by 1990 were undertaken, and special schemes to reduce the incidence of childhood diseases (such as diarrhea, dysentery and respiratory diseases) were implemented. An expanded program of immunizing children and oral rehydration therapy for treating diarrheal diseases was launched, especially in the least developed states, with assistance from the UNICEF.

Some state legislatures passed unanimous resolutions supporting the family welfare program, and this political commitment enhanced its credibility and boosted the morale of those engaged in the family planning field. It has been proposed to have similar resolutions adopted in other state legislatures. The involvement of political leaders in the program, through the forum of the Indian Association of Parliamentarians for Problems of Population and Development, offers considerable political credibility and stable conditions in which the program can be intensified in future years.

During 1990–91, the cost per sterilization was ₹1,205, reflecting the trend of rapid increase in cost since 1976–77 when it was lowest at only ₹200 per sterilization. With the setback to the program in 1977–78, after the national emergency in 1976–77, the cost per service to the acceptor rose sharply, reflecting the fears of the program personnel to act overcautiously. While the numbers of personnel working for the program and expenditures on infrastructural facilities have steadily increased since 1975–76, the poor performance between 1977 and 1980 has raised per capita expenditure on sterilizations during these years to very high levels. The infrastructure and expenditure on personnel already deployed were definitely capable of yielding a far better performance, given a proper political climate, motivation from local leaders and commitment of personnel.

Per capita governmental expenditure on the family planning program in India was still under ₹6 (US 50 cents) in 1984–85 as compared to per capita expenditures of US 79 cents in Malaysia (1979), 69 cents in Singapore (1981) and 62 cents in Philippines (1980) and South Korea (1979) (Ross et al. 1988). However, in relation to its per capita income, India spends a larger amount from its budget on family planning than most of the developing countries.

The incentives paid to acceptors of various family planning methods, motivators, and medical and paramedical personnel involved in performing the sterilizations or IUD insertions have also increased over the years but not to the extent that they play a key role in motivating couples to adopt these methods. Incentive money was introduced in 1957 in Tamil Nadu and Maharashtra as compensation to vasectomy acceptors for loss of wages during the compulsory postoperative rest period. Even now, it is maintained that compensation for the lost wages is not really an incentive. In 1985, an acceptor of sterilization got a total cash benefit equal to US$ 12–16 and medicines—hardly a major inducement for sterilization (see Table 3.2).

The intensity of the efforts undertaken by a country on various aspects of its family planning program is a more direct and sensitive indicator of program inputs than just the budget or expenditures. Efforts in various components of the program include formulating population policies and ensuring political leaders' commitment to them; setting demographic goals and family planning targets; information–education–communication activities; training and developing skilled medical and paramedical personnel; delivering contraceptive services and service-related activities; easy availability and accessibility of services to eligible couples; and record-keeping and evaluation activities. These efforts have to be of sufficient quality and coverage for the program to have a significant impact on the acceptance and use of methods and a corresponding fertility decline.

Table 3.2:
Family planning incentives offered by the Central Government: India (1964–83)

| | Incentives for Sterilization Acceptors (in Rupees) | | | | | | Incentives for IUD Acceptors | |
| | Men | | | Women | | | | |
Effective Date	Lost Wages	Drugs, Meals, Transport	Other	Lost Wages	Drugs, Meals, Transport	Other	Lost Wages	Other
12/1/1964	10	10	0	10	10	0	5	NA
10/1/1966	30	10	SA	40	10	SA	11	NA
6/1/1972	35	10	SA	45	10	SA	15	NA
4/1/1974	20	15	0	25	45	0	6	2
4/1/1976								
Acceptors with								
2 children	100	20	30	100	40	10	6	20
3 children	50	20	30	50	40	10	6	NA
4+ children	25	20	25	25	40	5	6	NA
1977	70	20	10	70	40	10	6	2
2/1/1983	100	40	30	100	70	30	9	25

Source: Ministry of Health of Family Welfare, Department of Family Welfare (1991).
Note: NA = not available; SA = small amount, varying slightly from state to state.

In a major attempt at an international evaluation of family planning programs, Lapham and Mauldin (1985) developed a 30-item list of specific program-related activities under four major components that are as follows:

- Policy and stage-setting activities (8 items).
- Service and service-related activities (13 items).
- Record-keeping and evaluation (3 items).
- Availability and accessibility of contraceptives (6 items).

They ranked every country's efforts on a scale of 0–4—from very little or no activity to maximum effort or activity on each item—based on responses to a questionnaire about the program. The respondents were about 400 informed judges selected from program administrators, population specialists and/or researchers in different countries in 1983–84. Based on the data collected, Lapham and Mauldin made detailed analyses of the influence of program efforts on the use of contraceptive method in different socioeconomic settings for 79 developing countries. For the 30 items, the maximum score possible for any country is 120 and the minimum is zero. The study was repeated by Ross and Mauldin in the same countries in 1989 and the change in the program effort scores in various components computed (Ross et al. 1992). We can presume that countries with a higher score on all the 30 items have a higher level of program effort than countries with lower scores.

Table 3.3 contains the data extracted from the work of Lapham and Mauldin, providing the scores for 1982, and Ross and Mauldin for 1989 on the program effort scores for the 12 largest developing countries of the world with populations of 50 million or more. The scores are given as percentages of the maximum possible score in each component or of the total. India's 1982 score ranked it fourth (after China, Indonesia and Mexico). In 1989, India improved its overall program effort score somewhat, but so did the other countries; therefore, India tied with Bangladesh for the fourth position, below the same three countries. Thus, program efforts have not shown much improvement in India as compared to other large countries.

Judging the scores of the countries in the four broad areas of program activity, while India fared relatively well in policy and stage setting (ranking second in both years) and service and service-related activities (third in 1982 but seventh in 1989), in the other areas the scores were somewhat poorer for India which ranked fourth (1982) and sixth (1989).

Table 3.3:

Program effort scores on family planning program components and contraceptive prevalence rate for 1990: Twelve large nations (1982 and 1989)

| Country | Total Score | | Program Effort Component Scores | | | | | | | | Contraception Prevalence Rate |
| | | | Policy & Stage Setting | | Service & Service-related | | Record Keeping & Evaluation | | Availability & Accessibility | | |
	1982	1989	1982	1989	1982	1989	1982	1989	1982	1989	1990
Maximum Possible Score	120	120	32	32	52	52	12	12	24	24	24
China	84	87	97	95	78	80	57	67	96	100	75
India	66	72	81	81	62	63	60	58	58	87	45
Indonesia	75	80	77	81	78	83	93	83	57	69	52
Brazil	43	32	36	41	36	20	67	0	53	61	69
Bangladesh	57	72	58	73	55	73	43	56	68	78	33
Nigeria	13	43	18	50	11	46	11	42	10	28	7
Pakistan	40	48	59	58	28	49	53	54	37	28	15
Mexico	66	77	71	71	60	73	65	82	75	93	58
Philippines	56	49	57	51	52	48	47	39	67	57	49
Thailand	61	80	52	69	53	79	72	89	84	94	74
Turkey	29	46	60	40	16	43	29	48	17	58	66
Egypt	40	66	50	71	38	65	25	67	36	60	41

Source: Ross et al. (1992).

Note: Scores for each country are percentages of maximum score possible in each component or total.

In availability and accessibility of services, India improved from 1982 to 1989. However, the level of contraceptive use in India—percentage of currently married women in the reproductive ages (15–44) using any method of artificial or natural contraception—was far lower in comparison to program efforts, estimated at 32.4 in 1982 and 45 in 1990, placing India eighth among the 12 large developing countries in both years. Only Egypt, Bangladesh, Pakistan and Nigeria recorded contraceptive prevalence rates below India's. Despite substantial efforts in every aspect of the family planning program in India, the impact achieved in increased contraceptive prevalence levels is not commensurate with its efforts. The impact appears to be significantly lower than expected as compared to other large developing countries.

The Eighth Five-Year Plan (1992–97)

This eighth plan should have logically covered the period 1990–95 as a follow-up of the Seventh Plan (1985–90). However, because of frequent changes in the central government in 1990 and 1991, its formulation was postponed and only annual plans were implemented during 1990–91 and 1991–92. The Eighth Five-Year Plan document was approved in July 1992 to cover the period 1992–97.

   The Eighth Plan marked a new turn in the era of planned development in India that had commenced with the First Five-Year Plan in 1951. The collapse of the Soviet Union and many centrally planned economies of Eastern Europe gave a new thrust to the democratic form of governance and the operation of the market forces as the more efficient form of economic development. India had to take account of these global changes in its planning process. To quote the Prime Minister who wrote the Foreword to the Plan Document:

> The Eighth Plan is being launched at a tune of momentous changes in the world and in India. The international political and economic order is being restructured every day, and as the 20th century draws to a close, many of its distinguishing philosophies and features have also been swept away. In this turbulent world, our policies must also deal with changing realities. Our basic policies have stood us in very good stead, and now provide us an opportunity to respond with flexibility to the new situation, so that we can work uninterruptedly towards our basic aim of providing a rich and

just life for our people, Human Development, in all its many facets, is the
ultimate goal of the Eighth Plan. (Government of India 1992)

It is a plan for managing the change, for managing the transition from a
centrally planned economy to a market-led economy without tearing the
socioeconomic fabric of the country. From a highly centralized planning system, a move has been made toward "indicative planning" wherein
efforts will be made to remove the bottlenecks in the growth of the
economy, with a clear prioritization of the goals. The state will be a facil-
itator in economic development but a main actor in the areas of poverty
alleviation, education, public health, human welfare and population
stabilization. Planning is still considered essential for creating a social
infrastructure to care for the poor and reduce regional disparities. While
the role of the public sector is sought to be reduced considerably, as
seen from the plan allocations, it will continue to play a leading role in
providing infrastructural facilities.

Keeping in view the above philosophy, six priority objectives for
the plan have been defined. The second objective is "containment of
population growth through active people's cooperation and an effective
scheme of incentives and disincentives" (Plan Document 9 of Eighth
Five Year Plan, 1992–97).

The country is committed to social and economic justice to the
millions of people living under conditions of poverty and deprivation.
Failure to do so within a reasonable period may generate social tensions
and unrest. Besides, the environmental degradation, which is associated
with unchecked growth of population, carries the inherent risk of natural
calamities and disasters. In this context, population control assumes an
overriding importance in the Eighth Plan (Plan Document 9 of Eighth
Five Year Plan, 1992–97: 331).

The Plan document has identified eight major constraints that
have inhibited the success of the family planning and fertility regulation
program in the earlier years in the country, and it seeks to remove them
as far as possible during the plan period. They are as follows:

1. Regulation of fertility in the population was perceived in the past as
   the main responsibility of the Department of Family Welfare of the
   Ministry of Health and Family Welfare in the central government,
   but experience has shown that this is a joint collective responsibility
   of all the departments of the government at all levels, NGOs and
   the society at large. The Eighth Plan seeks to remedy the situation

partly by developing an NPP, to be enunciated and adopted by parliament, in which the entire governmental machinery—at the center and in the states—and the society as a whole will be participating. "Given the political commitment at all levels, it must generate a cascading effect to become a people's movement" (Plan Document 9 of Eighth Five-Year Plan, 1992–97: 335).

2. Within the government, the program has not only remained with the Department of Family Welfare in the Ministry of Health and Family Welfare but has also suffered on account of centralized planning and target setting from the top. The major change in strategy through which this is sought to be remedied is decentralized planning and implementation of the program. Panchayati Raj and Nagar Palika systems, to be introduced in the country as a whole by the Constitution (72nd Amendment Bill of 1991), had planned to set in motion the process of democratic decentralization by providing more powers and resources to the elected representatives at the village, town, block, and district levels. In this context, these institutions will have to play a more important role in many aspects of development of their areas, including population control and family planning programs. The task of specification of targets of family planning acceptance and fertility and administering the programs will fall in the lap of these local governments. The roles of the central and state governments would be limited to general policy planning and coordination, providing technological and financial inputs where required, safeguarding critical areas and taking innovative leads. Decentralized planning and strategy formulation will become the hallmark of the Indian family planning program in the coming years, if the above scheme is implemented.

3. The quality of the contraceptive and the maternal and child health services offered in the program has been below standard in many parts of the country. The Eighth Plan sought to improve the situation by additional investments in the training of personnel; provision of additional facilities at the subcenter, PHC and the community health center levels; complete the infrastructural facilities initiated in the earlier plans; and expand the implementation of the globally accepted "Child Survival and Safe Motherhood" (CSSM) programs to cover the whole country.

From the beginning, the Indian government has sought to promote the program by giving incentives in cash and kind to acceptors of family planning methods, particularly for sterilization to motivators, medical and paramedical personnel and to the state governments for good performance in exceeding the targets set by the central government. The role that this incentive scheme has played in promoting acceptance among eligible couples and bringing above reduction in fertility has been questioned in the Eighth Plan. Studies have shown that acceptors who turn in for the sake of incentive money may not belong to the most fertile group, and the incentive scheme tends to erode at the quality of service statistics. The Eighth Plan sought to restructure the entire package of incentives and awards to make it more purposeful. It had been planned to promote community incentives in the form of priority consideration for rural development schemes for those rural areas that take a lead in population stabilization efforts.

Introducing Major Changes in the Indian Economy and Society: 1990–95

There were three major developments within and outside the country that marked the post-1994 period with regard to their influence on population policies and family planning programs in India. They were democratic decentralization within the country, economic liberalization and globalization and the rise of international women's groups expressing their strong voice on family planning in the ICPD held in Cairo in 1994. These are briefly discussed below from the point of view of their relevance to family planning.

Political and Economic Contextual Changes in India

A major change in the political scenario of the country was introduced in 1992 with the 72nd and 73rd Constitutional Amendments and enactments of Panchayat Raj and Nagar Palika Acts setting in motion the process of democratic decentralization. These acts ushered in a three-tier system of political governance in the country—central government, state government and the Panchayats in the rural areas and the Nagar Palikas in the urban areas up to the district level—by which, constitutionally, the powers, responsibilities and resources are to be shared by these three-tiers of elected bodies. The primary health care including family planning, primary education and provision of certain basic amenities such as drinking water and roads became the responsibility of the Panchayats. Another noticeable feature of this Act is the reservation of one-third of the seats in Panchayats for women members. Thus, at the grassroots level, the women are politically empowered by this act on all decision-making issues pertaining to social development, including family planning. This is a great leap forward for the Indian democracy and empowerment of women. The process of this demographic decentralization is still going on with varying speed and intensity in different states. Generally, the states are reluctant to share their powers and resources with the elected bodies of the Panchayats. Although such a reservation is sought to be made at the state and central levels, this would not been possible owing to strong objections from many political parties in the national parliament. Family planning and primary health care are, legally, as of now in the domain of the Panchayats and Nagar Palikas; however, funding for the same has to come from the state and the central governments. Family planning is still considered a matter in the concurrent list between the center and the state. This democratic decentralization has further infringed on the powers of state government to impose any strong family planning program through its PHCs and subcenters.

The second major change that took place in the late 1980s and pursued vigorously in the 1990s was the economic liberalization policies of the government and the slow but steady linking of the Indian economy with the global economy. Since independence, India followed the "socialistic pattern of society" with the economic modeling of the Soviet Union as the guideline with their seven-year plans modified to Indian five-year plans and developing a "command and control" economy. With the collapse of the Soviet Union in the late 1980s, India was almost lost without a model to follow and serious balance of payments arose from repayment of loans and interests thereon to World Bank, International Monetary Fund (IMF) and other donor agencies. The situation left the country with no choice but to open its doors for the foreign investors and shift to market economy. The "license raj" ended once and for all.

The launch of National Family Health Survey-1 (NFHS-1) in 1991–92, for which preparations were started in 1989, was symbolic of opening up of the Indian economy. Until 1988, data from the censuses and large-scale surveys in the country were not supposed to leave the country, and taking original data even on placid demographic variables out of the country was considered a crime. Now data from a number of large-scale surveys, such as the NFHS and Reproductive and Child Health (RCH) series, in the country are in the public domain through websites accessible to everyone and anyone in the world. This liberalization of the Indian economy and the society has also had its impact on population policies and programs in the country.

International Women's Movements and their Views on Family Planning

Another noticeable development, beginning in the early 1990s, was the organized intensification and expansion of the women's movements within and outside the country, questioning the policies and directions of the government with regard to the role of governments on their reproductive rights and organized national family planning programs in which women had to shoulder major responsibilities for fertility regulation and demographic transition. Setting up fertility goals and related family planning targets by the governments was considered as an infringement on human rights, women's rights and especially on their reproductive rights. All family planning programs, they argue, have been ultimately targeting women through propagation of female methods of family planning, in the context of a target-oriented and incentive-based system. The preponderance of female sterilizations as the dominant method of family planning in the country, it was argued, was because of the pressure brought on women by the officials in the health department who were keen to fulfill their quotas of family planning. This became tantamount to an infringement on their fundamental rights. Thus, family planning program landed itself in a quagmire where it could neither achieve its demographic goals of low fertility and population stabilization—through birth rate goals converted into family planning targets and pursuing these targets—nor withdraw from such a program in the context of a continuing rise in the yearly additions to its population.

4

Post-ICPD Phase (1996—2015): Ineffective Integration of Programs

International Conference on Population and Development at Cairo, 1994

The International Conference on Population and Development (ICPD), organized by the United Nations in Cairo in 1994, in its deliberations, by and large, was dominated by women's groups. The Program of Action (PoA) formulated at the end of the Conference, and for which India was a signatory, postulated that population policies should be viewed as an integral part of programs for women's development, women's rights, women's reproductive health, poverty alleviation and sustainable development. Women's concern dominated the discussions at the Cairo conference, which felt that population policies that are based on macro-demographic considerations and acceptor target-driven programs are unnecessarily and unevenly burdening women with the task of regulating reproduction to suit macro-level policies. They argued that, henceforth, population policies should not be viewed with the sole concern of reductions in fertility rates considered desirable by planners and demographers but by considerations of reproductive health, reproductive rights and gender equity. It was argued that developmental programs, which are not engendered, are not only sustainable but also endangered. The PoA adopted by ICPD recommends a set of qualitative and quantitative development goals: sustained economic growth in the context of sustainable development; education, especially for girls; gender equity, equality and empowerment of women; infant, child and maternal mortality reduction; and the provision of universal access to reproductive health services, including family planning and sexual health.

From many angles, the mid-1990s marked a major shift in the policies and programs of the government with economic growth agenda dominating the social welfare and equity agenda that prevailed till that time. Consequently, economic disparities widened, health of the people at large did not improve as expected, and the impact of public health programs was far lesser than anticipated and contraceptive use and fertility declines slowed down. Just as the year 1921 is considered the demographic divide, 1994 can be considered the family planning program divide, globally as well as in India.

Post-Cairo Policies: RCH Approach since 1995 and Second Slowdown of the Family Planning Program

The Government of India, one of the signatories of ICPD PoA, promptly followed up on the recommendations by abolishing the acceptor-based family planning targets in the country as a whole in April 1995. It had already experimented with the "target-free" approach in a few selected districts in the previous year, but the effectiveness of the approach was not properly assessed. Since 1997, officially, the reproductive health approach has been adopted as the national policy of the Government of India. The official RCH programs include the conventional MCH services including immunization of children and contraceptive services to couples; treatment of reproductive tract infections (RTIs) and sexually transmitted diseases (STDs); provision of reproductive health education and services for adolescent boys and girls; and screening of women near menopausal age for cervical and uterine cancer and treatment where required. Family Planning became "embedded" in a cocktail of other programs, totaling almost 13. It was called an integrated and decentralized approach to family planning. The budget required for these additional services intended to be covered under reproductive health were quite high, but only marginally higher amount was allocated. Although it was known that the emphasis on contraceptive services would be diluted when budgets are not adequately increased to cover the wider goals of RCH programs, but this was done. Population concerns go beyond reproductive health even though the latter is an important contributing factor for population stabilization.

Current Policies

At present, as of 2016, three policies seem to be in operation in the country that have a direct impact on population issues and availability of family planning services. These are the NPP 2000, the National Health Policy (NHP 2002) and the National Rural Health Mission (NRHM 2005). A comparative summary of the objectives, goals, strategies and inputs into the program are given in Appendix C and D. We will discuss them briefly.

National Population Policy 2000 (NPP 2000) and National Health Policy 2002 (NHP 2002)

NPP 2000 and NHP 2002 came up one after the other within a gap of two years. NPP 2000 was announced with a lot of fanfare in February 2000 after almost six years of preparation and discussion of drafts by various committees, starting with the M. S. Swaminathan Committee on population policy. Innumerable discussions were held on the appropriate population policy by various committees set up by the Planning Commission (of which the author happened to be a member of one committee) for a revised population policy for the country. The final policy document approved by a group of ministers and Planning Commission was launched in February 2000 by Sri A. R. Nanda (the then Secretary, Department of Family Welfare), approved by the newly set up National Commission on Population under the Chairmanship of the prime minister in its first meeting held in July 2000 and, later, by the Parliament in 2001. Parliamentary approval became mandatory since the policy recommended a continuation of a constitutional amendment made in 1976 that froze the seats in parliament and state legislative assemblies on the basis of 1971 census until 2001. In 2001, based on the recommendations of NPP 2000, the parliament extended this constitutional freeze of seats until 2021.

Compared to NPP 2000, NHP 2002 received much less fanfare and popular or professional discussions. Since independence, the population policies formulated from time to time, beginning with the policy in 1976, have aroused a high level of political interest and popular discussions compared to other policies, even health and development policies. This may be because of the long held mistaken view that population problem is the mother of all the problems in the country and once we clinch this problem, in the sense that the population growth rate is arrested and brought down close to zero, all other problems will automatically be solved or become amenable to easy resolution. No other country in the world, including China, had so many population policies as India. China had only one policy, the one-child policy, and just went ahead and implemented it.

NPP 2000 and NHP 2002 typify the impact or goal obsessed approach to policy rather than the inputs-, processes- and outcome-oriented approach to policy. Knowing full well that certain goals are impossible to realize, they are still being stated in the policy documents under the assumption that the goal in itself is half of the achievement of the goal. NPP 2000 has laid down 3 objectives—immediate, medium and long term—and 14 quantitative goals, called the national sociodemographic goals to be achieved by the year 2010. Most of the stated goals were known to be impossible to achieve, but the policymakers went ahead and put them in the document. For example, the goal for IMR stipulated in all the three policies was IMR of 30 by 2010 in NPP 2000 and NHP 2002 and the same by 2012 in NRHM 2005 as well, but it was not achieved by 2012. Constant shifting the goal posts seem to be an unending posture in the government programs.

National Rural Health Mission 2005/National Health Mission

NRHM 2005 launched by the then Hon'ble Prime Minister, Dr Manmohan Singh, is considered a flagship program in the country and is indeed a departure from the earlier policy and plan documents in two aspects. First, it takes the program in a "mission mode," probably encouraged by the success of the earlier missions such as the Technology Mission. Second, and more importantly, it is not obsessed by the desired goals of impact, rather it focuses on inputs, strategies and programs to be done and leaves the ultimate impact as an outcome of what is done. This is a more realistic approach for the improvement of the health of the people. The "preamble" to the "Mission Document" states that

> [r]ecognizing the importance of health in the process of economic and social development and improving the quality of life of our citizens, the Government of India has resolved to launch the National Rural Health Mission to carry out necessary architectural correction in the basic health care delivery system.

The Mission adopted a synergistic approach by relating health to determinants of good health, that is, segments of nutrition, sanitation, hygiene and safe drinking water. It also aimed at mainstreaming the Indian systems of medicine to facilitate health care. The plan of action included increasing public expenditure on health, reducing regional imbalance in health infrastructure, pooling resources, integration of organizational structures, optimization of health manpower, decentralization and district-level management of health programs, community participation and ownership of assets, induction of management and financial personnel into district health system, and operationalizing community health centers into functional hospitals meeting Indian Public Health Standards in each block of the country. The goal of the Mission is "to improve the availability of and access to quality health care by people, especially for those residing in rural areas, the poor, women and children." Appendix C and D state the objective and goals, respectively, of NPP 2000, NHP 2002 and NRHM 2005. After the first review of NRHM in 2009, it was designated as National Health Mission (NHM).

In 2013, in urban areas, an urban health mission was started in which the earlier programs under the Nehru Urban Health Mission, 2013 (NUHM) were integrated with NRHM stated in 2005 and called NHM. Additional funds were allotted. The endeavor would be ensuring achievement of the indicators mentioned below. Specific goals for the states would be based on the existing levels, capacity and context. State specific innovations would be encouraged. Process and outcome indicators would be developed to reflect equity, quality, efficiency and responsiveness. Targets for communicable and noncommunicable disease will be set at state level, considering local epidemiological patterns and the financing available for each of these conditions. The specific goals of NUHM for the urban areas with special focus on urban slums are as follows:

1. Reducing maternal mortality ratio (MMR) to 1 per 1,000 live births.
2. Reducing IMR to 25 per 1,000 live births.
3. Reducing total fertility rate (TFR) to 2.1.
4. Preventing and reducing anemia in women in the age group of 15–49 years.
5. Preventing and reducing mortality and morbidity from communicable and noncommunicable diseases, injuries and other emerging diseases.

6. Reducing household out-of-pocket expenditure on total health care expenditure.
7. Reducing annual incidence and mortality from tuberculosis by half.
8. Reducing prevalence of leprosy to less than 1 per 10,000 population and incidence to zero in all districts.
9. Annual malaria incidence to be less than 1 per 1,000.
10. Less than 1 percent microfilaria prevalence in all districts.
11. Eliminating kala-azar by 2015, less than 1 case per 10,000 population in all blocks.

With regard to inputs into the program, the emphasis of NHRM and NUHM, now jointly called NHM, is different from that of NPP 2000 and NHP 2002. Unlike the latter two documents that talk about percentage of GDP or percent of total government budget to be spent on public health, NHM talks about actual money to be spent, which was ₹65 billion in rural areas during 2005–06 and to be raised by about 30 percent, every subsequent year, of the sum spent in the earlier year. Similar increases are also made available to the urban health programs. Similarly, under inputs, it talks of committees to be formed at each level—village, district and state and national levels—and the activities, including training and monitoring programs, to be initiated. There would be a community liaison person (1 per 1,000 people) in every village called ASHA, an acronym for Accredited Social Health Activist, similar to the Anganwadi worker (AWW) but functioning under the control and guidance of the health department. An ASHA is usually selected from the young, ever-married women of the village with at least middle school education and interested in the community. They are provided with needed training in primary health care services, focusing on maternal and childcare, paid a monthly honorarium and monetary incentives for taking care of the pregnant women and arranging for and caring during institutional delivery. The success of the scheme is yet to be tested.

It is refreshing to note that NHM was more pragmatic in its approach and emphasizing more on inputs and strategies. The policy envisages a key role for the central government in designing national health programs with the active participation of state governments. Also, the Policy ensures the provisioning of financial resources, in addition to technical support, monitoring and evaluation at the national level by the Center. However, to optimize the utilization of the public health infrastructure at the primary level, a gradual convergence of all health programs under a single field administration is envisaged. Vertical programs for the control of major diseases like tuberculosis, malaria, HIV/AIDS, also RCH and universal immunization programs, would need to be continued until moderate levels of prevalence are reached. NRHM envisages that while the program implementation is effected through autonomous bodies at state and district levels, the interventions of state health departments may be limited to the overall monitoring of the achievement of program targets and other technical aspects. The setting up of an independent Health Trust of India, which will be financing NRHM, will give greater flexibility to the whole scheme. The relative distancing of program implementation at district level from state health departments will give the district team a greater operational flexibility. Moreover, the presence of state government officials, social activists, private health professionals and Members of Legislative Assembly (MLAs)/Members of Parliament (MPs) on the management boards of the autonomous bodies will facilitate well-informed decision-making. For the financial year 2015—16, the Government of India allocated a sum of ₹333 billion to the Ministry of Health and Family Welfare out of which, a sum of ₹188 billion was for NHM, about ₹168 billion for NRHM and the remaining ₹20 billion for the NUHM.

India's Commitment to FP 2020

A summit of leaders, family planning programmers and administrators from about 70 countries was held in London in July 2012 under the sponsorship of leading corporate donor agencies, such as Bill and Melinda Gates Foundation and UK Aid, and supported by the UNFPA and USAID, mainly to address the immediate but unmet need for contraception to space and limit births in these countries and to prepare a timeframe—possibly before 2020—to meet this need. Out of a global need for contraceptive services of 120 million couples, it was estimated that India had an unmet need of 48 million. Estimated date suggests that more than one-third of global need for contraception is in India. The officials of the department of family planning in the Ministry of Health and Family Welfare attended this meeting, presenting a road map of fulfilling this need by the year 2020. This program is called FP 2020 program. It suggests,

> India also pledged to commit over 2 billion USD to provide family planning services to 48 million additional women while sustaining the current coverage of over 100 million users till 2020. For achieving the above goals, it has been envisaged not only to strengthen the existing strategies

but also nurture innovations in the arena of family planning as well as other related sectors, for example, working to reduce teenage marriages and teenage births, increasing literacy of the girl child, addressing other socio cultural barriers etc. For this, India has established a national FP2020 structure with a 'National Steering Committee' and an 'India FP 2020 Country Coordination Committee'.

Achieving the goal of 48 million additional women would mean having a contraceptive prevalence rate of 63.7% necessitating contributions from all states of India. The projections charted out in the FP2020 country document reveals that the "share of the much preferred female sterilization will decrease substantially and that of spacing methods will increase significantly. The current focus on post-partum family planning (PPFP) and introduction of a new method in PPIUCD as well as a new device in Cu IUCD 375 will assist in accelerating India's march towards achieving the FP2020 goals.

The government has drawn out comprehensive national and state road-maps and also district action plans in EAG states adopting a decentralized planning approach focusing on operationalisation of facilities and delivery of services. (Government of India 2014)

The RCH program, now renamed as Reproductive, Maternal, Newborn, Child and Adolescent Health (RMNCH+A),

has provided a platform for addressing the reproductive rights while integrating the current FP services with maternal, child as well as adolescent health. Further impetus to Family Planning services would thus require more community based approach, demand generation together with provision of quality services.

[As such,] the current FP interventions include [a variety of services]: PPFP, Fixed day strategy, male participation, and community based schemes through ASHAs viz. home delivery of contraceptives, ensuring spacing at birth, pregnancy testing kits, family planning counsellors, compensation scheme, family planning indemnity scheme, public private partnership etc.

Under 'Vision FP2020' India has prepared a roadmap to accelerate the efforts in family planning program and enhance the budget allocation for the same. This is evident as huge money is being pooled by the Central government under NRHM. Since the advent of NRHM, total federal funding has been INR 1.3 lakh crore (17.32 billion USD) with annual funding of INR 16,800 crore (2.8 billion USD). The share of RMNCH+A activities is INR 94,320 crore (15.72 billion USD). The funding is projected to increase by INR 22,200 crore (3.7 billion USD) annually, incrementing over the next few years. This means from the advent of NRHM till 2020, the federal funding will amount to INR 2.04 lakh crore (34 billion USD) (including RMNCH+A).

The total Family Planning budget amounted to INR 1864.7 crore (282.5 million USD) in 2013–14, including INR 440 crore (73.3 million USD) for commodities and supplies. By the year 2020, the projected funding for Family planning will increase to INR 3003.2 crore (500 million USD). This indicates that from 2012 to 2020, the total allocation for family planning will amount to over INR 17,812 crore (3 billion USD). (Government of India 2014)

Thus FP 2020 has become a hotchpotch of a variety of programs integrated under one scheme and mostly driven strategically by some donor agencies. Our national agenda on family planning has largely been driven by the international agencies and donor agencies.

Convergence of all programs since 2005, at the field level, has not taken place as expected. Like "decentralization" and "integration," convergence is also a desired concept, but not implementable in the field, since these concepts are interpreted differently by different levels of workers. These confusions have adversely affected the impact of various programs, as we will see in the following section.

Impact of Post-1994 Policies on Reproductive and Child Health

Post 1995, the buzz words were "integration and decentralization." Both at the national and international levels such integration did not prove effective as we will see shortly in a review of reproductive, child health and family planning programs before and after integration. This did not work, as we will see shortly, in the case of RCH and family planning. The program of family planning or contraceptive education and services, post 1995, got a low priority because it was integrated with 13 other programs such as education of adolescent boys and girls, immunization services for children etc. The program was also decentralized to the Panchayat and Nagar Palika levels since, according to the 72nd and 73rd Constitutional Amendments, provision of basic health care, including contraceptive services, is the responsibility of the local institutions, but the entire funding was from the central and state governments. The Panchayat head also had a say in the program implementation through the involvement in the recruitment and supervision of the field workers—ASHA and AWW. There was a slowdown not only in the acceptance and use of family planning methods but also in the use of maternal and other RCH services in the post-RCH period. Let us examine it first by studying the state level trends in the percentage of couples effectively protected (CEP) by contraception, TFR and IMR, using official data from the family planning service statistics and sample registration system (SRS).

Tables 4.1a and 4.1b present data on CEP rate, TFR and IMR for the years between 1980 and 2014 for All India, two less developed state (Bihar and Uttar Pradesh) and two more developed states (Kerala and Tamil Nadu). The data was compiled from the official data sources, Family Planning Service statistics published by the Ministry of Health and Family Welfare, NFHS, AHS (Annual Health Surveys) and SRS of the Registrar General of India. The time trends in CEP, TFR and IMR values are depicted as line graphs in Figures 4.1, 4.2 and 4.3.

Conclusions drawn from the tables and the related graphs are discussed in the following sections.

Contraceptive Use

Quality of Data on Contraceptive Use

In India, until 2011, data on contraceptive use in populations at the state and national level for every year was calculated by acquiring service statistics, compiled by the Ministry of Health and Family Welfare from various state family planning departments, on the number of new acceptors of different family planning methods, and then converting this data to use under certain assumptions of continuation rates of different methods and age distribution of acceptors (Srinivasan 1995). This method which has been in vogue since the early 1960s for many decades has been called off, and the present data on contraceptive use or prevalence rates are compiled from national level surveys commencing from the NFHS-1, conducted in 1991–92. Various subsequent national level surveys, NFHS-2 (conducted in 1998–99), NFHS-3 (2005–06) and NFHS-4 (2014–15), various surveys conducted under the District Level Household Surveys (DLHS)—1, 2, 3 and 4—and the Annual Health Surveys carried out by the Registrar General of India have all been of varying data quality and added confusion to the actual levels of prevalence of contraceptive use in the country. For example, data from Table 4.1a and 4.1b—data on contraceptive prevalence rates (CPRs) for any modern methods of family planning over the years—do not have continuity with the pre-2011 prevalence data computed from the service statistics nor is it consistent with the trends in fertility values. For India as a whole, CPR estimated from the service statistics for 1992–93 was 43.6 compared to 36.5 from NFHS-1; for 1998–99, it was 45 compared to 42.8 in NFHS-2; and for 2005–06, it was 46 compared to 48.5 in NFHS-3. For some of the states, the

Table 4.1a:
Percent of couples effectively protected (CEP) by all methods, TFR and IMR, 1980–2013: India and selected states

Year	All India			Bihar			Kerala			Tamil Nadu			Uttar Pradesh		
	CEP	TFR	IMR	CEP	TFR	IMR	CEP	TFR	IMR	CEP	TFR	IMR	CEP	TFR	IMR
1980	22.3	4.4	114	12.4	5.7	118	28.9	3	40	28.2	3.4	93	11.5	5.9	159
1985	32.1	4.3	97	17.2	5.4	106	38.1	2.4	31	36.1	2.8	81	17.1	5.6	142
1986	34.9	4.2	96	18.9	5.2	101	41.1	2.3	27	41.1	2.7	80	20.6	5.4	132
1987	37.5	4.1	95	20.6	5.3	101	44.6	2.2	28	46.3	2.6	76	25	5.5	127
1988	39.9	4	94	22.9	5.4	97	46.4	2	28	52.6	2.5	74	28.8	5.4	124
1989	41.9	3.9	91	25.8	5.1	91	49.7	2	21	55	2.5	68	32.2	5.2	118
1990	43.3	3.8	80	26.3	4.8	75	54.4	1.9	17	57.1	2.3	59	33.3	5.2	99
1991	44.1	3.6	80	26	4.4	69	55.6	1.8	16	57.3	2.2	57	35.5	5.1	97
1992	43.6	3.6	79	24.7	4.6	73	55.7	1.7	17	57.3	2.2	58	33.7	5.2	98
1993	43.5	3.5	74	24	4.6	70	53.4	1.7	13	54.5	2.1	56	33.2	5.2	94
1994	45.4	3.5	74	24.1	4.6	67	51.5	1.7	16	54.9	2.1	59	36.5	5.1	88
1995	45.8	3.5	74	22.4	4.5	73	50.7	1.8	15	54.8	2.2	54	37.1	5	86
1996	46.5	3.4	72	23.1	4.5	71	48.8	1.8	14	53.5	2.1	53	40.7	4.9	85
1997	45.4	3.3	71	21.1	4.4	71	46.7	1.8	12	51.7	2	53	37.2	4.8	85
1998	45.4	3.2	72	20.9	4.3	67	41.3	1.8	16	50.8	2	53	39.1	4.6	85
1999	44	3.2	70	19.7	4.5	63	40.5	1.8	14	50.4	2	52	38.2	4.7	84
2000	46.2	3.2	68	21.2	4.5	62	39.6	1.9	14	50.4	2.1	51	38	4.7	83

(Table 4.1a continued)

(Table 4.1a continued)

Year	All India			Bihar			Kerala			Tamil Nadu			Uttar Pradesh		
	CEP	TFR	IMR	CEP	TFR	IMR	CEP	TFR	IMR	CEP	TFR	IMR	CEP	TFR	IMR
2001	45.6	3.1	66	17.4	4.4	62	40.3	1.8	11	50.3	2	49	37.9	4.5	83
2002	45.7	3	63	17.3	4.3	61	39.2	1.8	10	49.6	2	44	37.4	4.4	80
2003	47.1	3	60	17.3	4.2	60	38.9	1.8	11	49.1	1.9	43	37.1	4.4	76
2004	47.2	2.9	58	15.2	4.3	61	38.4	1.7	12	49.6	1.8	41	36.8	4.4	72
2005	46.3	2.9	58	14.1	4.3	61	37.6	1.7	14	49	1.7	37	36	4.2	73
2006	46.7	2.8	57	13.8	4.2	60	37.5	1.7	15	48.4	1.7	37	35.2	4.2	71
2007	46.2	2.7	55	13.5	3.9	58	36.3	1.7	13	47.3	1.6	35	34.6	3.9	69
2008	46.5	2.6	53	13.9	3.9	56	34.9	1.7	12	46.6	1.7	31	34.1	3.8	67
2009	42.9	2.6	50	14.4	3.9	52	33.9	1.7	12	45.6	1.7	28	30.1	3.7	63
2010	41.6	2.5	47	15.5	3.7	48	32.8	1.8	13	44.7	1.7	24	29.5	3.5	61
2011	40.4	2.4	44	16.5	3.6	44	31.8	1.8	12	41.5	1.7	22	27.7	3.4	57
2012	NA	2.4	42	43.4*	3.6	43	NA	1.8	12	NA	1.7	21	58.6*	3.4	53
2013	NA	2.3	40	41.2*	3.4	42	NA	1.8	12	NA	1.7	21	59*	3.1	50
2014		2.3	39		3.2	42		1.9	12		1.7	20		1.4	48

Sources: Registrar General of India (2009, 2013); Ministry of Health and Family Welfare (2011); NFHS-4 2015–16, IIPS, Mumbai.
Note: 1999 to 2011: Excludes Jharkhand.
*AHS Report 2014.

Table 4.1b:
Contraceptive prevalence rates estimated from NFHS surveys

		India	Bihar	Kerala	Tamil Nadu	Uttar Pradesh
NFHS-1	(1992–93)	36.5	NA	54.4	45.2	NA
NFHS-2	(1998–99)	42.8	21.6	56.1	50.3	20.8
NFHS-3	(2005–06)	48.5	28.9	57.6	60	29.3
NFHS-4	(2015–16)		23.3		52.6	

Source: NFHS-1, 2, 3 and 4, IIPS Mumbai.

differences were more significant. For example, in Bihar, the estimates of CPR are 21.6 for 1998 (NFHS-2), 28.9 for 2005 (NFHS-3), 43.4 for 2012 and 41.2 for 2013 (AHS) and 23.3 for 2015 (NFHS-4). However, during this period, 1992–2015, there has been a secular steady decline in the fertility levels in Bihar, as observed from SRS; these two trends are incompatible with each other. It seems advisable to reduce the number of national- or state-level surveys on fertility and family planning and improve the quality of any one survey. This criticism of unreliability of estimates computed on the basis of samples, however carefully designed but loaded with non-sampling errors, can be extended to many other surveys and estimates based thereon.

Inconsistencies Between Contraceptive Use and Fertility Trends

There should be a consistent relationship between CPRs and the fertility levels in any population, within subgroups in the population and over time in the same population. Higher the CPR, lower should be the fertility levels. When CPRs increase in any population, the fertility levels should decline within a margin of error. Unfortunately, this is not found to be the case in the Indian scenario in the recent years. The percentage of eligible CEP by contraception has actually declined between 1995 and 2011, as per official statistics, from 45.8 to 40.4. CEP level was stagnant until 2008 and there was a steep decline thereafter. This has happened in spite of spending huge amount of money on the RCH program between 1995 and 2011 under RCH and NRHM. However, TFR levels declined from 3.5 to 2.4 steadily during this period. This is a puzzle to be resolved. One assumption is that many couples had used private medical and health facilities to get their contraceptive services, including sterilizations, paying substantial money from their pockets. Their numbers may not be counted in the official statistics. This puzzle is as much applicable to

Kerala and Tamil Nadu as it is to Bihar and Uttar Pradesh. In Bihar, CEP declined from 24.1 in 1995 to 16.5 in 2011. However, during the same period, TFR declined significantly from 4.6 to 3.6. In Kerala, there was a continuous secular decline from 50.7 in 1995 to 31.8 in 2011, while TFR levels remained at 1.8 during this period. In Tamil Nadu, there was again a continuous secular decline from 54.8 in 1995 to 41.5 in 2011 in contraceptive use, and TFR levels declined from 2.2 to 1.7 during this period. In Uttar Pradesh, there was a continuous secular decline from 37.1 in 1995 to 27.7 in 2011, but TFR levels declined significantly from 5.0 to 3.4 during this period.

The fact that fertility levels also declined in most of the states even in the context of declining contraceptive use, officially reported data indicates that many of the users of sterilizations and temporary methods have switched over to the private sector paying a heavy price for such services. Table 4.1a and the Figures 4.1 and 4.2 reveal that, in the country as a whole, CEP declined substantially both in the developed and developing states post 1995, while huge additional investments were made in the program.

Figure 4.1:
Trends of percentage of couples effectively protected in India and selected states

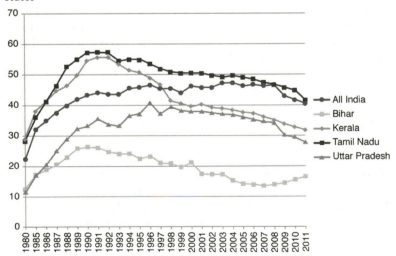

Source: Registrar General India (2013).

Figure 4.2:

Trends of total fertility rates in India and selected states

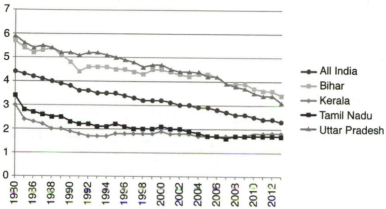

Source: Registrar General India (2013).

In the above context of unreliability of contraceptive use data compiled from official statistics as well as inconsistencies between estimates derived from different sample surveys and in the context of rapid declines in fertility already taking place in most parts of the country, there appears to be no need or justification to waste time and resources in conducting large-scale sample surveys in the country to collect data on contraceptive use in populations, especially where fertility has already declined to replacement or below replacement levels. There is a need to ensure the easy availability of good quality contraceptives at affordable prices and keep a track of the fertility levels in the population.

Comparative Analysis of Pre- and Post-1994 Performance in RCH

A comparative analysis of changes in 29 parameters pertaining to RCH were grouped into three categories—7 on marriage and fertility, 10 on family planning and desired family size and 12 on MCH—during the period 1992–2006 was carried out considering this period in two parts: 1992–98 and 1998–2006. The changes between 1992 and 1998 can be considered as changes in the pre-integration or RCH period and between 1998 and 2006 as post integration or RCH period. Comparisons of the changes

Figure 4.3:
Trends of infant mortality rate in India and selected states

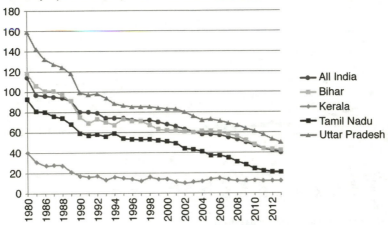

Source: Registrar General India (2013).

in each of the 29 parameters during 1992–98 was done using NFHS-1 and 2 data while comparison between 1998 and 2006 was done using NFHS-2 and 3 data. Such comparison revealed very interesting results.

Table 4.2 provides the annual change in percentage values, observed during 1998–99 and 2005–06 and computed from NFHS-2 and 3 data and also the annual change between 1992–93 and 1998–99 obtained from the NFHS-1 and 2. The last column of the table provides a summary picture whether the post-1998 changes were worse off (slowdown in progress) than the pre-1998 changes—"Yes" indicating that the pace of change post-1998 is worse off and "No" implying the opposite. This analysis refers to the country as a whole. It is remarkable to note that in most of the variables (25 out of 29) the pace of improvement from 1998–99 to 2005–06 is slower than the pace of improvement between 1992–93 and 1998–99. For example, take the case of the percentage of fully immunized children in the age group of 12–23 months. This increased from 35.5 percent in 1992–93 to 42 percent in 1998–99 (an annual increase of 1.08 percentage points), while in NFHS-3 the percentage was 43.5 (an annual increase of 0.21 percentage points) in the post-1998 period. This implies that the full immunization program has undergone a dampening effect from 1998–99 to 2005–06, and the reasons for the same have to be explored. Similarly, the increase in the percentage of couples using modern methods of contraception was 1.05 percentage points annually

Table 4.2:

Annual change in marriage and fertility, family planning and maternal and child health during pre- and post-1998, India

Indicators	NFHS-3 (2005–06)	NFHS-2 (1998–99)	NFHS-1 (1992–93)	Annual Change 1998–2005 (Percent Points)	Annual Change 1992–93	Annual Change (1992–98) > (1998–2005)
Marriage and Fertility						
1. Women aged 20–24, married by age 18 (%)	44.5	50	54.2	−0.79	−0.7	No
3. Total fertility rate (children per woman)	2.7	2.9	3.4	−0.02	−0.09	Yes
5. Median age at first birth for women, age 25–49	19.8	19.3	19.4	0.07	−0.02	No
6. Married women with 2 living children wanting no more children (%)	83.2	72.4	59.7	1.54	2.12	Yes
6a. Two sons	89.9	82.7	71.5	1.03	1.87	Yes
6b. One son, one daughter	88.1	76.4	66	1.67	1.73	Yes
6c. Two daughters	62.1	47	36.9	2.16	1.68	No
Family Planning (currently married women, aged 15–49)						
Current use						
7. Any method (%)	56.3	48.2	40.7	1.16	1.25	Yes
8. Any modern method (%)	48.5	42.8	36.5	0.81	1.05	Yes
8a. Female sterilization (%)	37.3	34.1	27.4	0.46	1.12	Yes
8b. Male sterilization (%)	1	1.9	3.5	−0.13	−0.27	No
8c. IUD (%)	1.8	1.6	1.9	0.03	−0.05	No
8d. Pill (%)	3.1	2.1	1.2	0.14	0.15	Yes

(Table 4.2 continued)

(Table 4.2 continued)

Indicators	NFHS-3 (2005–06)	NFHS-2 (1998–99)	NFHS-1 (1992–93)	Annual Change (Percent Points)		Annual Change (1992–98) > (1998–2005)
				1998–2005	1992–93	
8e. Condom (%)	5.3	3.1	2.4	0.31	0.12	No
Unmet need for family planning						
9. Total unmet need (%)	13.2	15.8	19.5	-0.37	-0.62	Yes
9a. For spacing (%)	6.3	8.3	11	-0.29	-0.45	Yes
9b. For limiting (%)	6.8	7.5	8.5	-0.1	-0.17	Yes
Maternal and Child Health						
Maternity care (for births in the last 3 years)						
10. Mothers who had at least 3 antenatal care visits for their last birth (%)	50.7	44.2	43.9	0.93	0.05	No
12. Births assisted by a doctor/nurse/LHV/ANM/other health personnel (%)	48.3	42.4	33	0.84	1.57	Yes
13. Institutional births (%)	40.7	33.6	26.1	1.01	1.25	Yes
Child immunization and vitamin A supplementation[1]						
15a. Children 12–23 months fully immunized[2] (%)	43.5	42	35.5	0.21	1.08	Yes
15d. Children 12–23 months who have received 3 doses of DPT vaccine (%)	55.3	55.1	51.7	0.03	0.57	Yes

15e. Children 12–23 months who have received measles vaccine (%)	58.8	50.7	42.2	1.16	1.42	Yes
Treatment of childhood diseases (children under 3 years)						
17. Children with diarrhea in the last 2 weeks who received ORS (%)	26.2	26.9	17.8	-0.1	1.52	Yes
18. Children with diarrhea in the last 2 weeks taken to a health facility (%)	58	65.3	61.9	-1.04	0.57	Yes
Child feeding practices and nutritional status of children						
20. Children under 3 years breastfed within one hour of birth (%)	23.4	16	9.5	1.06	1.08	Yes
25. Children under 3 years who are underweight (%)	45.9	47	51.5	-0.16	-0.75	Yes

Source: National Family Health Survey 1, 2 and 3.

Note: Numbering as given in Fact sheets of NFHS.

during 1992–98, and this declined to 0.81 points post-1998 until 2005. The unmet need for contraception (spacing and limitation) declined by 0.62 points annually during 1992–98 and slowed down to 0.37 points during 1998–2005, and TFR decline slowed down from an annual decline of 0.09 points to 0.02 points.

Table 4.3 provides state-level data for 22 states for which information was available in all three rounds of NFHS surveys for most of the 29 indicators. The indicators were segregated, as stated earlier, into three major categories: (a) Marriage and Fertility, (b) Family Planning and (c) MCH. At the all India level, numbers of indicators covered in these three categories were 7, 10 and 12 respectively. For the different states, number of indictors for which such time series data was available, and the number on which the pace of improvement in post-1998 period was less than the pre-1998 period, is also given in the table. The computations were similar to the one carried out at the national level. It can be seen from this table that in most of the states, the pace of improvement in the post-1998 period is less than the earlier period, with the median values of 50 percent in the first category, 60 percent in the second and 65 percent in the third. While in the country as whole, there was a slow-down on 72 percent of the indicators, it was 79 and 72 in Punjab and Karnataka respectively.

Thus, the RCH program implemented after 1998 has not been particularly successful on a number of RCH indicators. If we adjust the effects of per capita expenditures spent on the RCH programs in pre- and post-RCH period, the differentials will be accentuated since the expenditure on RCH after 1998, compared to 1992 to 1997 period, has almost doubled on the per capita basis.

Extent of Wastage of Condoms in Public Supply

During post-RCH period, there was unduly high program emphasis on the use of spacing methods, especially the condom, since the use of condoms was supposed to prevent transmission of HIV/AIDS in addition to preventing unwanted pregnancies. Beginning late 1980s, possibly because of international pressure, the prevalence of HIV/AIDS in the country was unduly and irrationally over-estimated, especially during the late 1990s until 2005–06 when NFHS-3 results on prevalence of HIV/AIDS, based on actual blood tests of a sample population, blew up these high prevalnce assumptions. The National AIDS Control Organization

Table 4.3:
State-wise total number of cases and percentages indicating pre-1998 changes greater than the post-1998 period in the three selected groups of indicators

	Marriage and Fertility A(7)	Family Planning B(10)	Maternal and Child Health C(12)	S=A+B+C	A/7*100	B/10*100	C/12*100	Overall S/29*100
India	4	7	10	21	57	70	83	72.4
Andhra Pradesh	3	5	9	17	43	50	75	58.6
Arunachal Pradesh	3	6	10	19	75	60	83	65.5
Assam	4	5	4	13	57	50	33	44.8
Delhi	2	5	11	18	29	50	92	62.1
Gujarat	1	7	10	18	14	70	83	62.1
Goa	2	3	9	14	29	30	75	48.3
Himachal Pradesh	5	5	9	19	71	50	75	65.5
Haryana	7	6	9	22	100	60	75	75.9
Karnataka	6	6	9	21	86	60	75	72.4
Kerala	4	2	10	16	57	20	83	55.2
Meghalaya	1	2	1	4	25	20	8	15.4
Maharashtra	3	4	7	14	43	40	58	48.3
Manipur	2	3	8	13	50	30	67	50
Mizoram	1	6	11	18	25	60	92	69.2

(Table 4.3 continued)

(Table 4.3 continued)

	Marriage and Fertility	Family Planning	Maternal and Child Health	S=A+B+C	A/7*100	B/10*100	C/12*100	Overall
	A(7)	B(10)	C(12)					S/29*100
Nagaland	2	5	10	17	50	50	83	65.4
Odisha	3	6	8	17	43	60	67	58.6
Punjab	6	8	9	23	86	80	75	79.3
Rajasthan	2	5	4	11	29	50	33	37.9
Tamil Nadu	2	0	11	13	29	0	92	44.8
Tripura	4	3	9	16	100	30	75	61.5
Uttar Pradesh	3	2	7	12	43	20	58	41.4
West Bengal	7	7	6	20	100	70	50	69
Median	5	5	9	17	50	50	75	61.5

Source: Srinivasan K. (1995).

(NACO) estimated that there were 5.26 million HIV+ cases in the country by 2006, but the actual blood tests of a representative sample population in the country (NFHS-3) estimated the prevalence at only 2.6 million. The use of condoms in the population was unnecessarily exaggerated by the condoms manufacturing and marketing companies, including government owned companies, in the country. A quantitative estimate of the extent of such wastage of condoms was made possible by using data on actual use reported by couples in NFHS-3, which collected information on the use of various methods of contraception by married couple, including current use, method used, duration of use and source from which the services and supplies were obtained. The data on condom use obtained from this survey is used as benchmarks, against which we compare the official data on condom distribution and condom users, published by the Ministry of Health and Family Welfare in their Yearbook.

The data analyzed from the two sources described above on the number of condoms used and number of condom users was analyzed in detail. Table 4.4 provides the estimated number of condoms used in different states, according to the source from which the condoms were procured, whether from free supply, through social marketing or those who purchase branded packs and extent of wastage as per the official service statistics in 2006–07 published by the government. "Free supply" connotes the condoms supplied free of charge by the government machinery directly to the needy couples. "social marketing" denotes the supply of condoms made by NGOs procuring condoms from the government sources free of cost and supplying to the needy couples on marginal cost, and "branded items" denote the sale of condoms in shops and pharmacies at market prices. Table 4.5 presents similar data compiled from an analysis of data from NFHS-3 (for details on the analysis of NFHS-3, see Srinivasan et al. 2005). Taking as the benchmark the more reliable data on the actual use of condoms the extent of wastage has been estimated.

We found that, out of interviews with married women in the country, during 2005–06 there were 11.571 million regular users of condoms, and at an estimate of 72 pieces per year per couple, a total of 833.14 million pieces were used. However, according to official service statistics for the same year, a total of 1,877.63 million pieces have been distributed in the country, giving an estimate of wastage/misuse of 1,044.49 million pieces or over a billion pieces. The percentage of wastage/misuse is very high at 55.63 percent. This is appalling since more than half of the condoms distributed or reported to be officially distributed to the couples are not used by them. Probably they were used for various other commercial

Table 4.4 :
Condom usage during 2005–06 according to NFHS-3 (women interviews)

Country/State	No. of Condom Users (000s)				No. of Condoms Used (000s)			
	Free	Social	Branded	Total	Free	Social	Branded	Total
India	2,248.68	5,129.81	4,192.86	11,571.36	161,905.31	369,346.49	301,885.95	833,137.76
Andhra Pradesh	0.31	11.88	74.99	87.18	22.22	855.45	5,399.32	6,276.99
Arunachal Pradesh	0.75	1.2	4.48	6.44	54.09	86.72	322.85	463.67
Assam	29.24	38.79	57.9	125.93	2,105.33	2,793.07	4,168.55	9,066.95
Bihar	20.96	69.48	56.6	147.04	1,509.35	5,002.41	4,075.24	10,586.99
Goa	2.36	3.13	14.64	20.13	170.15	225.04	1,053.86	1,449.06
Gujarat	110.3	88.11	146.04	344.45	7,941.38	6,344.23	10,514.56	24,800.17
Haryana	217.72	292.62	189.85	700.19	15,675.85	21,068.34	13,669.34	50,413.53
Himachal Pradesh	166.71	206.95	255.82	629.48	12,003.26	14,900.59	18,418.79	45,322.64
Karnataka	9.71	13.94	91.59	115.24	698.88	1,003.53	6,594.60	8,297.01
Kerala	82.92	24.39	197.05	304.36	5,970.18	1,755.93	14,187.95	21,914.06
Madhya Pradesh	64.28	153.92	81.94	300.14	4,628.39	11,082.06	5,899.57	21,610.01
Maharashtra	12.56	159.9	187.53	359.99	904.17	11,513.07	13,502.24	25,919.48
Manipur	61.91	32.46	82.29	176.66	4,457.33	2,337.38	5,924.98	12,719.69
Meghalaya	12	12.83	92.9	117.73	863.72	923.98	6,688.79	8,476.49
Mizoram	56.59	16.51	NA	73.1	4,074.27	1,189.06	NA	5,263.33
Nagaland	12.12	31.28	66.5	109.9	872.45	2,252.13	4,788.32	7,912.89

Odisha	36.66	113.19	21.36	171.21	2,639.70	8,149.76	1,537.69	12,327.15
Punjab	152.19	406.48	285.11	843.79	10,947.66	29,266.65	20,528.27	60,752.58
Rajasthan	153.67	142.95	67.39	364	11,064.06	10,292.15	4,852.01	26,208.22
Sikkim	11.69	84.78	107.8	204.27	841.92	6,103.95	7,761.49	14,707.37
Tamil Nadu	23.36	4.05	96.57	123.98	1,682.17	291.58	6,952.96	8,926.71
Tripura	59.07	59.07	67.55	185.69	4,252.82	4,252.82	4,863.85	13,369.49
Uttar Pradesh	83.24	362.67	77.29	523.2	5,992.98	26,112.28	5,564.91	37,670.17
West Bengal	54.15	42.99	161.89	259.03	3,898.80	3,094.93	11,656.22	18,649.95
Delhi	81.15	528.58	677.72	1,287.44	5,842.84	38,057.41	48,795.60	92,695.86
Jharkhand	23.49	83.19	58.73	165.41	1,691.30	5,990.00	4,228.24	11,909.54
Chhattisgarh	30.79	82.1	54.39	167.28	2,216.72	5,911.25	3,916.20	12,044.17
Uttaranchal	128.23	457.18	256.47	841.88	9,232.79	32,916.90	18,465.58	60,615.27
Jammu & Kashmir	9.07	99.76	290.22	399.05	652.99	7,182.92	20,895.78	28,731.69

Source: National Family Health Survey-3.

Table 4.5:
Condom usage during 2005–06 according to NFHS-3 and service statistics and excess reported

Country/State	Source	No. of Condom Users (000s)				No. of Condoms Used (000s)			
		Free	Social	Branded	Total	Free	Social	Branded	Total
India	NFHS-3	2,248.68	5,129.81	4,192.86	11,571.36	161,905.31	369,346.49	301,885.95	833,137.76
	Service Statistics	10,290.43	10,498.89	5,288.89	26,078.21	740,911	755,920	380,800	1,877,631
	Official Excess	**8,041.75**	**5,369.08**	**1,096.03**	**14,506.85**	**579,005.69**	**386,573.51**	**78,914.05**	**1,044,493.2**
Kerala	NFHS-3	82.92	24.39	197.05	304.36	5,970.18	1,755.93	14,187.95	21,914.06
	Service Statistics	185.93	328.39	141.86	656.18	13,387	23,643.86	10,213.93	47,244.79
	Official Excess	**103.01**	**304**	**–55.19**	**351.82**	**7,416.82**	**21,887.93**	**–3974.02**	**25,330.73**
Rajasthan	NFHS-3	153.67	142.95	67.39	364	11,064.06	10,292.15	4,852.01	26,208.22
	Service Statistics	1,677.47	632.19	243.89	2,553.55	12,0778	45,517.78	17,559.85	183,855.62
	Official Excess	**1,523.8**	**489.24**	**176.5**	**2,189.55**	**109,713.9**	**35,225.63**	**12,707.84**	**157,647.4**

Source: National Family Health Survey-3.

purposes reported in the papers or just been dumped and reported to have been distributed to the couples.

From the analysis reported in Srinivasan, Chander Shekhar, and Arokiasamy (2007), we find that for the country as a whole, the wastage figures are the highest among the "free" supplies (78.15 percent), better in "social marketing" (51.14 percent) and the least in "branded/commercial" category (20.72 percent). For Uttar Pradesh (which is considered the low-risk state for the prevalence of HIV/AIDS), the wastage figures were 95, 81 and 88, respectively, for the three sources of supply. For Tamil Nadu (which is considered the high-risk state for the prevalence of HIV/AIDS), the wastage figures were 89, 99 and 82, respectively, for the three sources of supply. The wastage levels were equally high in the high prevalence of HIV and low prevalence of HIV states. It has to be pointed out here that NFHS did not ask for the balance of condom pieces kept in the users' households, and this can be estimated at the maximal level as the difference between the survey and official figures from "branded/commercial" source (i.e., 20.72). If we assume that the same percentage is kept as a stored supply in the "free" and "social markets" category, then the wastage in the "free" category is 57.43 percent and 30.42 percent in the "social marketing" category.

An Overview of Population Policies and Programs Implemented Until 1995

Based on the description and analysis of the family planning programs in India since its inception in 1952 till date, presented in Chapters 3 to 5, a summary and an overview is presented in this section.

1. To understand the sterilization as the dominant method of family planning in India, we need to know the following:

    i. Since the very inception of family planning program in India in 1952, sterilization of the male was promoted as a method of family planning and, for the first time in human history, incentives were given to the acceptors of this method. The first to begin this incentive method was the Madras State (now Tamil Nadu). Mr R. A. Gopalaswamy, the Chief Secretary of the State, started such a policy by providing an incentive of ₹10 per acceptor in 1954. He even postulated that, over a 10-year period, sterilization of all married men with wives in reproductive and over four children would bring down the birth rate from 40 in 1956 to 25 in 1966. Children above birth order 4 were considered improvident maternity. Similar incentives were provided the next year in Maharashtra and it became a national policy in 1961. Tamil Nadu led the sterilization movement in the country.

ii. Vasectomy over the following years became the dominant method of family planning, partly because of increased incentive amount to acceptors, canvassers and service personnel. It became a commercial endeavor and a culture of family planning in India, initially targeting couples with four children, then with three children and then with two children. During the Emergency period, 1976, a few states even passed an act, making sterilization compulsory for couples with two children. Such a procedure was even recommended in the NPP of 1976. Vasectomy camps, small and large, were conducted throughout the country, and states and districts which did the best were rewarded by the central government. During the Emergency, many vasectomy camps were conducted at railway stations, bus stands and other places. There were mini and major camps. The three camps held in Ernakulum, Kerala, made history. There were three camps held in this city: the first during November–December 1970 in which 16,006 vasectomies were done; the second during July 1971 in which 63,416 vasectomies were done; and the third in July–August 1972 in which 15,536 vasectomies were done. People from all over Kerala were brought to these campsites for sterilization, and it was done in a festive mood. The international organizations were very vocal in praising these camps and a good and supportive article was published in the *Studies in Family Planning*, a publication of the Population Council, New York (Krishnakumar 1974). After 1994 with the ICPD PoA adopted by many countries, the same and many other international organizations began to play a low-key on family planning, hold the flag of women's rights and women's empowerment and even started criticizing many national family planning programs as infringing on these rights.

iii. However, in the country, because of many forced sterilizations carried out during the Emergency where ineligible couples were forcefully sterilized, the program came into popular disrepute and popular agitations were organized. It became one of the major planks on which the Emergency had to be lifted, elections were called up and the then ruling party suffered a crushing defeat. It was written that these large vasectomy camps, instead of bringing down the birth rates, brought down the government.

iv. As discussed earlier, family planning program suffered its credibility of vasectomy campaigns, and the program almost totally collapsed after the Emergency was lifted in 1977. It goes to the credit and foresight of the women of this country to have come forward for tubal ligations in large numbers after 1977, and the female sterilizations have replaced the male sterilizations for preventing unwanted births. Sterilizations, tubectomy and laparoscopic tubal ligation have now become the dominant methods of family planning in India. The measures taken by the state and the central governments with various temporary and reversible methods, such as conventional IUD, Copper T, oral pills, condoms etc., have not been that successful. The motto of an average Indian couple seems to have as many children as desired and then go for sterilization. They do not want to mess around with temporary methods.

v. Table 4.1a gives data on the percentage of CEP by all methods and the percentage effectively protected by sterilization during the recent years 2007–11 for India as whole and for the four selected states.

vi. In the country as a whole, in 2007, CEP was 46.7 and CEP owing to sterilization was 27 or 58 percent of the total protection, and it was 66 percent in 2011. In the developed states, Kerala and Tamil Nadu that have already achieved replacement levels of fertility, the percentage protection owing to sterilization in 2007 were 86 and 81 respectively, and 90 and 82 in 2011. In Bihar, it was 81 percent in 2007 as well as 2011. Thus, sterilization is as much the dominant method of contraceptive protection in high fertility states as in low fertility states.

2. Because of the rigidity in the organizational pattern for MCH and family planning programs throughout the country and the strong insistence of the government at all levels (center, state and district) on achieving the targets on sterilization, the delivery of MCH services suffered.

3. The offer of incentives to acceptors, motivators and medical and paramedical personnel involved with the sterilization program gave a commercial touch to the whole program. Also, in the hands

of unscrupulous administrators, many "ineligible cases" were sterilized to gain monetary benefits at the individual or state level. On
many occasions, in order to get awards from the central government as the best performing state in the family planning program,
the number of sterilizations done was manipulated. The quality of
services at the time of sterilizations and follow-up care for cases
with complications left much to be desired. The program lost
much of its popularity among the people; however, the motivational and educational programs on small family norms have been
fairly successful.

4. The performance of the different states in family planning even
   under a common population policy, organizational scheme for
   financial assistance to the program over the past three decades
   varied widely. States such as Kerala, Tamil Nadu and Maharashtra
   were most successful in their family planning programs and reduction in the fertility level in comparison to states such as Uttar
   Pradesh, Rajasthan, Bihar and Madhya Pradesh. The factors underlying the differential performance of the states are the bureaucratic
   efficiency of the states; political commitment to the program at
   the state level; progress of the states in selected areas of socioeconomic development, especially female literacy, which increases
   the desire for small family norm and demand for family planning
   methods; and the cultural aspects of populations, particularly the
   status of women in the states.

5. The program implicitly assumed that all married women in
   reproductive ages are equal partners or contributors to the fertility
   of the population. No attempt was made to identify relatively more
   fecund couples and target the program to them.

6. Narayana and Kantner (1992: 129–52), in their critical study of
   the population policy in India, have observed that the processes
   of decentralization of political power and decision-making through
   "Panchayati Raj" system (wherein locally elected leaders at the
   level of a village or a group of villages are given authority to raise
   taxes, plan and implement local development programs with
   assistance from higher levels) will contribute to better quality of
   services, including health and family planning services. Further
   analysis renders support to their conclusions.

7. Demographically, the impact of the program on fertility has been
   towards reduction in the fertility rates among women above the
   age of 30 because of the emphasis on sterilization as the major

method of family planning. The program was nibbling as it were on the tail end of the fertility curve. Further, as we will demonstrate in the next chapter, the natural fertility or fertility of women in the absence of contraception has been on increase during the past three decades among women below the age of 30 because of the forces of modernization. We have thus a peculiar situation wherein the fertility rate of married women in the age group 20–29 has been increasing for the past three decades in a number of states, and significant declines in fertility have been observed only among women above the age of 30. The combination of these two factors contributed to a near stagnating TFR level even in the context of a rise in contraceptive use. These observations will be discussed in detail in the subsequent chapters.

5

Culture and Natural Fertility

Cultural and Social Values Related to Nuptiality and Fertility

This chapter marks a substantive departure from the earlier chapters. While the previous chapters discussed the nature of government interventions through public policies and programs aimed at a desired reduction of fertility and population growth rates through increased use of modern methods of contraception by the married couples, mainly the sterilization of the males until 1977 and of females thereafter, this chapter focuses on the basic cultural and social checks on fertility and the institution of marriage that were influencing the society for hundreds, if not thousands, of years in the past and are still operating in the Indian society. These are by no means small effects, as we will see later in this chapter, and are still very much in force. While some of the policies and programs have been consistent with these and hence magnified their effects, some of them have run counter to the cultural and social norms and hence had a diminished impact. When we assess the impact of the organized family planning program in India, the effects of these factors and changes in them caused by modernization should also be considered. A very brief review of the culture of India as it impinges on marriage and fertility may be in the order.

Cultural Factors Affecting Marriage and Fertility

India, with its unbroken history of over 4,000 years, has developed its own philosophical and cultural systems that consciously or unconsciously influence the emotions and behaviors of its people. The epics of Ramayana and Mahabharata, stories from which parents and grandparents narrate to every child in India, and now through television channels in the past two decades, inculcate directly and indirectly the values of life and the criteria for judging the opposites—good and bad, vice and virtue, and so on. Similarly, various philosophical works, such as the Upanishads and Bhagavad Gita, and the holy books of other religions, Islam and Christianity, impart the goals of life, the doctrines of reincarnation and Karma or other systems, the roots of happiness and sorrow, and various duties of individuals to their parents, teachers, gods and fellow human beings. All the major religions of India are observed in letter and spirit more in India than anywhere else in the world.

Cultural values and norms for marriage and sexual activities and duties to parents, spouse and children are very elaborate and demanding and influence Indian fertility levels and patterns. When life expectancy at birth was quite low, perhaps 20–25 years, it was necessary, for the survival of the people, for the Indian culture to incorporate specific values that would ensure moderately high fertility—early marriage of girls, bearing the first child as early as possible after marriage, ensuring the survival of children already born, care and nurture of pregnant women to enable successful parturition and various practices of infant and child care. Many of these values and norms have been institutionalized and given religious sanctity to ensure adherence by as large a section of the people as possible.

Over the centuries, the Indian social system has also recognized that the optimal path of survival, in the face of high mortality, is one of having moderately high fertility levels—neither very high nor very low. When infant and child mortality levels were very high, population learned from experience that closely spaced births reduced further the chances of survival of the child already born and of the mother. Hence came the custom of a pregnant woman going to her mother's home for delivery (especially for the first two or three children). She had better attention and rest at her mother's home, and returned to her husband's home only a year or two after delivery. Long periods of postpartum abstinence were recommended and found socially desirable as a means of protecting children's health. Similarly, prolonged breastfeeding was also recommended and practiced.

Couples have practiced periodic abstinence for religious and health reasons and terminal abstinence after reaching a certain age or a stage of the life cycles, such as after the son or daughter's marriage. These traditional and cultural checks on fertility were directed and institutionalized to optimize child survival.

Although there was a social and cultural stigma attached to an infertile woman, a woman with a larger family and poorly spaced births was also an object of ridicule and sarcastic remarks popular in most of the Indian languages. For example, in Tamil, there is a popular saying that "even a king will become a pauper if he has five daughters."

On the other hand, there was a strong religious and social pressure for couples to have a male child as quickly as possible after marriage. Couples who had a baby boy first were considered the luckiest. Roots of the patriarchal and patrilineal system of family life and inheritance can be traced back to the Vedic periods and can be considered part of the collective consciousness of the Hindu society. A son was considered necessary not only for the continuation of the family line or *gotra* (clan or lineage) but also for the liberation of the departed souls of parents and grandparents by offering prayers and gifts every year on their death anniversaries. Life in this world, and the other after death, was considered incomplete and unfulfilled without a son. Those who had no son were permitted to adopt a daughter's child as their son after an appropriate religious ceremony. After the adoption, the grandson used to take over the religious duties of a son.

Thus we see that in the Hindu society, the cultural and social systems developed over the ages, which have come to be adopted in other religious groups as well, have contributed to maximize children's health and longevity in the face of a high-mortality situation. The values and norms developed to realize this goal were oriented toward early marriage, having the first child as soon as possible after marriage, good birth spacing by observing lengthy postpartum abstinence, prolonged breastfeeding, periodic abstinence for religious and social reasons, and emphasis on having a son and terminal abstinence at a relatively early age.

It is interesting to observe a number of built-in traditional and religious checks on fertility, along with the emphasis on early marriage, the preference for a son and the stigma related to infertility. Owing to women's low status, assigned in *The Laws of Manu* (*Manusmriti*), one of the earliest texts in Sanskrit written over 2,000 years ago, the book placed high emphasis on a girl marrying as early as possible and having a son very quickly to raise her social status. The net effect of various positive and negative checks on fertility fluctuated over time with the intensity they were practiced, but it can be inferred from historical records that extramarital fertility was insignificant and within marriage, it never reached the biological maximum levels.

Framework for Study

The variables through which the social, economic and cultural environment influences fertility have been termed the "intermediate variables" (see Table 5.1) by Davis and Blake (1956). These are also useful in

Table 5.1:
Intermediate variables influencing human fertility

1. **Factors affecting exposure to intercourse**

Intercourse Variables

A. Those governing the formation and dissolution of unions in the reproductive period

    i. Age of entry into sexual unions

    ii. Permanent celibacy: proportion of women never entering sexual unions

    iii. Amount of reproductive period spent after or between unions

        (a) When unions are broken by divorce, separation or desertion

        (b) When unions are broken by death of husband

B. Those governing the exposure to intercourse within unions

    iv. Voluntary abstinence

    v. Involuntary abstinence (from impotence, illness or unavailable but temporary separations)

    vi. Coital frequency (excluding periods of abstinence)

2. **Factors affecting exposure to conception**

Conception Variables

    vii. Fecundity or infecundity, as affected by involuntary causes

    viii. Use or non-use of contraception

        (a) By mechanical and chemical means

        (b) By other means

    ix. Fecundity or infecundity as affected by voluntary causes (Sterilization, sub incision, medical treatment etc.)

3. **Factors affecting gestation and successful parturition**

Gestation Variables

    x. Fetal mortality from involuntary causes

    xi. Fetal mortality from voluntary causes

Source: D. Kingsley and J. Blake (1956).

studying the effects of culture on nuptiality and fertility. They categorize and list these 11 variables in a framework that has become an important aspect of demographic analyses of fertility studies. According to this framework, any change in the fertility levels of a population can be brought about only by changes in one or more of 11 intermediate variables. The variables are grouped into following three categories:

- Factors affecting exposure to intercourse (intercourse variables).
- Factors affecting exposure to conception (conception variables).
- Factors affecting gestation and successful parturition (gestation variables).

The effects of cultural and traditional norms on each of the intermediate variables in India are not necessarily unidirectional. For example, prohibition on widow remarriages, socially and culturally imposed on many segments of the Indian society, tends to reduce fertility below the biological maximum by withdrawing women from reproduction over a considerable span of their fertile period when they are widowed. In a high-mortality situation, when girls marry very young and husbands are considerably older than they are, the span of female reproductive life eliminated because of widowhood can be considerable. On the other hand, the universality of marriage for women and the young age at marriage can be expected to contribute to increased fertility.

Impact of Culture on Fertility

The fertility-enhancing or depressing effects of the dominant norms of a Hindu society on each of the intermediate variables appear in Table 5.2.

The fertility effects of the norms of the traditional Indian society on various intermediate variables have been taken from different studies on the culture of India in its relation to marriage, pregnancy, value of children especially a son, widowhood, etc. (Basham 1963; Nag 1982; Srinivasan, Reddy and Murthy Raju 1978). There were minor variations of these norms between different sections of the society such as Hindus and Muslims and different caste groups within the Hindu religion, but the overriding impact of the norms on fertility is as given in Table 5.2. A positive sign (+) indicates that the effect of the particular norm is increased fertility and a negative (–) sign indicates the opposite. In a traditional Hindu society, many of the norms on intermediate variables, such as prohibiting widow remarriages, voluntary abstinence for religious

Table 5.2:

Effects of Indian culture on the proximate determinants of fertility

Intermediate Variable	Cultural Value	Traditional Norm	Effect on Fertility
Intercourse Variables			
(Those governing union formation and dissolution)			
The age of entry into sexual union	Premarital sex forbidden strictly for females	Early age at marriage, preferably before puberty	Positive (+), by increasing reproductive span
Permanent celibacy— proportion of women not entering sexual union	All women obligated to marry and beget children	Practically no woman remained single voluntarily	Positive (+), by ensuring almost 100% of females marry by age 20
The amount of reproductive period spent after union or between unions			
After unions are broken by divorce, separation or desertion	Formal divorce sanctioned only in extreme circumstances	Separation and desertion of married women not infrequent	Negative (−), by reducing exposure to intercourse for women after separation or desertion
When unions are broken by husband's death	Widow remarriage prohibited for higher castes, not for lower castes	Widows ill-treated, socially condemned in higher castes; in lower castes, remarriage of young widows not infrequent	Strongly negative (−); in high mortality situation, prevents high proportion of widows aged 15–44 from reproducing
Exposure to intercourse within unions' voluntary abstinence	Highly cherished value—preserving semen considered good for body and soul	Sexual taboo several days per month based on moon phases; expected on most religious occasions	Strongly negative (−), by reducing coital frequency in menstrual intervals, postpartum and encouraging terminal abstinence at relative young age

(Table 5.2 continued)

(Table 5.2 continued)

Intermediate Variable	Cultural Value	Traditional Norm	Effect on Fertility
	Women cherished abstinence during lactation, fearing semen might pollute breast milk	Long periods of lactation, postpartum abstinence common	
	Couples not to have children after their own children marry	Terminal abstinence practised at relatively young age by couples	
Involuntary abstinence (impotence, illness, unavoidable and temporary separations)	Sexual intercourse during illness considered unhealthy; separations not frequent	Impotence not reason for divorce or separation; sex considered blasphemous if smallpox, chicken pox, measles in household; sex felt to invite wrath of goddess controlling these diseases	Strongly negative (−), in context of high morbidity from febrile diseases (malaria, TB), viral epidemics (smallpox, chicken pox, measles); sex during child's illness felt to worsen disease prognosis
Coital frequency (excluding period of abstinence)	High value placed on preserving semen; in some caste groups, coitus considered necessary only for procreation	Low coital frequency desired	Negative (−)

Conception Variables

Fecundity or infecundity as affected by involuntary cases	Female sterility a great social stigma; a great social and religious significance in begetting a son	Bride's first pregnancy eagerly awaited; inability to conceive for several years sufficient reason for husband to remarry; birth of sons welcomed and celebrated	Positive (+)

Intermediate Variable	Cultural Value	Traditional Norm	Effect on Fertility
Use or non-use of contraception mechanical or chemical methods	Permitted when spacing or limitation necessary	Nothing seems to have been practised as commonly accepted method	Positive (+)
Other Means	Permitted	Some herbals used as contraceptives, with unknown effectiveness	Positive (+)
Fecundity or infecundity by voluntary as affected causes (sterilization, medical treatment, etc.)	Permitted as long as woman has son; fecundity after daughter is grown or son married considered shameful	Terminal abstinence practised at young age as 'grandmother complex'	Strongly negative (–)
Gestation Variables			
Involuntary fetal mortality	Considered curse or wrath of god	Various appeasement procedures and traditional forms of treatment woman in mother's home	Positive(+)
Voluntary fetal mortality (induced abortion)	Not condemned in high-parity women	Traditional methods available with unknown effectiveness	Negative (–)

Source: Srinivasan K. (1995).

or social reasons, decreased coital frequency because of men's value on preserving semen and impaired fecundity because of febrile illnesses, tended to depress fertility; norms on other variables (age at marriage, universality of marriage and taboos on induced abortion) tended to enhance fertility.

Historical Natural Fertility Levels in India

Based on studies of historical demographic data, various scholars of Indian demography have recognized that fertility levels in India have never been very high at any time in the past because of the social and cultural effects mentioned previously. Such a conclusion is supported from independent analysis of data from the following three sources:

- Indirect estimates of fertility from the population age distributions acquired from the decennial censuses conducted since 1881, applying the techniques of generalized stable population theory.
- A careful analysis of data from pre-1962 sample surveys when there was very insignificant contraceptive use in the country.
- Data on vital registration in the selected areas where the registration system for births and deaths was considered to be of fairly high quality with complete and accurate registration of vital events.

Based on the data from the population censuses in India, conducted at regular intervals of 10 years since 1881, using their age distributions and applying generalized stable population theory, Mari Bhat (1989) derived estimates of CBR, age-specific fertility rates (ASFRs) and CBRs, for various intercensal periods from 1881 to 1961 (see Table 5.3).

It can be seen from the table that TFR estimates vary around 6 within a narrow margin, and the stability of the value over time is astonishing. The period, 1881 to 1961, witnessed many famines and epidemics, especially during 1911 to 1921 as described in Chapter 2, and even during those decades, TFR was around 6. Although the CBRs were high, ranging between 46 and 48 during 1881 and 1951, because of the changes in the age distributions of the population that had a significantly high

Table 5.3:
Fertility estimates: India (1881–1961)

Period	CBR	CBR^c	CBR^d	TFR^d
1881–91	48.9[a]	NA	46.6	5.76
1891–1901	45.8[a]	49	46.2	5.73
1901–11	49.2[a]	50	46.4	5.72
1911–21	48.1[a]	50	45.6	5.7
1921–31	46.4[a]	48	45.9	5.81
1931–41	45.2[b]	46	46.2	5.93
1941–51	39. 9[b]	44	45	5.91
1951–61	41.7[b]	45	45.4	6.06

Sources: Adapted from Srinivasan (1988, Table 5); a. Kingsley Davis (1951); b. Registrar General of India (1951–61); c. Mukherjee (1976); d. Mari Bhat (1986).

proportion of women in reproductive ages, the fertility rates per woman was relatively low.

The finding of 5–6 children born per woman during the periods before organized family planning programs, when the biological limits were around 9 children per woman as observed in the European populations in the eighteenth century, indicates that cultural factors played a dominant role in shaping fertility patterns and levels. It is also borne from 10 carefully conducted sample surveys by different scholars in various parts of the country. After reviewing data on fertility schedules from a number of surveys and studies from different parts of the country, data on age-specific marital fertility rates were compiled from 10 surveys or studies in different rural parts of India prior to 1962, when contraceptive practice was low and insignificant and it can be presumed that women had close to natural fertility levels. The surveys included a 1958–59 All India National Sample Survey, a local survey in Bengal in 1945–46, three south Indian surveys in 1950–52, three datasets from Punjab, a survey from central India and one from western India. These studies were felt to be carefully conducted inquiries yielding relatively high-quality data and quoted frequently in the Indian demographic literature. Table 5.4 provides these values. A brief statement on the surveys is also included. The mean value of the total marital fertility rate (TMFR) for the age group 20–49, averaged over the 10 datasets, is 5.5, which is quite close to the estimates based on the census age distributions by Mari Bhat (1978).

Another validation of relatively low levels of TFR and CBR are obtained from the registered births and related populations in areas where birth registration was supposed to be very good and complete even during the British rule. Dyson and Murphy (1986) compiled data from four districts of Berar and Madhya Bharat—Akola, Amravati, Buldana and Yeotmal—presently in Maharashtra, and computed the birth and fertility rates based on the vital registration data on the estimated population for the decades 1881–1970 (see Table 5.5).

From Table 5.5, it can be seen that TFR ranged from 4.8 in 1891–90 to 6.0 during 1911–20 and CBR ranged from 38 to 47. Thus, the variations in CBR were larger than the variations in TFR as per the census-based estimates, sample surveys and birth registration data collected from areas where registration system was fairly good and complete. These datasets establish the fact that the fertility levels of populations in India have been historically only at moderate levels—TFR between 5 and 6— and many cultural checks on fertility have been effectively operating in the society. These are the natural fertility levels of the Indian society.

Table 5.4:
Age-specific marital fertility rates from ten selected studies compared with European pattern of natural fertility in rural India (1945–62)

Study Area	Survey Dates	Age Group								Total Marital Fertility Rate
		15–19	20–24	25–29	30–34	35–39	40–44	45–49	
Bengali Rural Hindu Women*	1945–46	0.118	0.323	0.288	0.282	0.212	0.1	0.033	6.19
Ramanagaram Health District	1950	0.117	0.314	0.264	0.201	0.146	0.024	0.001	4.75
Mysore Rural Hill	1952	0.282	0.337	0.317	0.232	0.163	0.057	NA	5.53
(Zones 1 & 2)									
Mysore Rural Plains*	1952	0.277	0.293	0.302	0.17	0.157	0.061	NA	4.92
Poona District*	1952	0.231	0.29	0.267	0.212	0.142	0.071	0.027	5.05
Banaras Tehsil	1956	0.22	0.34	0.32	0.24	0.16	0.12	0.06	6.2
Punjab Chamars*	1959	0.277	0.37	0.357	0.346	0.259	0.113	NA	7.22
Punjab Rural*	1961–62	0.209	0.303	0.295	0.254	0.164	0.087	NA	5.52
Madhya Pradesh Rural*	1961–62	0.186	0.27	0.253	0.208	0.152	0.086	NA	4.85
NSS Rural 14th Round[a]	1958–59	0.195	0.283	0.258	0.205	0.147	0.064	0.025	4.91

Average (India)[b]	Prior to 1962	0.211	0.312	0.292	0.235	0.17	0.078	0.014	5.51
Average of 13 schedules[c]	1600–1955	NA	0.435	0.403	0.371	0.298	0.152	0.022	8.42
Average of 9[d]	1600–1920	NA	0.47	0.442	0.404	0.329	0.173	0.025	9.21

Sources: Adapted from Srinivasan (1988, Table 1); *: Chandrasekaran (1954); United Nations (1961); Dandekar and Dandekar (1953); Rele (1962); Potter et al. (1965); Kumar (1971); a: Registrar General of India (1964); b: Indian Statistical Institute (1963); c: Henry (1961); d: computed from Henry (1961) omitting Iran, India, Taiwan and Guinea and including only schedules of European fertility.

Note: NA = not available.

Table 5.5:
Fertility estimates: Berar (1881—1970)

Period	Crude Birth Rate	Total Fertility Rate
1881–90	39.4 (40.8)	5.1
1891–1900	38.3 (38.4)	4.78
1901–10	47.1 (49.3)	5.65
1911–20	45.6 (46.8)	6.02
1921–30	44.1 (46.5)	5.79
1931–40	40.7 (41.0)	5.12
1941–50	38.6 NA	4.75
1951–60	38.4 NA	4.75
1961–70	41.1 NA	5.66
Average	41.5 —	5.29

Source: Estimates from Dyson and Murphy (1985) based
essentially on vital registration data.
Notes: Averages are corresponding averages of official rate for
Maharashtra; figures in parentheses are corresponding averages
of official rates; NA = not available; Berar comprises the four
districts of Akola, Amravati, Buldana and Yeotmal in parentheses;
figures in parentheses are corresponding averages of official rates.

Louis Henry (1961) defined natural fertility as the marital fertility
prevailing in a population in the absence of any deliberate birth control.
Based on an analysis of data on age-specific marital fertility rates collected
from 13 populations with no use of contraception, 9 from European
populations and 4 from other regions, including one from India (which
Henry considered to be under natural fertility conditions), he derived
certain properties of such fertility schedules. The nine schedules relating
to European origin populations were mostly French speaking and for
whom data were compiled from parish registers, some as early as 1600 AD.
The other four schedules were from Guinea, India, Iran and Taiwan,
using data from surveys considered reliable. The estimates of marital
fertility rates that he made on the basis of these datasets are given in the
last row of Table 5.4. Henry made following two major observations from
his analysis of fertility schedules:

1. Populations can differ widely in their natural fertility levels.
   For example, in the 13 schedules Henry studied, TMFRs among

women aged 20–49 ranged from 6.1 in Hindu villages of Bengal in 1945–46 to 10.9 among Hutterite women (French–Canadian) married during 1921–30. The natural fertility of the Hindu women was only 57 percent of that of the Hutterite women.

2. In spite of substantial differences in natural fertility levels among the 13 groups included in the study, their age patterns of fertility were essentially the same. The curves of age-specific marital fertility rates were almost parallel for different populations. Data on natural fertility levels and patterns, available from different parts of India, reveals not only substantially lower levels of natural fertility than in Western populations but also substantial regional variations. Indian TMFR, even in the absence of contraception, was only 65 percent of the average of the 13 schedules. Henry did not include women aged 15–19 in his analysis of marital fertility because of significant numbers of premarital pregnancies in this group in the European populations that he studied. If we relate Indian TMFR of the age group of 20–49 to the average TMFR of only the 9 European schedules of marital fertility that he studied (Table 5.5), yielding a TMFR value of 9.2, the ratio works out to only 60 percent. While for the age group of 20–24, the average Indian marital fertility rate is 66 percent of European fertility and for 35–39 and 40–44, rates were still lower at 52 and 37 percent as compared to European fertility. Not only was the level of Indian natural fertility lower but also the age pattern differed from European fertility. Indian women seem to have completed their childbearing earlier by resorting, possibly, to terminal abstinence based on a "grandmother complex."

While the average marital fertility rate for age group 15–44 is 65, they varied from 5.3 in Mysore to 8.5 in Punjab as per the 10 datasets for India. Thus, even under natural fertility conditions, with no use of modern contraception, there is substantial variation in fertility in different areas of the country. The major proximate determinants of natural fertility are breastfeeding duration, norms of sexual abstinence, biological levels of fecundity and extent of spontaneous fetal loss. Any differences in observed natural fertility should be explained in variations in one or more of these proximate determinants. Unfortunately, since we do not have data on these proximate variables for different parts of the country where the surveys were conducted and for the same periods, it is difficult to separate out their contributions to variations in natural fertility. We can only conclude that one or more of these determinants varied among different regions of the country.

Modernization and Natural Fertility Changes

Modernization can be defined as the process of transforming a society from its traditional values to a modern set of values and associated behavioral changes (Inkeles and Smith 1974). In Europe, modernization seems to have begun in the late seventeenth century and swept through country after country then it spread in North America and Oceania, changing religious beliefs and dogma, occupational structure, economic conditions and almost all other aspects of life. In Asia, Japan led the process of modernization in the late-nineteenth century. Modernization has brought macro-level economic and social changes.

On the economic side, modernization involves a sustained rise in real output per head and wide-ranging changes in techniques of producing, transporting and distributing goods in the scale and organization of productive activities and in types of outputs and inputs. It also embraces major shifts in the industrial, occupational and spatial distribution of productive resources and in the degree of exchange and monetization of the economy. On the social and demographic side, it involves significant alterations in fertility, mortality and migration in place of residence, family size and structure, educational system and provision for public health. Its influence extends to the areas of income distribution, class structure, government organization and political structure. In terms of human personality, modernization is characterized by an increased openness to new experience, increased independence from parental authority, belief in the efficacy of science and ambition for oneself and one's children (Easterlin and Crimmins 1985: 3–4).

The process of modernization, as defined above, was ushered into India on an extensive scale in the middle of the last century, with Macaulay introducing Western-style education in 1835 (Allen et al. 1969; Biswas and Agarwal 1985) and census taking in 1872. Western-style education has modified many traditional values for marriages, family ties, kin and caste relationships and attitudes on various religious beliefs and dogmas. These changes have had an impact on Indian fertility by altering natural fertility and nuptiality patterns. With the attainment of political independence in 1947 and the launch of various developmental plans for economic and social betterment of the people, modernization has accelerated in India with varying degrees of impact in different parts of the country. Many of the proximate determinants of natural fertility are changing with modernization.

Empirical Support for Increased Natural Fertility Levels in India during the 1950s and 1960s

The substantial body of empirical data on marital fertility patterns in India, compiled at different times over a period of three decades, supports the hypothesis that natural fertility increased systematically in a number of states. From a detailed analysis of data on age-specific marital fertility rates, compiled from two large-scale rural sample surveys conducted in 1959 and 1972 in 11 major states in India (see Table 5.6), Srinivasan and Jejeebhoy (1981) observed:

> The results consistently indicate an increase in the total marital fertility rates in eight of the eleven states (the exceptions being Kerala, Orissa and Punjab) between 1959 and 1972. The most striking increases in total marital fertility have been observed in those states where there has been practically no prevalence of contraception. The increase is 28 percent in Uttar Pradesh, 26 percent in Rajasthan, 13 percent in Madhya Pradesh—and all these states were practically under natural fertility conditions... (1981: 103)

In rural Karnataka, despite substantial increase in contraceptive practice during the 13-year period, total marital fertility increased by 2.3 percent. Srinivasan and Jejeebhoy concluded that natural fertility levels may vary widely among populations within nation at a given time and, in general, those levels are likely to rise during the early stages of modernization.

Ten Indian states were analyzed to test the synthetic framework that Easterlin (1978) has developed to explain the transition from natural to controlled fertility. The analysis by Srinivasan et al. (1984) suggested a procedure for estimating natural fertility based on the number of children born to married women aged 35–44 who had at least two living children (at the time of the survey in 1970), and observed that in the process of modernization, natural fertility levels tended to increase (see Table 5.7).

Table 5.6:
Observed age-specific marital fertility schedules, rural areas of selected states: India (1959 and 1972)

Staff	Year	20–24	25–29	30–34	35–39	40–44	TMFR (20–44)	No. of Households Sampled
Andhra Pradesh	1959	0.2742	0.2804	0.1756	0.1034	0.0452	4.394	27,492
	1972	0.3068	0.2236	0.1783	0.1221	0.0484	4.396	11,186
Gujarat	1959	0.3275	0.3302	0.2759	0.1951	0.0765	6.026	11,376
	1972	0.3731	0.3615	0.2694	0.1954	0.1110	6.552	10,070
Karnataka	1959	0.2773	0.2846	0.1867	0.1359	0.0465	4.655	11,103
	1972	0.2812	0.2572	0.1839	0.1342	0.0902	4.734	8,928
Kerala	1959	0.3294	0.3468	0.2436	0.1989	0.0637	5.912	8,584
	1972	0.3631	0.3105	0.2303	0.1571	0.0742	5.676	9,712
Madhya Pradesh	1959	0.2930	0.2777	0.2582	0.1867	0.0908	5.532	18,468
	1972	0.2978	0.3266	0.2853	0.2098	0.1346	6.270	5,974
Maharashtra	1959	0.2945	0.2361	0.2071	0.1340	0.0500	4.609	21,906
	1972	0.2988	0.2920	0.2039	0.1400	0.0577	4.912	8,752
Odisha	1959	0.2971	0.2777	0.1805	0.1369	0.0445	4.683	7,298
	1972	0.2538	0.2876	0.1848	0.1269	0.0803	4.667	5,350
Punjab*	1959	0.3706	0.3081	0.2983	0.1981	0.1289	6.520	7,351
	1972	0.3684	0.3554	0.3073	0.1837	0.0954	6.551	7,913

Rajasthan	1959	0.2971	0.2770	0.187	0.2151	0.0747	5.255	10.327
	1972	0.3231	0.3798	0.2839	0.2039	0.1242	6.574	0.6797
Tamil Nadu	1959	0.2871	0.2267	0.1447	0.0965	0.0295	3.923	24.773
	1972	0.3298	0.2577	0.1926	0.1113	0.0511	4.713	11.875
Uttar Pradesh	1959	0.2896	0.2174	0.2492	0.1763	0.0829	5.347	25.465
	1972	0.3259	0.3673	0.3125	0.2276	0.1307	6.820	7.772

Sources: Srinivasan (1988, Table 6); 1959—Rao (1967); adjusted marital fertility rates obtained from age-specific fertility rates in Indian Statistical Institute (1963); 1972—Registrar General of India (1976a).

Notes: *The 1972 rates for Punjab include Haryana to make them comparable with 1959. The remaining states have been excluded for the following reasons: (1) poor 1959 and 1972 data in Assam, Bihar and Jammu & Kashmir; (2) no 1959 data available for Himachal Pradesh, Meghalaya, Manipur, Nagaland, Sikkim and Tripura; (3) no 1972 rural data available for West Bengal; (4) boundary changes—Haryana, part of the Punjab in 1959, has been incorporated into the Punjab.

Table 5.7:
Estimates of natural fertility, child survival, children ever born and proportion ever practising contraception for currently married women, married only once aged 35–44 with two or more living children at the time of survey for ten Indian states (1970)

State	NF	CS	CEB	PEPC
Andhra Pradesh	5.86	0.763	5.87	23.8
Gujarat	6.19	0.8	6.04	34.1
Karnataka	6.05	0.813	5.99	17.5
Kerala	5.96	0.864	5.85	5.7
Madhya Pradesh	5.47	0.779	5.49	15.4
Maharashtra	5.86	0.817	5.57	41.1
Punjab	6.4	0.797	5.94	42.4
Rajasthan	6.06	0.746	5.91	19
Tamil Nadu	6.18	0.777	5.89	39.1
Uttar Pradesh	6.01	0.72	5.94	12.8

Source: Based on Easterlin and Crimmins (1985: 154–60).
Notes: NF = natural fertility; CS = child survival; CEB = children ever born; PEPC = proportion ever practising contraception.

Natural fertility levels vary even among the fertile women in the same age group (35–39) from 64 in Punjab to 5.5 in Madhya Pradesh (Table 5.7). Levels are generally higher in states relatively more advanced in various developmental criteria. The correlation coefficient between the observed fertility levels (children ever born; CEB) and the percentage using contraception (CPR) is low at 0.02 and not significant from zero. Higher contraceptive use should theoretically imply lower fertility, but since states with greater use also tended to have higher natural fertility in the early 1970s, the relation of use and actual marital fertility is not empirically observable. On the other hand, the correlation coefficient between natural fertility (NF) and observed fertility (CEB) is quite high at 0.80 and statistically significant. Observed fertility levels seem to have been more influenced by changes in natural fertility than by changes in contraceptive use until 1970, supporting the view that marital fertility may not decrease during the early phase of fertility transition (it may even increase in some situations) because increased contraceptive use does little more than offset increased natural marital fertility.

The point brought out by the analysis of Srinivasan et al. (1984) is that the relative levels of observed marital fertility, by themselves, are not good indicators of the stage of demographic transition. Some Indian states are considerably more advanced in motivation for fertility control and show more response in actual use of contraception, even though their comparative levels of marital fertility may differ a little from the average. Studying the association among state-level differences in the use of contraception and actual fertility, Srinivasan et al. (1984) conclude:

> This conforms to our expectation that, in the early stages of transition from natural to controlled fertility, observed marital fertility may be constant, or even rising, as the positive effect of higher natural fertility offsets the negative effects of control through contraception. In some states, unregulated fertility may result in greater than average numbers of surviving children because of increase in natural fertility. (1984: 292)

Data from a number of localized, large-scale sample surveys conducted in different parts of the country, at different times, reveals a similar finding of increasing marital fertility in the early stage of modernization.

Srinivasan, Reddy and Raju (1978) compared cumulative and current fertility patterns of largely overlapping and comparable areas covered by the Mysore Population Study conducted in 1951–52 and the Bangalore Population Study in 1975 in Karnataka. Cumulative fertility rates of ever-married women failed to show any decline in any age group in the reproductive span during this 24-year period in spite of substantial increases in contraceptive use in every group during the period. Similarly, marital fertility rates of women in 1975 revealed a change in the age pattern from the 1951 rates that cannot be fully accounted for by the phenomena of rising age at marriage and higher contraceptive use at older ages. The natural fertility of married women increased substantially at ages 20–29.

For example, the average number of children ever born to ever-married and recently married women in Bangalore city rose from 1951 to 1975 even as the proportion ever using contraception grew substantially in all ages in this period (see Table 5.8). The fact that the greater percentages of couples were using contraception in 1975 than in 1951 had very little apparent impact on the observed mean number of children born in the age groups of 15–24 and 25–34.

For age groups 20–24 and 25–29, there was also a sharp increase in age-specific marital fertility between 1951 and 1975 in spite of a substantial increase in the percentage of those who had ever used contraception. Particularly intriguing is the increase at age 25–29, where the proportion practicing contraception rose by 203 percentage points in

Table 5.8:
Mean number of children ever born and level of contraceptive practice for ever married and currently married women: Bangalore city (1951 and 1975)

Mean No. of Children Ever Born			Percentage Practising Contraception Among Currently Married (aged 15–34) Only					
	Ever Married		*Currently Married*		*AU Methods*		*Modern Methods*	
Age Group of Women	*1951*	*1975*	*1951*	*1975*	*1951*	*1975*	*1951*	*1975*
15–24	1.3	1.4	1.3	1.4	8.5	18.5	2.8	18.5
25–34	3.2	3.4	3.4	3.4	18.7	36.1	6	36.1
35–44	4.9	5.2	5.4	5.2	NA	NA	NA	NA
45+	5.3	5.7	5.9	5.8	NA	NA	NA	NA

Sources: Adapted from Srinivasan, Reddy and Raju (1978, Table 12) and UN (1961, Table 10.1).
Note: Data on contraceptive practice were collected only for currently married women aged 18–33 in 1951, hence, the comparison is restricted to the age group 15–34.

24 years. If we consider only modem methods of contraception, the increase was 31.3 points among ever users. Since the methods used in 1975 were quite efficient (mostly sterilization and IUDs), one should expect at least a 20 percent decline in fertility between 1951 and 1975 (from 36.2 to 15.9), assuming that the potential fertility of acceptors was same as that of all women in the age group. The quality of data collected in the surveys conducted in 1951 and 1975 have been found to be exceedingly good since both the surveys were large-scale studies, carefully designed and field managed; the former carried out under the auspices of the United Nations Population Division and the latter with financial assistance and support from the World Bank. There appears to be no reason to attribute the increase in the marital fertility rates in age groups of 20–24 and 25–29 between 1951 and 1975 to variations in quality of data. (A number of studies show that potential fertility of acceptors is actually higher than the average for their age group.) The 14 percent increase in marital fertility at age group 25–29 suggests that natural fertility should have increased substantially from 1951 to 1975. Thus, any analysis of statewide fertility differentials of family planning program impacts on fertility should consider the variations in natural fertility levels and patterns among states at different modernization levels.

6

Nuptiality and Stability of Marriage[*]

Norms on Marriage in India

The term "nuptiality" connotes the dimension of marriage and related status of an individual. It includes the marital status—single, widowed, divorced or separated—age at marriage and the other conditions of marital status and factors affecting such conditions. The levels and patterns of natural fertility described in the previous section pertain only to the fertility of married women, with husbands alive during the periods for which the population has been studied. A population's overall fertility, computed in measures such as CBR or TFR, is a function of marital fertility levels, proportions married at different ages and the age–sex distribution. Total fertility in a population can have substantial variation, even under a specified natural fertility schedule, depending on the variation in the proportions of women married at different ages within the reproductive span. Similarly, CBRs, under a specified natural fertility regime, can vary substantially depending on the age–sex–marital distribution of the population.

In Indian culture, cutting across all the religions, marriage of one's daughter is one of the prime responsibilities of the parents. Marriage is always viewed as a relationship between two families and not just

---

[*] *This chapter is an expanded and updated version of an earlier paper of mine co-authored with K.S. James "The Golden Cage: Stability of the Institution of marriage in India" published in Economic and Political Weekly, March 28, 2015; Vol. L No.13.*

between two individuals, husband and wife. In the Hindu belief system, giving one's daughter in marriage, as a virgin, called *Kanyadan*, is one of the great merits of a person. Prepubertal and child marriages were widely practiced in India from time immemorial and, even now, it is practiced in sizeable number (but in decreasing proportions in many communities) especially in the northern states. This custom of child marriage was institutionalized in the Hindu religion by ascribing a good deal of *punya* (merit) to parents who gave their daughter in prepubertal marriage to an eligible bachelor. Early age at marriage and universality of marriage are typical of Indian societies and very different from the practices in the Western culture. In Western societies, even in the seventeenth and eighteenth centuries, the bridal age was quite high, above 25, according to historical demographic data. A small proportion of women remained single throughout their lives (see Table 6.1). On the other hand, historically, the age at marriage for girls in India was quite low and prepubertal marriages were very common. There was generally a cultural prohibition on widow marriages, even of girls widowed at very young age.

Even as early as 1700, the mean age at marriage for many European women was much higher than that of Indian women two centuries later. The proportions of women remaining single had always been lower in India (about 1–2 percent) than in European societies (10–20 percent). The effect of the Indian customs of early and universal marriage has been to maintain relatively high fertility levels as mentioned earlier. In the previous paragraphs, we found that the natural fertility levels of

Table 6.1:

Mean age at marriage of women: Selected European countries (18th–19th centuries) and India (20th century)

Country	Time Period		
	Pre-1750	*1740–90*	*1780–1820*
Belgium	25	24.8	27.9
England	25	25.3	24.2
France	24.6	26	26.7
Germany	26.4	26.9	27.5
Scandinavia	26.7	25.5	29.8
India	1901–11	1941–51	1971–81
	12	15.4	18.4

Source: Srinivasan (1988c, Table 2).

women in India were substantially lower than those of Western women. This low level of natural fertility was compensated to some extent by the high proportions of younger women married in India.

Universal marriage and the low age of brides ensured that the proportions married in each age group (especially up to 30 when marital fertility rates were maximal) were very high. High mortality in the past and the prohibition of widow remarriages among the higher castes contributed to a reduction in the proportions currently married women over 30 years of age. Overall, the universality of marriage and the low age at marriage contributed to raising CBR and TFR to moderately higher levels. Had the nuptiality patterns in India remained at European levels, CBR and TFR, coupled with India's low natural fertility, would have resulted in a much lower birth rate, putting TFR and population survival in jeopardy.

Legal Provisions Against Child Marriages

British were very much aware of the health and life hazards of young girls marrying in their childhood ages and exposing themselves to the risks of child bearing at tender ages when their reproductive systems were not fully developed. For them, MMRs were well above 1,000 maternal deaths per 100,000 live births (Mari Bhat 1989). In 1929, they brought in the Child Marriage Restraint Act, 1929, also called the Sarda Act to restrict the practice of child marriages. It became a law on April 1, 1930 extended across the whole nation, except Jammu and Kashmir, and applied to every Indian citizen. Its goal was to eliminate the dangers placed on young girls unnecessarily exposing themselves to the stress of married life and avoid early deaths. The Sarda Act was very instrumental in restricting, to a large extent, the incidences of child marriages, girls getting married before the age of 14.

After the independence and adoption of Indian Constitution in 1950, the child marriage act has undergone several revisions. NPP 1976, described in Chapter 3, stated that the minimum legal age for marriage should be 18 for girls and 21 for boys. This was implemented as a separate law in 1978. Under the Hindu Marriage Act passed in 1955, the minimum age at marriage was already 18 for girls and 21 for boys, but it was restricted to Hindu marriages only. The 1978 Act extended this minimum age to all religions; however, this has been challenged in Indian courts, with some Indian Muslim organizations seeking no minimum age and that the age matter should be left to their personal laws. Since 1978 until 2015, child marriage and age at marriage was an active political subject as well as a subject of continuing cases under review in the highest courts of India. According to the 1878 Act, a minor is a child of either sex of 18 years or younger. The punishment for a male between 18 and 21 years marrying a child was an imprisonment of up to 15 days or a fine of 1,000 rupees, or both. The punishment for a male above 21 years of age marrying a minor was an imprisonment of up to three months and a possible fine. The punishment for anyone who performed or directed a child marriage ceremony was an imprisonment of up to three months and a possible fine, unless s/he could prove the marriage performed was not a child marriage. The punishment for a parent or guardian of a child taking part in the marriage was an imprisonment of up to three months and/or a possible fine. These penalties have been amended time and again.

Continued Prevalence of Child Marriages

The age at marriage has been steadily rising in every part of the country during the past five decades because of modernization, education of women, changing cultural norms on age at marriage, and legislations of minimum age at marriage act stipulating that it is illegal for a woman to get legally married before the age of 18 and for men before the age of 21. However, marriages of girls below the age of 18 are still widely prevalent in many parts of the country. Many of them are child marriages but may not be reported as such fearing the persecution by the law. According to the censuses of 1981, 1991, 2001 and 2011, the percentage of women married before the age of 18, has declined steadily from 43.4 percent to, 35.3, 14.4 and 3.5. According to NFHS-3, conducted during 1998–99, 43.4 percent of the women in the age group of 15–19 were reported as married; the value was higher than the 1991 census figures. There is always a caution in the reporting of ages of young married women because of fears of severe penalties under the law.

A careful study on the prevalence and trends in child marriages in different parts of the country has recently been conducted by the International Center for Research on Women (ICRW; Srinivasan et al. 2015). Authors conclude that although the incidence of child marriages have been declining over time, it is still widely prevalent in some parts of the country. They used the data from the population by age and marital status given in the censuses of 1991, 2001 and 2011 and also the data from the District Level Household Surveys (DLHS) and various rounds conducted by

IIPS, Mumbai. The most recent census of 2011 reveals that 22 percent of females aged 15–19 in rural areas and 15 percent in the urban areas are ever married, and most of them can be categorized as child marriages, that is, below the age of 18. Although there has been appreciable decline in the prevalence of such marriages in all the states in the last two decades (comparing the censuses of 1991, 2001 and 2011), the changes over time have not always been smooth and consistent in many states. There are marked rural–urban differences in prevalence trends. As per Srinivasan et al. (2015), there were steep declines in the marriage rate among 15–19 year old females between 1991 and 2001 in both rural and urban areas, followed by very little variation in the trend between 2001 and 2011. Some states, such as Gujarat and Andhra Pradesh, have seen much slower reductions in child marriage prevalence, while others have experienced rapid declines. In others, the marriage rate in this age group seems to have experienced an upturn between 2001 and 2011, in both rural and urban areas. In rural Maharashtra, for example, between 1991 and 2001, there was significant decline in the marriage rate, by about 13 percentage points, among 15–19 year old females; however, between 2001 and 2011, there was slight increase in the percentage of 15–19 year old ever-married females in both rural and urban areas. Gujarat makes for a curious study because although there was a substantial decline between 1991 and 2001 in percentage of 15–19 year old ever-married females, the trend took an upturn between 2001 and 2011, markedly in urban areas. The increase in many states, though slight, needs to be investigated, especially in the light of the rapid social and economic development that many states, including Gujarat, have experienced in the last 15 years.

Although the practice of child marriage exists in every part of the country, without exception, district level analysis of percentage of women married in the age group 15–19 using the census data revealed interesting findings. Figure 6.1 gives the map of India by districts, indicating by shading the intensity of child marriages, defined as the proportion of women married in the age group 15–19 as per the 2011 census. Figure 6.2 gives a shaded map of the Indian districts according to the proportion of women married before the age of 18, among them the recently married women aged 20–24, according the DLHS-3 survey conducted during 2007–08. According to the authors who made a detailed study on this topic, there are two prominent clusters of districts with high levels of child marriage within the country. A large cluster is found in the belt comprising Uttar Pradesh, Madhya Pradesh, Rajasthan, Bihar and

Figure 6.1:
District-wise percentage of ever-married women aged 15–19 years, India (Census 2011)

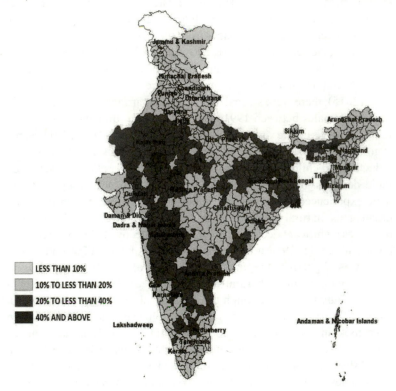

LESS THAN 10%

10% TO LESS THAN 20%

20% TO LESS THAN 40%

40% AND ABOVE

Source: Padmavathi Srinivasan et al. (2015).
Notes: Reproduced from ICRW publication with permission from the first author. Figure is not scaled.

Chhattisgarh, and a smaller one comprising southern parts of Andhra Pradesh, Southeastern Maharashtra and Northern Karnataka. Almost two-thirds of the districts in Madhya Pradesh, Uttar Pradesh, Bihar, Jharkhand and Rajasthan have more than 50 percent of women who are married before the legal marriage age. However, the smaller but significant cluster in the South needs further investigation. Although the southern states have moderate or low levels of child marriage, there are one or two districts in each of these states with high levels of child marriage that are significant.

Figure 6.2:
District-wise percentage of currently married women aged 20–24, married before the age of 18 years (DLHS 2007–08)

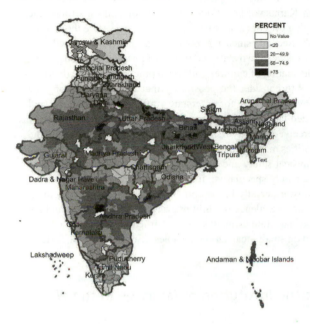

Source: Padmavathi Srinivasan et al. (2015).
Notes: Reproduced from ICRW publication with permission from the first author. Figure is not scaled.

There are 16 districts in the country where 75 percent or more of currently married women ages 20–24 years are married before the age of 18 years. Among these districts, six are in the state of Bihar, six in Uttar Pradesh, one each in Madhya Pradesh, Jharkhand, Orissa, and Karnataka. Most of these districts curiously lie along state borders [Figure 6.1]. The district of Gulbarga in Karnataka, where 77 percent of women are married before the age of 18, lies along the border between Andhra Pradesh and Karnataka. The district of Buduan in Uttar Pradesh, where about 80 percent of women are married before the age of 18, lies on the state line between Uttar Pradesh and Bihar. (Srinivasan et al. 2015)

There may be several plausible reasons for the high child marriage prevalence in the border districts. First, the border districts typically imbibe
cultural and social customs and practices characteristic of the adjoining
states. Although Karnataka has moderate levels of child marriage, the
custom of marrying off girls at an early age remains pervasive throughout
Andhra Pradesh. Second, since the populations in towns and villages
along the border between two states comprise of people from both states,
there is an amalgamation of cultures and social practices in these districts.
Third, one needs to consider the possibility that towns lying along the
borders are convenient hubs for interstate trafficking of children and
women for bonded labour, prostitution, and forced marriage. Because of
either real or perceived security risks to adolescent females, parents in the
state border localities may feel compelled to marry their daughter off early
to ensure her physical safety and protect her chastity. However, as these
explanations are purely speculative, it is important that these districts be
studied thoroughly, especially in the context of their geopolitical setting,
to discern the exact prevalence of child marriage in these regions and the
causes. Child marriage rate estimates vary significantly between sources,
with some based on small local survey samples. (Srinivasan et al. 2015)

Breakdown of the Institution of Marriage in the West

As is well known and well documented in the published literature, the
institution of marriage under which reproduction is expected to take
place across most cultures and religious groups over centuries, is found
to be breaking down, rather pretty fast, in the Western societies and there
is a growing concern that similar situation may spread across the globe
(Inglehart 1970, 1985; Lesthaeghe 2002; Srinivasan and James 2015;
Weiss 1975, 1979). The recent article by Srinivasan and James (2015),
based on an analysis of data on the percentages of women remaining
single in different age groups over time periods in different states in
India and comparing them with four selected developed countries, it
was found that while modernization has pushed up the age at marriage in
India across the states, the ultimate proportion of women marrying by
age 30–34 remained high and almost constant at about 90 percent, and
the divorce or separation rates were also low unlike in the West. This
was found in more developed states as Kerala and Tamil Nadu and less
developed states as Bihar and Uttar Pradesh. Through an analysis of
household level data made available from NFHS-3 (2005–06), the authors

found that religion and caste, in which the institution of marriage is rooted in India, are the most crucial determinants of the status of marriage in any age. In this context, a brief overview of the extent of marital break-down in the West is in order. Some of the major findings of this study are given below in order to establish that the institution of marriage is relatively more stable in India than in the West and is likely to remain so in the near future.

According to statistics compiled by the United Nations on marriage (United Nations 2012), a very high proportion of women in the age group 30–34 are reported to be single or unmarried in many West European countries. Around 2010, it was 53.8 percent in Sweden, 49.4 in Norway, 48.9 in Ireland, 48.7 in France and 47.8 in the United Kingdom. A trend line, showing the pace of increase in the proportion of women single during the past 30 years for Sweden and France is given in Figure 6.1.

Many of these women who have reported to be unmarried legally are living with their partners in conjugal relationships called "live-in" arrangements. Live-in arrangements are cohabitations without formal marriage between the sexes and even of persons in the same sex and have become an alternative to formal marriage, at least, on a temporary basis in many Western countries. A majority of births to women in the Scandinavian and other European countries occur under such live-in arrangement or for single women. During the year 2012, 59.1 percent of births in Estonia, 57.6 in Slovenia, 55.7 in France and 54.1 in Bulgaria occurred to unmarried women. A line graph of percentage of births to single women to total births in France and Sweden showing the pace of increase in such births during the past 30 years is given in Figure 6.3.

Even among married women, divorce rates are rising rapidly. In the United Kingdom, 5.8 percent of the women in the age group 30–34 reported themselves as divorced, and in France this figure was 4.7 in the year 2009. Around 2010, the percent of women reported as divorced in the age group 30–34 was very high among the states separated from the former Soviet Union—17.2 in Ukraine, 12.5 in Belarus, 14.7 in Russian Federation, 16.4 in Estonia and 9.9 in Lithuania. Divorce rates among the countries separated from the former Soviet Union seem to be much higher than in the rest of the European countries, such as France, United Kingdom and Germany, that had divorce rates of 4.7, 5.8 and 6.4 respectively. The breakdown of the Soviet Union as an authoritarian political entity seems to have contributed to a sharp increase in the breakdown of marriage as an institution, implying a relationship between the institution of marriage and the political system. A trend line showing the percentage

Figure 6.3:
Trends in single women in the age group 30–34 in France and Sweden

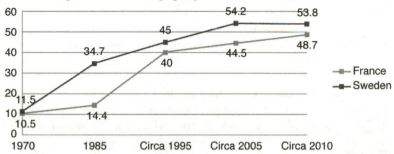

Source: World Marriage Prospects of United Nations: 2012 Revision.

of women divorced in ages 30–34 for Ukraine and France is given in Figure 6.3.

Figures comparing the living arrangements of children aged 0–14 in 30 Organization for Economic Cooperation and Development (OECD) member countries in 2007 found that the United Kingdom has one of the highest rates of family breakdown in the Western world for countries for which such data were available, with just 68.9 percent of children living with both parents. The proportion of children living with their mother and not their father in the United Kingdom was 27.6 percent, while for those living with only their father is 2.4 percent. The data also indicates that in terms of proportion of children living with both the parents, the United Kingdom is fourth lowest among the OECD countries behind Belgium, Latvia and Estonia. Finland had the most children living with both parents, 95.2 percent. The lowest percentage of all was in Latvia at 64.9; Germany stood at 82, Italy at 92.1, Spain at 91.5 and the United States on 70.7 percent, and the average was 84 percent (Eurostat Data Base 2012).

Thus, it is evident from data on reported percentages of women remaining single, divorced, children to unwed mothers and children living with only one parent that the institution of marriage is breaking down in Europe and in populations of European origin. The dimensions of percent of women remaining single in ages 30–34 (expected to be in marriage in a stable marriage environment), percent of women divorced in the same age group (need to stay in marriage in a stable environment) and percent of children born out of wedlock (considering reproduction within marriage as an essential function of marriage) seem to represent three different dimensions of the institution of marriage and changes in them indicates a breakdown of marriage.

Causes of Marital Breakdown

Many studies have been carried out on the pace of breakdown of marriages in the Western countries and the underlying causes for the same. Literally, thousands of scholarly research articles on marriage, divorce and family have been written, and this topic is one of the most debated topics in the society from the sociological, economic and gender perspectives. The prestigious *Journal of Marriage and Family* published in United States of America since 1939 is completely devoted to this phenomenon. It is difficult to make a comprehensive review of all these studies in this article but, in order to be relevant to our study, we review a few important recent studies that have relevance to the objectives of this paper, that is, for measuring the stability of the institution of marriage at the country or macro level and relating them to selected causal factors for which information is available in published records in the public domain.

Historically, the fall in fertility below replacement level has been considered as one of the triggers for the breakdown of marriages. The formulation of second demographic transition (SDT) theory to explain why fertility levels doggedly refuse to go up even after reaching well below replacement levels has been based on the empirical examination of such trends across Western European countries (Lesthaeghe and Neidert 2006) and marriage breakdown is a logical consequence of such low fertility levels. To quote Lesthaeghe (2006),

> during the first demographic transition (FDT), the decline in fertility was 'unleashed by an enormous sentimental and financial investment in the child' (i.e., the 'king child era' to use Ariès's term), whereas the motivation during the second demographic transition (SDT) is adult self-realization within the role or lifestyle as a parent or more complete and fulfilled adult.

The breakdown in the institution of marriage seems to have commenced in the 1960s and is continuing unabated in the Western societies.

In the recent article by Srinivasan and James (2015), cited earlier, they observed,

> The form and nature of marriage and family life have . ..nged over the past few decades in Western societies and in East Asia, but they have

taken different pathways. Reproduction is becoming delinked from marriage in the West, while in East Asia remaining single has become more of a norm. Looking at how the various factors operating in these societies impinge on marriages in India, this paper finds that while development has contributed to a significant rise in age at marriage, it has not altered the ultimate proportion of the population getting married by 30–34. These figures are in stark contrast to what is observed in the West and Japan. Deeply rooted in religion and caste, and with marital breakdown facing punishing social and economic costs, the institution of marriage is strong in India and unlikely to show signs of a breakdown in the near future.

For the measurement of marital stability, they used the age group 30–34 for women and the proportion of single and the proportion of divorced in the same group to study the marital stability and found that the major factor contributing to this stability is the high prevalence of marriages within the same caste and religion and the high costs—economic and social—of marrying outside the caste and religion of divorce and marital separation. Most of the studies on the measurement of the extent of breakdown of the institution of marriage have focused on the levels in divorce rates in the population, on the levels and trends in births to unmarried women, on the prevalence rates and trends in live-in arrangements among men and women, and their causes and consequences. On the topic of divorce, the seminal and well-quoted work by W. J. Goode (1993) analyses that the world changes in divorce patterns, which does a lucid comparative analysis of international trends in divorces over the past four decades. The author studied the relationships between divorce and a variety of socioeconomic factors such as age and social class.

> We want to know whether the duration of marriage has changed with the increase of divorce rates, whether a higher percentage of divorcing parents are childless, and the likelihood of remarriage. How is the rise in cohabitation linked with the lessened stability of marriage? We must also consider the absence of child support by ex-husbands and the burden on the state as a consequence, and why there is a rise in mother-headed families.

Similarly, on the topic of marriages, the seminal studies by Goldstein and Kenney (2001) have studied the declines in marriage rates in the United States of America and test the hypothesis if these declines predict just the avoidance of marriage as an institution or just delay the events. According to their analysis,

Our forecasts for cohorts born in the 1950s and 1960s suggest that marriage will remain nearly universal for American women—close to 90 percent of women are predicted to marry. However, separate forecasts by educational attainment reveal a new socioeconomic pattern of first marriage: Whereas in the past, women with more education were less likely to marry, recent college graduates are now forecast to marry at higher levels despite their later entry into first marriage.

Thus, while there is recognition of the breakdown of marriages in the United States of America, there is also a hope that the institution will survive the onslaughts on the system. However, they concluded, "that marriage is increasingly becoming a province of the most educated a trend that may become a new source of inequality for future generations."

Recently, there have been many studies by scholars and intelligentsia at large that marriage as an institution is precious and vital to the societal harmony, peace and stability. A group of prominent sociologists have come together and published a well-researched volume (Wilcox et al. 2005), *Why Marriage Matters: Twenty-Six Conclusions from the Social Sciences*. The original study started in 1996, and many subsequent reports have come out.

The National Bureau of Economic Research, USA, has undertaken a series of studies on factors affecting marriage and divorce in different socioeconomic strata and found different trends in different groups. The working paper by Isen and Stevenson (2010) examines how marital and fertility patterns have changed over the years along racial and educational lines for men and women. Historically, women that were more educated were more likely to remain single and even marrying late in life and had fewer children. However, this has changed over time. Recently, marriage and remarriage rates have risen for women with a college degree relative to women with fewer years of education. The institution of marriage is becoming more acceptable to women in the higher economic strata and with higher education. Thus, the study found,

> College educated women marry later, have fewer children, are less likely to view marriage as "financial security", are happier in their marriages and with their family life, and are not only the least likely to divorce, but have had the biggest decrease in divorce since the 1970s compared to women without a college degree. In contrast, there have been fewer changes in marital patterns by education for men.

Higher education of women seems to be a driving force in restoring the institution of marriage.

According to available literature, among the major causes for break-down of marriage four have been emphasized, though not exhaustive: (a) rise of individualism (b) the economic independence of women and rising cost of marriage for women (c) skill specializations and (d) movement towards gender equality. All of these were facilitated by the discovery and easy availability of female contraceptives. These are briefly described below:

1. **Rise of individualism:** The spread of individualism in the most aspects of one's life was observed by many as early as in the middle of the last century. While studying the American families, Kuhn (1955) observed that individualism is not just limited to one cause but is the result of several factors. According to him,

   > Protestantism laid great stress on individual worth, individual moral responsibility, and individual rather than corporate relationships with God. Concomitantly, the rise of commercial relationships and capitalism began to break down all the old settled, feudal relationships that rested on inherited, ascribed, and group-sanctioned status, and to build in their stead relationships of a highly individualistic sort resting on personally achieved status.

   According to Maslow (1954), a leading proponent of this perspective and the famous exponent of hierarchy of needs of human beings,

   > Self-actualization is defined in various ways but a solid core of agreement is perceptible. All definitions accept or imply, (a) acceptance and expression of the inner core or self, i.e., actualization of these latent capacities, and potentialities, "full function", availability of the human and personal essence; (b) they all imply minimal presence of ill health, neurosis, psychosis, or loss or diminution of the basic human and personal capacities....If this essential core (inner nature) of the person is frustrated, denied or suppressed, sickness results, sometimes in obvious forms, sometimes in subtle and devious forms, sometimes immediately, sometimes later.

   Thus we see that as human beings evolve from meeting the basic needs to higher levels, the institution of marriage is only an intermediary stage; self-actualization is the final goal, and marriage may become a hindrance in achieving this goal. According to this theory, each individual has to pursue his/her own inner and external goals, and bondages of marriage may be a hindrance in this direction. Individualism is a necessary step toward self-actualization and marriage an impediment.

2. **Costs of marriage:** Yet another reason identified for the break-down of marriage is the cost of family formation. According to Becker (1960, 1996) and many other economists, all human decisions, including personal ones, are ultimately based on an economic cost-benefit analysis if done overtly or not. When the society is economically backward, it makes economic sense to marry and have children to add to the labor force of the family and living in one house reduces costs. When the society develops and cost of rearing children rises, parents want to control their family size and the decisions are euphemistically put as "baby" or "Baby Austin." When the society becomes economically more advanced and women have good employment potential with specialized skills, the cost of marriage for a woman far outweighs the economic benefits, and the choice may be "marriage" or "Mercedes Benz." Couples used contraception to space and limit their family size in the earlier stage, and when the economy develops further, the choice for women will be when to stop contraception to have a child.

3. **Specialization of skills:** There is growing specialization of skills occurring as the natural byproduct of rapid economic development and consumerism that is taking place in the Western societies, and this trend is occurring in the developing countries as well with a time lag. Specialization is seen in terms of employment, education and health care and social services. Even in schools and colleges, the courses offered for study are becoming varied and specialized. The same is happening in manufacturing, distribution of goods and services, health care, banking and other services. Many responsibilities have been transferred from families to these specialized services such as homes for the aged, security services, maintenance services etc. (Desai and Dubey 2011). The traditional functions of a family have been taken over by nonfamilial institutions as a part of the social and economic development of the country, and marriage has become the casualty of this over specialization.

4. **Gender equality:** Most of the societies in the world in the East or in the West have been based on patriarchy for centuries, where women played a secondary or subordinate role to men. This situation has dramatically changed in the Western societies over the past century, with women getting more and more educated,

economically gainfully employed, politically empowered and women's movements throughout the world arguing for gender equality in all aspects of human existence. Their equity and equality have been demanded as a fundamental aspect of human rights. Reproductive rights and reproductive health have been agreed to by all the nations of the world as an integral part of human rights. Powerful feminist movements in Europe and the United States of America have written about and argued for women's freedom to shape their own lives. The institution of marriage was considered by many of them to be a hindrance on securing gender equity and equality. Many argue that marriage and family have intended to contribute to gender inequities, and those who aspire for female autonomy and gender equity found the institution of marriage a remnant of patriarchal system.

Analysis of Nuptiality in India in Recent Years

It is possible that each of the four contributory factors that operated toward the decline of the institution of marriage in the West are not relevant to the Indian cultural context, and the institution of marriage is relatively stable in India as yet. However, fears have been expressed from different quarters that what happened in the West will definitely occur in India, and signs and symptoms can already be seen. For instance, a web-based survey of the population professionals in India was carried out from October 2013 to January 2014 by the author, mainly to ascertain their views on various population-related issues and policies and programs in the country since 1951 (Srinivasan 2014). A question was also asked about their view or perception on the stability of the institution of marriage in India. The survey was carried out using the SurveyMonkey, and a sample of 242 professionals in the field, which was just 15 percent of the professionals to whom the questionnaire was sent, was covered. Later, a sample of nonrespondents was also surveyed through Google Direct, or personally interviewed, to get just their background details in order to assess the differences between the distributions of the respondents and nonrespondents. Since there were no significant differences between the two distributions on a number of variables, the author decided to proceed with an analysis of the unweighted sample of the respondents as representing the perception of the population professionals.

On the question about the institution of marriage, slightly more than half of the respondents (53 percent) perceived that marriage as "an institution within which child bearing should take place" will break down in India also, and childbearing will eventually be delinked from marriage. Almost 47 percent perceive that this will not happen at any time in the future. The average score is 0.53 with a coefficient of variation of 94.3 percent. This perception is negatively correlated with the respondents' age, marital status, educational qualification, years of association with population policy and the regional association of their working institute. Hence, a graduate male who is single working for around a decade in population policy from the northern state of India is more likely to perceive that marriage as an institution will break down.

Although this finding is based on a small sample of population professionals, it has rung some alarm bells on the future of marriages in India. This chapter, therefore, looks into the patterns of marriage in India with twin objectives in mind. First, it analyses the changes in the marital distributions in India, especially the proportions single and currently married and previously married among women, to study the secular trends in their distributions and explore whether there is already a trend or imminent breakdown in the institutor of marriage, as is happening in Western societies. Second, the chapter compares the trends in marital status distributions in India and Japan with those in France, the United Kingdom and the United States of America. We wish to interpret the data on later age at marriage and larger proportion of women remaining single until the end of the reproductive period. As marriage has deep cultural roots and origin and has foundation in the caste system, the factors that are contributing to the breakdown of marriage observed in the Western societies may not be relevant to India and Asian societies.

Data Used and Methods of Analysis

In this study, we analyze the data on marital status distributions at two levels: macro and micro. At the macro level, we used the data compiled from the population censuses in India and four selected states from 1961 to 2011. For state-level analysis, we selected Bihar, Kerala Tamil Nadu and Uttar Pradesh. Kerala and Tamil Nadu are considered more developed states, socially and economically, while Bihar and Uttar Pradesh represent the less developed states. In terms of Human Development Index (HDI) values estimated at the state level for 23 states of India by the

Planning Commission of India in March 2014, which was based on 2007–08 values, Kerala ranked number one, Tamil Nadu 8, Uttar Pradesh 18, and Bihar 21. For the micro-level analysis, we used the data collected at the individual level in the All India National Sample Survey-3 conducted during 2005–06 for India and the four selected states. The proportions of single women at different ages within the reproductive age group 15–49 from the year 1961 that has been taken from the censuses are given in Table 6.2 for India and the four states. The singulate mean age at marriage (SMAM), computed by the standard Hajnal's method, for India and the sates are given in Table 6.3.

We have also compiled data on the reported marital status of women in four developed countries—France, Germany, Japan and the United Kingdom—as available in the datasets published by the United Nations in their latest set, *World Marriage Prospects 2014*, for the years 1970–2010. The data based on their population censuses and surveys carried out between 1970 and 2010 are tabulated (see Table 6.4). The exact years to which these data relate for India and other countries are in given at the end of Table 6.4. Based on the data on percent of single women in different age groups, we computed SMAM for women (again using the Hajnal's method), and these are given in Table 6.5.

Table 6.2:
Percentage of females remaining single in different age group: India, Bihar, Kerala, Tamil Nadu and Uttar Pradesh (1961–2011)

Year	15–19	20–24	25–29	30–34	35–39	40–44	45–49	50–54
				Age Group				
				India				
1961	29.2	6	1.9	1	0.7	0.6	0.5	0.5
1971	43.7	9.5	2.3	1	0.8	0.6	0.5	0.5
1981	55.9	14	3.3	1.2	0.6	0.5	0.4	0.4
1991	64.3	17	4.2	1.8	0.9	1	0.7	0.8
2001	75.2	23	5.7	2.2	1.3	1.2	0.9	0.9
2011	87.8	37.3	12.2	4	1.4	1.7	0	0
				Bihar				
1961	15.6	3	1.3	0.9	0.7	0.6	0.6	0.6
1971	23.1	3.6	1	0.5	0.4	0.3	0.3	0.3
1981	35.3	5.2	1.3	0.5	0.3	0.3	0.2	0.2
1991	44.2	7.1	1.6	0.9	0.4	0.7	0.5	0.8

Year	Age Group							
	15–19	20–24	25–29	30–34	35–39	40–44	45–49	50–54
2001	60.4	9.5	1.5	0.7	0.6	0.3	0.2	0.3
2011	86	27.8	5.1	1.5	0	0	0	0
Kerala								
1961	69.6	22.7	8	4.5	3.2	2.9	2.2	1.8
1971	81	32.7	9.3	5.3	3.7	3.5	3.1	2.9
1981	85.4	40.2	12.5	5.8	3.5	3.4	2.9	3.1
1991	88.5	43.4	13.9	6.2	3.9	3.7	3	3.2
2001	86.7	41.6	13	5.8	3.9	3.5	3.2	3.4
2011	93.1	48.1	14.6	6.3	3.9	2.6	2.8	3.5
Tamil Nadu								
1971	72.7	17	2.7	1.2	0.7	0.7	0.6	0.5
1981	76.8	22.9	4.8	1.7	0.8	0.7	0.5	0.4
1991	81.9	28.5	6.8	2.5	1.1	1.1	0.7	0.7
2001	84.3	34.8	8.4	3	1.6	1.5	1.1	1.1
2011	94.6	47.9	15.2	4.7	1.3	1.4	1.6	0
Uttar Pradesh								
1961	17	2.5	1	0.6	0.4	0.4	0.3	0.4
1971	26.6	3.8	1.1	0.6	0.7	0.4	0.3	0.3
1981	39	5.8	1	0.3	0.2	0.2	0.1	0.2
1991	53	8.1	1.5	0.7	0.3	0.7	0.6	0.6
2001	72.6	16.1	3	1	0.6	0.6	0.4	0.5
2011	89.9	42.6	10.8	1.6	0	0	0	0

Source: Census of India.

Table 6.3:
Singulate mean age at marriage (SMAM) (15–49 age group) in India and selected states

Selected States	1961	1971	1981	1991	2001	2011
Bihar	15.93	16.37	17.08	17.56	18.59	21.02
Kerala	20.05	21.07	21.84	22.27	21.96	22.71
Tamil Nadu	18.45	19.61	20.27	20.91	21.41	23.12
Uttar Pradesh	15.99	16.57	17.28	18.06	19.57	22.25
India	16.84	17.76	18.66	19.26	20.2	22.22

Source: Census of India.

Table 6.4:
Percentage remaining single among females in each age group in France, Japan, Germany and the UK 1970–2010

Age	1970s				1980s				1990s				2000				2009–10			
	France 1970	Japan 1970	UK 1971	Germany 1970	France 1985	Japan 1985	UK 1981	Germany 1980	France 1999	Japan 1995	UK 1991	Germany 1990	France 2005	Japan 2005	UK 2001	Germany 2000	France 2009	Japan 2010	UK 2009	Germany 2009
15–19	93.7	97.9	91.3	NA	97.9	99.1	95.5	NA	99.4	99.3	98.2	97.8	99.1	99.2	95.2	99.7	99.5	99.4	99.6	97.9
20–24	46.1	71.7	40.3	NA	65	81.6	53.7	NA	93.1	86.8	75.4	74.3	90.8	88.7	69.1	91.4	92.9	89.6	93.3	76.9
25–29	16.5	18.1	13.9	NA	27.2	30.6	19.2	NA	66.2	48.2	38.4	36.6	66.8	59.1	38.1	61.2	70.8	60.3	71.9	45.7
30–34	10.5	7.2	7.8	NA	14.4	10.4	8.8	NA	40	19.7	18.2	17	44.5	32	21.9	38	48.7	34.5	47.8	26.2
35–39	8.9	5.8	7.2	NA	9.4	6.6	6.2	NA	26.2	10.1	10.2	9.8	32.4	18.8	14.3	25.4	36.5	23.1	31.8	16.7
40–44	8.4	5.3	7.7	NA	7.5	4.9	5.6	NA	16.7	6.8	6.4	6.4	23.4	12.2	9.8	16.4	27.9	17.4	22	13.4
45–49	8.3	4	8.3	NA	6.7	4.3	6	NA	11.6	5.6	5.2	5.2	16.2	8.3	7.1	13.2	20.7	12.6	15.1	10.5
50–54	8.1	2.7	9	NA	7	4.4	6.8	NA	8.5	4.6	5	5.3	11.5	6.2	5.2	8.4	14.4	8.7	10.2	8

Sources: United Nations (2012), World Marriage Prospects—2014.

Table 6.5:
Singulate mean age at marriage in India and developed countries

	1961	1970 Circa	1980 Circa	1990 Circa	2000 Circa	Latest
India	16.84	17.76	18.66	19.26	20.2	21.75
France		22.3	24.7	30.7	31	31.6
Germany		NA	NA	26.1	30.1	27.3
Japan		24.7	25.8	27.7	29.4	29.7
UK		21.3	23	26.4	26.3	31.8

Source: United Nations (2012), World Marriage Prospects—2014.

Comparing the figures on SMAM for India and the states given in Table 6.3 and for the developed countries in Table 6.5, reveals that there is a 10-years gap in SMAM values in India compared to the West (22 and 32).

As indicated earlier, we have used mainly three indicators for assessing the breakdown of marriage, that is, proportion of single women in the age group 30–34, SMAM values and the proportion divorced or separated in this age group. Data on the proportion of births to single mothers is not reliably known in India but is expected to be small, based on data available from NFHS surveys.

Single or Unmarried Women in India

Table 6.2 presents the percentage of females remaining single classified in five year age groups from 15–54 for all India along with the four states, two states mentioned above. It can be seen that in terms of percentage of single women that there has been a steady secular increase in the values in the age groups 15–19 and 20–24 and even in 25–29 implying a rise in the age at marriage but afterwards from the age group 30–34 onwards there is a secular decline. This is true with respect to states with advanced demographic transition and early demographic transition as Kerala and Tamil Nadu, and early demographic transition, as Bihar and Uttar Pradesh implying a rapid rise in the incidence of marriage across the country. For example, in Kerala, the percentage of females remaining single in the age group 30–34 in 2011 was 6.3, and in Bihar, it was 1.5. In the same year, in the age group 50–54, the percentage of females remaining single in Kerala was 3.4 compared to 0.00 in Bihar (approximated to the second decimal). Figure 6.4 gives a pictorial representation of the

Figure 6.4:
Trends in percentage of births outside wedlock

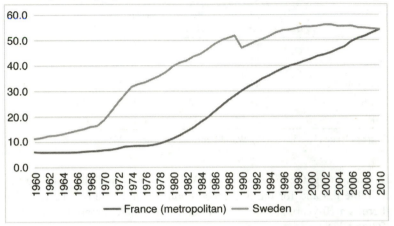

Source: Eurostat Data (2011).

trend lines in the percentage females remaining single in India and the four states for the age groups 30–34. We can see from this figure, how the percentage of females remaining single in all the states seem to converge over time to Kerala's value of 5 percent. While Kerala had 5.3 percent single women in 2011, all other states had somewhere between 1 and 4 percent, but rising to the levels of Kerala. Women in Kerala marry quite late, usually in their mid-20s, and by the age of 30–35, most of them do get married. Marriage is as much universal in Kerala as in other states in spite of its higher literacy rates, much better health conditions and high status of women.

SMAM Values

SMAM for women computed on the basis of data on percentage of females remaining single is presented in Tables 6.3, 6.4 and 6.5. For India as a whole (Table 6.3), it increased from 16.8 in 1961 to 18.7 in 1981 and to 22.22 in 2011. For Bihar, the increase was from 15.9 to 17.0 to 21.0; for Kerala, the rise was from 20.1 in 1961 to 21.8 in 1981 and to 22.7 in 2011; for Tamil Nadu, the figures were 18.5 to 20.3 to 23.1 and in UP it was from 16.0 to 17.3 to 22.2. Thus, the increase in SMAM values over the 50-year period, 1961–2011, was just 2.6 years in Kerala, 4.6 years in Tamil Nadu, 5.1 years in Bihar and 6.2 years in Uttar Pradesh. Figure 6.5

Figure 6.5:
Percentage of women divorced and separated in ages 30–34

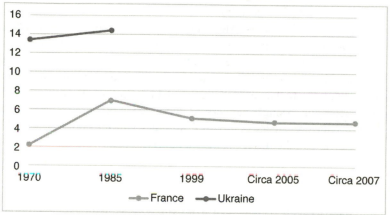

Source: World Marriage Prospects of United Nations (2012).

gives the trend lines pictorially. Again, there is a rapid convergence of all the states in their SMAM values to the Kerala level. This means, the less developed states are catching up with the advanced states in the SMAM values. While the marriage age in the less developed states is rising rapidly, there is a slowdown in the rate of increase in the more developed states.

Comparison with Situation in the Four Developed Countries

The data on marital status distribution of Germany, France, Japan and the United Kingdom for the period around 1970–2010 in each age group (from 15 to 54, divided into eight groups) and the SMAM values are presented in Tables 6.4 and 6.5, respectively. The data for these four developed countries presents a completely different picture from India. In the 30–34 age groups, while the percent of single women in India in 2011 was 4.0, it was 48.7 in France (2009), 34.5 in Japan, 47.8 in the United Kingdom and 26.3 in the United States of America. It is obvious that a high proportion of women reported as "single" in these four countries in the age group 30–34 may be having "live-in" arrangements and are living in conjugal relationships with their spouses but not legally married. Even in the age group 50–54, the percentage of women reported single in these four countries were 14.4, 8.7, 10.2 and 10.0, much higher than what is reported for Kerala (3.5) and India (0.00). This suggests that the institution of marriage has been on the decline in these developed countries for over four decades.

The scatter plot of SMAM values of India compared with other four developed countries is given in Figure 6.5. From this scatter plot, it can be seen that SMAM values are also steadily increasing in these four developed countries, implying a steady rise in "live-in" arrangements in these countries. In Japan, in the context of a very small proportion of births occurring to single mothers, as compared to other three developed countries, the prevalence of "live-in" arrangements may not be that wide spread as in the other three Western countries.

Incidence of Divorces

From the data on percentages of women reported "divorced" in the four developed countries in Figure 6.6 the percentages of women in different age groups reported "divorced" around 2010 in the four developed countries, is presented. For India, the extent of divorces among married couples is not known and cannot be known since very few marriages are registered and divorces are reported only on registered marriages. There is a likelihood of more of "separations" reported in India than formal divorces. In the 1991 census, data on the separated couples have been provided, and it was seen that for all age groups, the reported percentage of divorced women as less than 1 might not represent the true picture. On the other hand, for the four developed countries, this data is more reliable since most of the formal marriages are registered; however, separations from "live-in" arrangements may not be reported as divorces irrespective of the duration of "live-in" life. Since the duration of "live-in" life is also increasing even in developed countries, the reported rates of divorce may actually be higher than what is reported for these countries. Thus, there is a problem of quality of data on the percentage of women reported as "divorced" both in India and the developed countries, and both may be grossly underestimated. However, the order of differences may indicate a picture not far from reality.

From Table 6.5 and Figure 6.6, it can be seen that while the marriage rate is declining, the percentage of women reported as divorced within this declining group is increasing over the years. In France, it was 4.9 in 1970 that increased to 16.3 by 2010; in Japan, it increased from 3.8 to 9.2; in the United Kingdom, it rose from 2.0 to 19.0 and in the United States

Table 6.6:
Percent single, divorced/separated and births to single mothers, circa 2010

Country	PS	DS	BS
India	1.9	1.8	NA
France	48.7	9.2	54.1
Germany	46.8	12	33.3
United Kingdom	47.8	11.1	46.9
Japan	34.5	6.9	2.1

Sources: United Nations (2012), World Marriage Prospects—2014.

Figure 6.6:
Percent of single women in the age group 30–34 in India and four states, 1950–2010

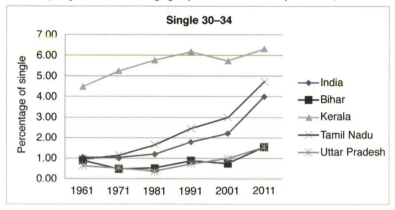

Source: Census of India, 1970–2011.

Figure 6.7:
Singulate mean age at marriage in India and four developed countries, 1950–2010

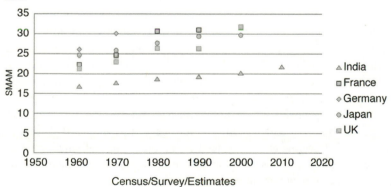

Source: United Nations "Marriage Prospects" (2012).

Figure 6.8:
Percentage of divorced women in age group 30–34 in India and developed countries

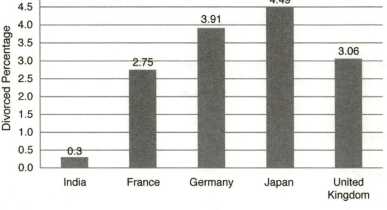

Divorced distribution in
age group 30–34 of women

Source: United Nations (2012).

of America, from 5.5 to 17.4. The rise in divorce rates is the lowest in Japan compared to France, the United Kingdom and the United States of America. Figure 6.8 gives a bar diagram of the percentage of women reporting divorced in these four countries and India around 2010 and 1991.

Single Status among Men

When we study the universality of marriage and its stability in India, it is better to corroborate the findings-based data on females with similar data on men. Table 6.7 provides data on the percentage of single men in the year 2011 (based on SRS age–sex–marital status distributions) for India as a whole and the four states. We find that in India, the percentage of single men was 97 in the age group 15–19, which declined sharply to 14 in the age group 30–34 and to 3 in the age group 50–54. In Kerala, the percentages of single men in these three age groups were 100, 27 and 2. The trend of decline can be noticed in the percentage of single men in these four states, and it is clear that all the states are converging to almost zero percent of men remaining single by age of 55.

Table 6.7:
Percentage of single men in India, Bihar, Kerala, Tamil Nadu and Uttar Pradesh, 2001

Age	India	Bihar	Kerala	Tamil Nadu	Uttar Pradesh
15–19	97.2	95.9	100	100	97.64
20–24	74.47	65.48	94.94	90.36	73
25–29	37.78	27.85	66.67	54.26	34.44
30–34	13.51	6.67	27.03	19.32	11.11
35–39	4.35	1.69	9.59	6.41	4.92
40–44	3.39	0	4.17	2.86	4.26
45–49	1.85	0	2.94	1.56	2.27
50–54	2.5	0	1.69	1.89	3.23
55–59	0	0	1.82	0	3.57

Source: SRS India.

Findings from Micro-level Analysis

The analysis contained in the above sections is based on aggregate level data at the state and national levels within India and across selected developed countries for comparative purposes. They provide only broad patterns on the distributions of women by marital status for comparison across selected states in India and countries over time. In the micro-level analysis, we use the data collected in the third round of NFHS, coordinated by the IIPS, Mumbai, under the aegis of the Government of India, which has been conducted in 2005–06. In this survey, all women in the reproductive ages, 15–49, were enquired unlike in NFHS-1 and NFHS-2 where only ever-married women were interviewed. NFHS-3 collected information from a nationally representative sample of 109,041 households, 124,385 women aged 15–49, and 74,369 men aged 15–54. NFHS-3 sample covers 99 percent of India's population living in all 29 states.

We analyzed the data on the marital status of women reported in the survey, grouping them as "never-married/single." "Ever-married" includes "currently married" and "previously married" included widowed, divorced and separated women. We used a simple binomial logit regression of these two states using as five predictors five—age, rural/urban status, education level of women, wealth index of the household and the variables of religion and caste, combined as "religio-caste" variable. While age is used as a continuous variable, the other four are used as discrete or categorical variables. For "religio-caste," we used a single ascribed variable that combines religion and caste among Hindus. We used dummies for the four states. The categorization of religio-caste variable that we used was (a) Christians, (b) Muslims, (c) Hindi Scheduled caste, (d) Hindi Scheduled tribe, (e) Hindi Other backward caste, (f) Hindu others and (g) Other religions.

The reason for combining religion and caste into a single variable was that even among Christians and Muslims, religious groups that are not supposed to have any caste categorization, reported a significant proportions among them as scheduled castes, scheduled tribes and other backward castes, probably from the caste categories in Hindu religion from which they got converted, and mentioning them in surveys in order to benefit from many government privileges that are given to these caste categories by the state and central government. Caste, which is predominantly an ascribed nomenclature, assigned at the time of birth for a child born in the Hindu religion is now becoming increasingly prevalent in other religious categories in India. This is a matter for further study. In the present analysis, it has been found that the presence of caste categorization among religions other than Hindus confounds the effects of caste and religion on the marital status and this required the formation of a new variable "religio-caste" as given above. The categorization of other variables was taken as given in the coded dataset of NFHS-3, and these are described in the bottom of Table 6.8. The values and significance of the odds ratios of these predictors for India as a whole and using state codes for the four selected states are given in Table 6.8.

From Table 6.8, it can be seen that all the variables selected as predictors have a highly significant odds ratios on the probability of getting married. Age, used as continuous variable, has an odds ratio of 1.5 and indicates that for controlling other factors, it increases the odds of marrying by 50 percent. Even controlling for age and other achieved variables of place of residence, education and wealth index, the effects of the "religio-caste" variable has the maximum impact among the Hindus in all caste categories with odds ratios over 2, compared to Christians. The highest odds ratio of 2.94 is among the Hindu other backward classes (OBCs). The odds ratios in all categories of the three achieved variables of rural/urban residence, wealth index and education of women are below 1, indicating that the maximum probability of marriage is among the rural, illiterate and poorest women, and any changes in these variables contributes to upward mobility and reduces the odds ratios. The dampening effect on the probability of getting married or moving from single status to the ever-married status of the three ascribed variables is revealed from this analysis. Most important finding is the high odds ratios of the

Table 6.8:
Logistic regression result on the odds of being married, 2005–06 (0 = unmarried; 1 = ever married)

Background Characteristics		India	
		Coefficient	Odds Ratio
Type of place of residence	Rural		
	Urban	–0.401	0.670***
Age of women	Current Age	0.407	1.503***
Religion and caste	Christians		
	Muslims	0.601	1.823***
	Other Religions	0.295	1.343***
	Hindu—SC	0.983	2.674***
	Hindu—ST	0.7	2.014***
	Hindu—OBC	1.078	2.937***
	Hindu—Others	0.733	2.082***
Educational level of women	Illiterates		
	Primary	–0.587	0.556***
	Secondary	–1.409	0.244***
	Higher	–2.819	0.060***
Wealth index	Poorest		
	Poorer	–0.014	0.986***
	Middle	–0.177	0.837***
	Richer	–0.234	0.791***
	Richest	–0.398	0.672***
State	All Other States		
	Bihar	0.454	1.574***
	Kerala	–0.168	0.846***
	Tamil Nadu	–0.594	0.552***
	Uttar Pradesh	0.041	1.042***
Constant		–7.263	0.001

Sources: Estimated from National Family Health Survey 3 (2005–06); Micro Data, IIPS and Macro International (2007).
Note: *** statistically significant at 1 in 1000 p value.

"religio-caste" variable. Use of state dummies in the logit reveals that the sates of Tamil Nadu (0.55) and Kerala (0.85) have odds ratios below 1 while Bihar (1.57) and Uttar Pradesh (1.04) have above 1, with all the other states combined and used as base for comparison.

The main inference we can draw from this analysis is that the ascribed variables of religion and caste are more important factors in the probabilities of marriage for a single women even after controlling the achieved variables of rural/urban residence, education for women and index of wealth of the family. As we will be arguing in the discussion section, the institution of marriage is strongly embedded over centuries within the religious and caste fold. Intercaste marriages and interreligious marriages are socially condemned and frowned upon. Hence, we wanted to find out whether the two ascribed factors dominate over the achievement factors in determining marriage and age at marriage.

Summary and Discussions on the Institution of Marriage in India

In the earlier section, we listed four major factors that have contributed to the breakdown of the institution of marriage in the West and briefly discussed them. We wish to argue in brief that in none of these factors the population of India is moving currently in the direction of the West. The first of the four factors is the "rise of individualism" and its negative impact on marriage in the West. In India, this is not likely to happen in the near future since any individual in the Indian culture is a part of a larger network of family, *gotra*, caste and religion. From its birth, a girl child is brought up as a daughter to be married off at a later age, fully dependent on the parents till marriage, later a dependent on her husband, and if unfortunately to be widowed after marriage, to be dependent on son and after death to be lit in the funeral pyre by a son to get merit in the other world. There appears to have no major changes in such norms in India even with considerable demographic and socioeconomic changes. The Vedas and Upanishads emphasize the utter dependence of a female on male from birth to death among the Hindus, and this sense of dependency has spilled over among other religious groups in India. One example of this is the dowry system which is practiced across all religious groups in India. Similarly, a boy is told from very young age of his responsibilities to his family, parents, sisters and various evils (*papa*s) that will descend on him if he ignores his parents or his family in their old age. Thus, there is no question of anyone born in India declaring that he is an "individual" bereft of all his familial connections and concentrating on his own personal development. At least for many decades to come, this is not likely to happen.

On the second factor of cost–benefit analysis of girls marrying within and outside the same caste, many studies have brought out the economic and emotional benefits of a girl marrying within the same caste. In an interesting study of marriages that took place based on a follow up of advertisements in the "matrimonial columns" of the *Anandabazar Patrika* (a daily newspaper in Kolkata) in 2009, Banerjee et al. (2013), made an interesting and detailed analysis of the data collected and published in 2013 by follow up visits to a large number of marriages that took place over many decades on the basis of these matrimonial advertisements. Their analysis included a detailed econometric analysis of the data collected from the women interviewed in this study and concluded that marrying within the same caste is socially and economically advantageous to both the bride and the bridegroom. To quote from their major findings,

> One of our key empirical findings is that there is a very strong preference for within-caste marriage. However, because both sides of the market share this preference and because the groups are fairly homogeneous in terms of the distributions of other attributes, in equilibrium, the cost of wanting to marry within-caste is low. This allows caste to remain a persistent feature of the Indian marriage market.

The extent of prevalence of same caste and intercaste marriages in India has been studied by Das et al. (2010) using data collected from the NFHS-3 which was conducted during 2005–06 in India. In this study, information on the caste category of each member of the household was obtained by the interviewer through a structured questionnaire. The caste categories used in this analysis is only four, that is, scheduled caste (SC), scheduled tribe (ST), OBC and others. Thus, only when the husband and wife belonged to a different category among these four groups, it was considered an intercaste marriage. Such a broad caste categorization can be expected to grossly underestimate the magnitude of intercaste marriages that take place within each broad category. Many intercaste marriages do take place within the broad caste category as OBC, SC and ST. However, the order of magnitude of intercaste marriages found in this study is quite revealing.

The study found that in India as a whole the percent of married women in the age range 15–49 reporting marriage within the same caste category was 89; in Bihar, 89; in Kerala, 80; in Tamil Nadu, 97, and in Uttar Pradesh, 88 (Das et al. 2010). It is really surprising that in Tamil Nadu, which had a strong Dravidian movement for over six decades and the

Dravidian parties in power for over four decades and which officially promoted and rewarded intercaste marriages, the percent of marriages reported within the same caste is as high as 97. However, the data quality on caste reported in NFHS-3 may be called to question: The order of magnitude of percent of intercaste marriages reported across all the states, more developed or less developed, can be considered quite low.

The third factor that contributed to the decline of marriages in the West is the over specialization of skills and almost each person becomes unique in his/her skills. In India, with more than 75 percent of the labor force employed in agriculture, this is not likely to happen in the near future. Even in the secondary and tertiary sectors, such a level of specialization of skills as observed in the West is not found and in IT sector, most of the jobs are outsourced from the developed countries because of the differences in the cost of labor.

The fourth factor is "gender equality and parity," and India is far from this goal. Based on various measures of gender disparity such as sex selective female feticides, education, employment, freedom to marry one whom she loves, domestic violence, employment, economic freedom and many others, Indian women rank very low compared to other women not only in developed countries but also in Asia. The poor status of women is reflected in highly skewed sex ratio (0–6) among children, high maternal mortality rates, high level of malnutrition, morbidity rates etc.

According to the Global Gender Gap Report released by the World Economic Forum (WEF) 2011, India was ranked 113 on the Gender Gap Index (GGI) among 135 countries polled. During the past three years, India has improved its rankings on the WEF's Gender Gap Index (GGI) to 105/136 in 2013, but is still quite low in the comity of nations. This index measured the gap in education, longevity, employment and political representation between men and women. Various gender empowerment measures have scaled India almost close to 130–40 rank out of 175 countries, and in spite of various efforts made by the governments, NGOs and a few political parties, the gender inequalities on the scale achieved in the West cannot be realized in the near future. Indian women tend to be valued by society in relation to their role in the family, namely, as a wife, daughter-in-law, and mother. Women who fall outside of these roles— widows and single women—face discrimination and in many cases, loss of property. Since a woman is considered incomplete without being married, a strong social stigma exists for unmarried adult women, widows and divorcees. A detailed discussion on gender inequalities and demograph:c behavior in India can be seen in a book with the same title authored by Desai (1997) in which she argues that marrying and having a son as early as possible is the only choice available for most of the women in India for social acceptability and upward mobility. Thus, marriage seems to be the only saving grace for restoring the status of women in Indian society.

The aforementioned study also reveals that the low percentage of intercaste marriages is equally observed among the more educated as among the poor educated, among the better economic groups as in the poorer groups and among those exposed to the mass media as among those not exposed. Same religion marriages were 85 percent among Hindus, 89 percent among Muslims and 90 percent among others. It was almost constant among those with different standard of living index (SLI), and among those exposed to mass media or not at was 89 percent. Thus, there appears structural caste rigidity in relation to marriages in India that cuts across education and economic groups. It can be inferred that as long as caste system is not disturbed, the institution of marriage as it is prevailing now may not undergo any radical changes.

Thus, based on the proportions of women at different age groups remaining single and trends in them over the past fifty years in India as whole and two more advanced and two less advanced states in terms of socioeconomic development, it was found that while development in India has contributed to a significant rise in age at marriage, it has not significantly altered the ultimate proportions getting married by age 30–34. Most of the women (97 percent) get married by the age of 45–49 even in the most developed state of Kerala, and more than 98 percent in the other three states. The percentage of women reported divorced or separated is very low at all ages, less than 1 percent. These figures are in complete contrast with what is observed in the developed countries of the West and Japan. We have compared the levels and trends in single, married and divorced states of women in different ages in three developed countries of the West—France, the United Kingdom and the United States of America and Japan—with India and the states and drew the conclusion that the institution of marriage is strong in India and is not showing nor likely to show, as feared by some professionals in a survey, to break down in the future. Micro-level analysis using NFHS-3 data shows the strongest linkage between age shift in marital status from single state to married state over riding all other factors. The ascribed factors of religion and caste have more effects on the odds ratios than education or wealth status of the household.

A strong contributing factor behind the stability in the institution of marriage is that marriages are still taking place within the same caste, and there is a strong caste support behind every marriage. This is rather unfortunate because the social evils and economic impediments of the rigid caste structure are well known, and many leaders including Mahatma Gandhi and Narayana Guru, and Periar in the South, have fought relentlessly against it for over many decades. The efforts of many social and political movements, such as the Dravidian movement in Tamil Nadu, that were in power and encouraging intercaste marriages over the past seven decades, does not appear to have any impact since even in Tamil Nadu the reported percentage of intercaste marriages is only about 3 percent during 2005–06 as found from NFHS-3. Similarly, the analysis of data on requirements of a spouse as published in the advertisements in the matrimonial columns of newspapers and websites specify the requirement of the same caste as an essential condition for marriage by most of the applicants, irrespective of their socioeconomic background. The caste based vote bank politics supported by many national and regional political parties even in the latest elections in 2014 have strengthened the caste system. One of the positive contributions of the caste system seems to be the stability it has brought to the institution of marriage in India. The costs and benefits of the caste system requires a Beckerian analysis—whether disruptions at the family level maintained by increased live-in arrangements, high divorce rates, children reared by single parents avoided by the caste based marriage system will be the tradeoff for achieving a more egalitarian and faster going nation. However, women in India seem to be safely trapped, as of present and for the near future, in the golden cage of marriage set up by religion and caste.

Modernization tends to improve women's status in the society by expanding their literacy and educational levels and their involvement in productive employment outside the household by giving them equal opportunity with men in political, administrative and managerial roles in the society, and by increasing longevity and health through improved maternal and childcare services. Consequences of such a modernization process are an increased age among brides, a greater proportion remaining single throughout their lifetime and changes in nuptiality and fertility patterns. Indian women's age at marriage has systematically increased since the beginning of the century, though the institution of marriage has stood up the processes of modernization or westernization thus far.

7

Demographic Levels, Trends, Differentials and Challenges

Cultural Background to Diversity

In this chapter, we present the broad trends, differentials and challenges at the national and state levels on selected demographic parameters of population such as size, growth, age structure, sex ratios, fertility, mortality, health and infrastructural facilities in India and the states, not from the point of view of any detailed demographic analysis on each of these topics (which in itself can take a separate volume) but from the point of view of population concerns and challenges they indicate and need our attention.

Trends in Basic Demographic Parameters

Population Size

As per all the three assumptions of fertility projected by the United Nations Population Division, India's population is rapidly heading towards the unenviable position of it being the topper in population size among the countries of the world and is expected to exceed the population size of China (1,400 million) in as early as 2022. Of course, the United Nations Population Division has always overestimated the population of

India since 1951, compared to the Indian census. The UN estimated India's population for 1951 at 376.32 million compared to census figure of 361.09 million; in 1971 at 566.61 compared to census figure of 548.16; in 1991 at 906.40 million compared to the 1991 census that totals to 846.42 million and in 2011 at 1,247.45 million compared to our latest census figure of 1,210.86 million. The gap between the UN population estimate and the census figure was highest in 1991 at 60 million but in 2011, the gap has come down to 37 million. Our censuses are conducted usually on March 1, of the year, while the UN projections refer to the middle of the calendar year. However, the differences between the two estimates even in 2011 (about 37 million) is so large that one of the immediate challenges of census officials of the country is to sit with the officials of the United Nations Population Division and sort out the differences and come up with an internationally and nationally acceptable figure on our population size. This, in my view, is of high priority. However, for our further analysis in this chapter, we use the census of India figures.

Table 7.1 provides the population figures of India and for the 29 states and the union territories as one entity in the censuses of 1951, 1971, 1991 and 2011 (at 20-year intervals) and the annual growth rates during these intervals.

In the first population census conducted after independence, India's population size was 361.09 million, and the most recent census conducted in 2011 placed its population at 1210.85 million, or more than three times the 1951 population size. What India has added in 60 years, from 1951 to 2011 (849 million), is almost equal to the combined population of six large countries—the United States of America, the United Kingdom, France, Germany, Brazil and Indonesia (totaling 884 million in 2011)—with only one-eighth of their combined land area. From any space station above, the sensors tracing human heat will find the Indian subcontinent the reddest on the planet, and India's density of the human population is a sight for the gods to see!

India is currently politically constituted into 29 states and 7 union territories, with the latest state of Telangana separated from Andhra Pradesh in 2014. The states vary enormously in population size, density, and other characteristics. The most populous state, since independence, is Uttar Pradesh with a population of 199.8 million in 2011 and the smallest is Sikkim with 0.61 million. Such enormous differences in the population sizes of the states make the political and administrative management of the affairs of the states highly difficult and inefficient in any form of organization. One of the population concerns from the points of view

Table 7.1:
Population trends and growth of India and states from 1951 to 2011

S. No.	States/Union Territories	Population Totals ('000)				100*P('11)/P('51)	Annual Growth Rate (in percent)			
		1951	1971	1991	2011		1951–71	1971–91	1991–2011
	INDIA	361,088	548,160	846,421	1,210,570	335.3	2.10	2.20	1.80
1	Andhra Pradesh	31,115	43,503	66,508	84,581	271.8	1.70	2.10	1.20
2	Arunachal Pradesh	NA	468	865	1,384	295.7		3.10	2.30
3	Assam	8,029	14,625	22,414	31,206	388.7	3.00	2.10	1.70
4	Bihar	29,085	42,126	64,531	104,099	357.9	1.90	2.10	2.40
5	Chhattisgarh	7,457	11,637	17,615	25,545	342.6	2.20	2.10	1.90
6	Delhi	1,744	4,066	9,421	16,788	962.6	4.20	4.20	2.90
7	Goa	547	795	1,170	1,459	266.6	1.90	1.90	1.10
8	Gujarat	16,263	26,697	41,310	60,440	371.6	2.50	2.20	1.90
9	Haryana	5,674	10,036	16,464	25,351	446.8	2.90	2.50	2.20
10	Himachal Pradesh	2,386	3,460	5,171	6,865	287.7	1.90	2.00	1.40
11	Jammu & Kashmir	3,254	4,617	7,837	12,541	385.4	1.70	2.60	2.40
12	Jharkhand	9,697	14,227	21,844	32,988	340.2	1.90	2.10	2.10
13	Karnataka	19,402	29,299	44,977	61,095	314.9	2.10	2.10	1.50
14	Kerala	13,549	21,347	29,099	33,406	246.6	2.30	1.50	0.70
15	Madhya Pradesh	18,615	30,017	48,566	72,627	390.2	2.40	2.40	2.00

(Table 7.1 continued)

(Table 7.1 continued)

S. No.	States/Union Territories	Population Totals ('000)				100*P('11)/P('51)	Annual Growth Rate (in percent)		
		1951	1971	1991	2011		1951–71	1971–91	1991–2011
16	Maharashtra	32,003	50,412	78,937	112,374	351.1	2.30%	2.20%	1.80%
17	Manipur	578	1,073	1,837	2,570	444.7	3.10%	2.70%	1.70%
18	Meghalaya	606	1,012	1,775	2,967	489.6	2.60%	2.80%	2.60%
19	Mizoram	196	332	690	1,097	559.8	2.60%	3.70%	2.30%
20	Nagaland	213	516	1,210	1,979	928.9	4.40%	4.30%	2.50%
21	Odisha	14,646	21,945	31,660	41,974	286.6	2.00%	1.80%	1.40%
22	Punjab	9,161	13,551	20,282	27,743	302.8	2.00%	2.00%	1.60%
23	Rajasthan	15,971	25,766	44,006	68,548	429.2	2.40%	2.70%	2.20%
24	Sikkim	138	210	406	611	442.4	2.10%	3.30%	2.00%
25	Tamil Nadu	30,119	41,199	55,859	72,147	239.5	1.60%	1.50%	1.30%
26	Tripura	639	1,556	2,757	3,674	574.9	4.40%	2.90%	1.40%
27	Uttaranchal	2,946	4,493	7,051	10,086	342.4	2.10%	2.30%	1.80%
28	Uttar Pradesh	60,274	83,849	132,062	199,812	331.5	1.70%	2.30%	2.10%
29	West Bengal	26,300	44,312	68,078	91,276	347.1	2.60%	2.10%	1.50%
30	Union Territory	484	1,013	2023	3,335	689.1	3.70%	3.50%	2.50%

Source: Census of India.

of efficiency in political and administrative management is to reduce the population sizes of the large states to manageable levels. This is the next population and development concern.

Since 1901, when the population within India's present boundaries was enumerated at 238.4 million, the population has increased by 972.4 million in 110 years within the same boundary. No region or country of the world has added so many people within its geographical area during this period. Almost 90 percent of the increase (849.7 million) came after 1951. This addition is massive for any region of the planet. India adds more people within its boundaries every year than what China adds with a population of slightly more than 1.30 billion because China has drastically reduced its population growth rate during the past three decades with its successfully implemented one-child policy.

Growth Rates

During the first 20-year period (1951–71), the annual percent rate of population growth for the country as whole was 2.1 per year, increasing to 2.2 during the second 20-year period (19971–91) and declined to 1.8 in the latest 20-year period (1991–2011). During the first period, the maximal growth rate among the states was found in Nagaland (4.4) followed by Tripura (4.4) and Delhi (4.2), and the minimum was found in Arunachal Pradesh and Jammu and Kashmir (both at 1.7 percent). During the latest 20-year period, the maxima were in Delhi (2.9), Odisha (2.5) and Meghalaya (2.6), and the minima were in Goa (1.1), Tamil Nadu (1.3) and Kerala (0.7). During 1991–2011, Kerala, Goa, Andhra Pradesh and Tamil Nadu registered low annual growth rates at 0.7, 1.1, 1.2 and 1.3 percent, while at the other end of the spectrum, the states of Bihar, Rajasthan, Madhya Pradesh and Uttar Pradesh registered annual growth rates of 2.4, 2.0, 2.2 and 2.1 percent respectively, almost double the growth rates of the former states. Since these states together constitute almost one third of India's population, the prevalence of such high growth rates in such a vast area largely determines the national scene.

Delhi is an urban metropolitan city, capital of the country and became a separate state (although not full statehood) in 1995. While high growth rate of around 4 percent per year for Delhi is understandable and attributable to high level of migration from other states to Delhi, but such an explanation for high growth rates in Nagaland, Assam, Tripura and Arunachal Pradesh during 1951–91 cannot be given and has to be explained in terms of large immigration from across the borders from Bangladesh. Figures 2.1 and 2.2 give the latest population size and density map of India.

Concerns on Political Representations from Indian States

Table 7.1 reveals that the states of India have been growing at different levels, especially after 1971 when the southern states led the country in drastic reductions in their mortality and fertility levels because of relatively more efficient implementation of public health and family planning programs, increasing age at marriage of women, faster economic and social development and women's empowerment making a large family undesirable within the family and at the macro level. For example, during the period during 1951–60, CBR of Kerala was 39.0 compared to 42.0 of the country as a whole and by 1988, CBR of Kerala had declined to 20.3 (below replacement level) compared to 31.5 of India as a whole. The rate of growth of population of Kerala in 1987 was 1.56 percent compared to 2.13 of India as whole. These sharper declines in the growth rates of the southern states, Goa, union territories and selected areas of Maharashtra and West Bengal have made their relative share of the population in the country decrease over time. This decline is continuing to this day. One implication of this is at the political level. With universal adult franchise guaranteed to every citizen above the age of 18 years, the states that have higher rates of growth of population will have a proportionately larger representation in the Indian parliament and in their state legislatures. Since the programs of family planning with targeted reductions in fertility levels of the population since 1951 were national programs implemented with central funds, it will be unwise that the states with relatively more success in these programs have relatively lesser seats in parliament and in political power just because of their successfulness in these programs. Hence, in 1976, the Indian parliament passed a constitutional amendment freezing the seats in parliament and state legislatures on the basis of 1971 census until 2001, after which the census of 2001 would form the basis (hoping that by that year the differentials in growth rates would largely disappear; see Chapter 3). However, it was observed in 2000 that relative differentials in population growth rates were still persisting, and hence the freeze was extended by another constitutional amendment in 2000, extending the freeze until 2026.

Table 7.2 presents figures on the present number of seats in parliament in the Lok Sabha (lower house) for each state (based on the 1971 census)

Table 7.2:
Share of political representation based on 2011 census population, voters' population and literate voters' population

S. No.	State/UT	Lok Sabha Seats	1971 Population	P/LSS	2011 Population	P2/LSS	Voters in 2011	Literate Voters in 2011	Expected Number of Seats if Ban is Lifted			Loss or Gain		
									Based on 2011 Population	Based on 2011 Voters Population	Based on 2011 Literate Voters Population	For 2011 Population	For 2011 Voters Population	For 2011 Literate Voters Population
	INDIA (2,3,4)	543	548,160	1,009.5	1,210,855	2,229.9	762,212	513,370						
1	A & N Islands	1	115	115	381	380.6	268	225	0.2	0.2	0.2	-0.8	-0.8	-0.8
2	Andhra Pradesh	42	43,503	1,035.8	84,581	2,013.8	57,324	34,216	37.9	40.8	36.2	-4.1	-1.2	-5.8
3	Arunachal Pradesh (1)	2	468	234	1,384	691.9	793	469	0.6	0.6	0.5	-1.4	-1.4	-1.5
4	Assam (2)	14	14,625	1,044.6	31,206	2,229	19,109	12,850	14	13.6	13.6	0	-0.4	-0.4
5	Bihar	40	42,126	1,053.2	1,04,099	2,602.5	56,193	29,715	46.7	40	31.4	6.7	0	-8.6
6	Chandigarh*	1	257	257	1,055	1,055.5	731	615	0.5	0.5	0.7	-0.5	-0.5	-0.3
7	Chhattisgarh	11	11,637	1,057.9	25,545	2,322.3	15,774	9,900	11.5	11.2	10.5	0.5	0.2	-0.5
8	Dadra & NH*	1	74	74	344	343.7	218	154	0.2	0.2	0.2	-0.8	-0.8	-0.8
9	Daman & Diu*	1	63	63	243	243.2	176	150	0.1	0.1	0.2	-0.9	-0.9	-0.8
10	Delhi*	7	4,066	580.9	16,788	2,398.3	11,234	9,428	7.5	8	10	0.5	1	3
11	Goa	2	795	397.5	1,459	729.3	1,074	936	0.7	0.8	1	-1.3	-1.2	-1

(Table 7.2 continued)

(Table 7.2 continued)

Members of Parliament, Number Existing and Number Expected Under Assumptions of Lifting the Freeze on Representation Imposed from 1971

S. No.	State/UT	Lok Sabha Seats	1971 Population	P/LSS	2011 Population	P2/LSS	Voters in 2011	Literate Voters in 2011	Expected Number of Seats if Ban is Lifted			Loss or Gain		
									Based on 2011 Population	Based on 2011 Voters Population	Based on 2011 Literate Voters Population	For 2011 Population	For 2011 Voters Population	For 2011 Literate Voters Population
12	Gujarat	26	26,697	1,026.8	60,440	2,324.6	39,284	28,854	27.1	28	30.5	1.1	2	4.5
13	Haryana	10	10,036	1,003.6	25,351	2,535.1	16,200	11,334	11.4	11.5	12	1.4	1.5	2
14	Himachal Pradesh	4	3,460	865	6,865	1,716.2	4,701	3,714	3.1	3.3	3.9	-0.9	-0.7	-0.1
15	Jammu & Kashmir	6	4,617	769.5	12,541	2,090.2	7,530	4,532	5.6	5.4	4.8	-0.4	-0.6	-1.2
16	Jharkhand	14	14,227	1,016.2	32,988	2,356.3	19,035	10,967	14.8	13.6	11.6	0.8	-0.4	-2.4
17	Karnataka	28	29,299	1,046.4	61,095	2,182	41,701	29,235	27.4	29.7	30.9	-0.6	1.7	2.9
18	Kerala	20	21,347	1,067.4	33,406	1,670.3	23,966	22,313	15	17.1	23.6	-5	-2.9	3.5
19	Lakshadweep	1	32	32	64	64.5	44	40	0	0	0	-1	-1	-1
20	Madhya Pradesh	29	30,017	1,035.1	72,627	2,504.4	43,784	26,862	32.6	31.2	28.4	3.6	2.2	-0.6
21	Maharashtra	48	50,412	1,050.3	112,374	2,341.1	75,855	59,942	50.4	54	63.4	2.4	6	15.4
22	Manipur	2	1,073	536.5	2,856	1,427.9	1,814	1,349	1.3	1.3	1.4	-0.7	-0.7	-0.6
23	Meghalaya	2	1,012	506	2,967	1,483.4	1,581	1,121	1.3	1.1	1.2	-0.7	-0.9	-0.8

No.	State							Total						
24	Mizoram	1	332		1,097	1,097.2	674	613	0.5	0.5	0.6	-0.5	-0.5	-0.4
25	Nagaland	1	516		1,979	1,978.5	1,157	897	0.9	0.8	0.9	-0.1	-0.2	-0.1
26	Odisha	21	21,945	1,045	41,974	1,998.8	27,442	18,580	18.8	19.5	19.7	-2.2	-1.5	-1.3
27	Pondicherry	1	472	472	1248	1,248	889	742	0.6	0.6	0.8	-0.4	-0.4	-0.2
28	Punjab	13	13,551	1,042.4	27,743	2,134.1	18,962	13,536	12.4	13.5	14.3	-0.6	0.5	1.3
29	Rajasthan	25	25,766	1,030.6	68,548	2,741.9	40,142	22,986	30.7	28.6	24.3	5.7	3.6	-0.7
30	Sikkim	1	210	210	611	610.6	404	312	0.3	0.3	0.3	-0.7	-0.7	-0.7
31	Tamil Nadu	39	41,199	1,056.4	72,147	1,849.9	51,418	39,082	32.4	36.6	41.3	-6.6	-2.4	2.3
32	Tripura	2	1,556	778	3,674	1,837	2,444	2,075	1.6	1.7	2.2	-0.4	-0.3	0.2
33	Uttaranchal	5	4,493	898.6	10,086	2,017.3	6,270	4,604	4.5	4.5	4.9	-0.5	-0.5	-0.1
34	Uttar Pradesh	80	83,849	1,048.1	1,99,812	2,497.7	112,855	67,145	89.6	80.4	71	9.6	0.4	-9
35	West Bengal	42	44,312	1,055	91,276	2,173.2	61,164	43,878	40.9	43.6	46.4	-1.1	1.6	4.4
								Total	543	543	543			

Source: Census of India.

with the freeze still in vogue, and what would happen to this picture if the freeze is lifted before 2020 and seats determined on the basis of 2011 population census. Just for exercise, we estimated the number of seats for each state under three assumptions: (a) number of seats estimated based on the census of 2011 keeping the total number of seats in the Lok Sabha at the existing size of 535 (excluding the two seats for Anglo-Indians that are to be nominated by the President), (b) on the basis of population of the number of eligible voters, that is, population above the age of 18 in each state and (c) the literate population above the age of 18 in 2011 census. The seven states of Andhra Pradesh, Himachal Pradesh, Karnataka, Kerala, Odisha (under assumption 1), Tamil Nadu and West Bengal would lose 4, 1, 1, 5, 2, 7 and 1 seats respectively, totaling a loss of 21 seats. In addition, three large Hindi speaking states—Bihar, Uttar Pradesh and Rajasthan—would gain 7, 6 and 10 seats, totaling 23, 2 seats more than the loss suffered by the seven states together.

The balance of political power fills shifts in the favor of the Hindi-speaking states. Under assumption 2, if the number of seats is based on the voter population (18 years and above), the differentials are much less, and if it is based on literate voter population, the differential will be wider. In assumptions 2 and 3, the population with higher literacy rates and higher proportion in voter population would lose fewer seats, for example, Kerala would lose 3 seats instead of 5 under assumption 1, and it would gain 4 seats under assumption 3. Similarly, Bihar, under assumption 2, will not gain any seats compared to the gain of 7 seats under assumption 1, and it will lose 9 seats under assumption 3 because of very high illiteracy among its adults. Thus, consideration of parliamentary seats based on the voter population and literate population in this age group is viable alternatives in the allocation of parliamentary and legislative seats. Since higher literacy implies a lower fertility with a higher proportion of adult population compared to those with lower literacy rates, allocation of parliamentary seats based on this criterion favors the states with higher literacy rates. Another solution to this problem is to permanently freeze the seats in parliament and state legislatures at its present level by another constitutional amendment (similar to the representations to the senate in the United States of America) or to extend the freeze by another 25 years or to give voting rights only to persons with a minimum education of 10 years of schooling and above and decide the number of seats on the basis of this population size.

Fertility

As discussed in Chapter 6, a unique characteristic of the Indian population is that its natural fertility has been only moderately high and well
below the levels observed in many developing countries. Levels were
significantly lower than the possible biological maximum and were
observed in populations such as the Huttrites in Canada (Srinivasan
1989). Despite early universal marriages in India, social practices such
as protracted periods of sexual abstinence for religious and cultural
reasons, prolonged breastfeeding, and prohibition of widow remarriage
in certain communities have contributed to a significantly lower natural
fertility among Indian women. For known periods of history, the average
number of children born to Indian women has hardly exceeded six. Total
fertility for various decades from 1901, estimated indirectly, has rarely
exceeded six for any decade before 1951 when there was hardly any
practice of modem contraception (see Chapter 6).

As stated earlier, India can take legitimate pride in having been the
first country to launch an official program of family planning as a part of
its First Five-Year Plan (1951–56). During the successive plans, investments in the program have substantially increased from 1951 to 2012.
During the Eleventh Plan period, from 2007 to 2012, an outlay of ₹906
billion was made on the Family Welfare Program compared to ₹0.25
billion only in the third plan, 1961–66. In spite of a substantial increase
in investments in the program, fertility has declined only slowly since
1951, from a TFR of 5.87 during 1951–61 to 5.1 during 1971–73, 3.6
during 1991–93 and 2.4 during 2001–13. This 60 percent decline in
fertility over a 60-year period is tardy compared to a decline of 50 percent
in TFR values within a 10-year period in China and similar declines over
a 20–25 year period in Korea, Thailand, Indonesia and other Southeast
Asian countries.

Table 7.3 gives CBR values as three-year moving averages for the
years 1971–73, 1991–93 and 2011–13, and for the latest available year
2015 for the major states of India for the rural, urban and combined
populations. Data is taken from the SRS. It can be seen from the table
that the national CBR was 20.8 in 2015, slightly lower than replacement
level of 21 (21.6 during 2011–13). It was 22.4 in rural areas and 17.3 in
urban areas respectively in 2015. CBR ranged from a high of 26.7
in Uttar Pradesh and 26.3 in Bihar to a low of 14.8 in Kerala and 15.2 in
Tamil Nadu. The range of variation was of 11.9 points. When we look
back, during 1971–73, national CBR was 36.3 with a high of 43.2 in

Table 7.3:
Crude birth rate

S. No.		1971–73			1991–93*			2011–13			2015		
		Total	Rural	Urban	Total	Rural	Urban	Total	Rural	Urban	Total	Rural	Urban
	India	36.3	37.7	30	29.1	30.7	23.7	21.6	23.1	17.4	20.8	22.4	17.3
1	Andhra Pradesh	34.1	34.3	33.1	24.9	25.4	23.4	17.5	17.8	16.6	16.8	17.1	16.1
2	Assam	36	36.8	28.7	30.4	31.2	22.5	22.6	23.7	15.5	22	23.2	15.3
3	Bihar	NA	NA	NA	31.7	32.5	25.3	27.7	28.3	21.6	26.3	27.1	20.6
4	Chhattisgarh	NA	NA	NA	NA	NA	NA	24.6	26	18.1	23.2	24.8	18.3
5	Delhi	31.1	42.7	29.8	24.5	27.8	24.2	17.3	19.1	17	16.4	17.9	16.4
6	Gujarat	38.6	40.1	34.2	27.9	28.9	25.5	21.1	22.5	18.7	20.4	22.4	18
7	Haryana	40.6	42.5	32	32	33.6	26.3	21.6	22.6	19.2	20.9	22.3	18.4
8	Jammu & Kashmir	31.1	33.8	21.7	NA	NA	NA	17.6	18.9	12.8	16.2	18	10.7
9	Jharkhand	NA	NA	NA	NA	NA	NA	24.6	26	18.6	23.5	25	19.2
10	Karnataka	30.7	32.3	26.4	26.2	27.3	23.4	18.5	19.4	16.9	17.9	18.8	16.5
11	Kerala	30.5	30.7	29.2	17.8	17.8	17.8	14.9	15.2	14.2	14.8	14.8	14.8
12	Madhya Pradesh	38.6	39.6	33.4	34.7	36.7	26.8	26.6	28.5	19.8	25.5	27.6	19.7
13	Maharashtra	31.1	32	29	25.6	27.5	22.4	16.6	17.3	15.6	16.3	16.6	15.9
14	Odisha	34.7	34.8	32.5	27.9	28.6	22.2	19.9	20.7	14.6	19.2	20.3	14.1
15	Punjab	34.1	35.1	30.4	27	28.2	24.1	15.9	16.5	14.9	15.2	15.9	14.2
16	Rajasthan	NA	NA	NA	34.6	36	28.7	25.9	27.1	22.2	24.8	25.7	22
17	Tamil Nadu	31.3	33.4	26.2	20.3	20.5	20	15.7	15.8	15.6	15.2	15.3	15.2
18	Uttar Pradesh	43.2	44.6	34	36	37.5	29.6	27.5	28.4	23.5	26.7	27.9	23
19	West Bengal	NA	NA	NA	25.8	28.9	17.7	16.1	17.9	11.4	15.5	17.3	11.6

Source: SRS India.

Uttar Pradesh and a low of 30.5 in Kerala, a difference of about 13 points. Kerala has continuously and steadily led the way in fertility decline in India. The rural–urban differential in Kerala during 2011–13 was of just one point while it was 6.7 points in Bihar. Thus, Kerala has become demographically a homogenous state with very small rural–urban differentials. This is consistent with the theory of demographic transition that for the states that are at the final stage of transition, the differentials largely disappear or become insignificant.

Similar observations can be made from Table 7.4 that gives TFR values for the same periods, 1971–73, 1991–93 and 2011–13, for rural and urban areas. In 2011–13, national TFR was 2.4 with urban at 1.8 and rural at 2.6. The range among the states varied from 1.7 in Tamil Nadu, Punjab and West Bengal and 1.8 in Kerala to a high of 3.5 in Bihar and 3.3 in Uttar Pradesh. Only Bihar, Chhattisgarh, Madhya Pradesh and Uttar Pradesh have TFR values over 3, and the rest have already achieved or nearing the replacement level of fertility of 2.1. Most of the Southeast and East Asian countries, euphemistically called East Asian Tigers, have achieved replacement levels of fertility about two decades earlier than India, and it has been found that this reduction has significantly contributed to their faster economic development, contributing to 20–30 percent of rise in the GDP per capita because of demographic dividends, relative rise in their economically productive populations in relation to their dependent populations.

There are two major reasons have been attributed to this apparently tardy impact of the family planning program in India. First, undue emphasis has been given to permanent methods of family planning (sterilization) in the program from its beginning, and this has reduced fertility only among older women after their desired family sizes have been achieved. The second major factor is that many of the traditional checks on fertility, such as prolonged sexual abstinence for religious or social reasons and taboos on widow remarriage, have been weakened by modernization, and marital fertility levels among younger women have been increasing since 1951. Marital fertility among women aged 15–29 rose almost by 20 percent between 1959 and 1972 (Srinivasan and Jeeebhoy 1981), despite an increased contraceptive practice and increased bridal age from about 13 to 18 years. The fertility-decreasing effects of sterilization among married women aged 30 and above have been almost neutralized by the increases in natural fertility among women under 30.

Besides rural–urban differentials, more detailed analysis of fertility data in populations within the rural and urban areas classified by various

Table 7.4:
Total fertility rates

	1971–73			1991–93*			2011–13			2014		
	Total	Rural	Urban	Total	Rural	Urban	Total	Rural	Urban	Total	Rural	Urban
India	5.1	5.3	4	3.6	3.9	2.7	2.4	2.6	1.8	2.3	2.5	1.8
Andhra Pradesh	4.5	4.6	4	2.8	2.9	2.4	1.8	1.9	1.7	1.8	1.8	1.6
Assam	5.2	5.3	3.9	3.4	3.5	2.2	2.4	2.5	1.5	2.3	2.5	1.6
Bihar	NA	NA	NA	4.5	4.7	3.5	3.5	3.6	2.5	3.2	3.3	2.4
Chhattisgarh	NA	NA	NA	NA	NA	NA	2.7	2.9	1.8	2.6	2.8	1.9
Delhi	NA	NA	NA	NA	NA	NA	1.8	1.9	1.8	1.7	1.8	1.7
Gujarat	5.4	5.7	4.4	3.2	3.3	2.9	2.3	2.5	2	2.3	2.5	2
Haryana	6.6	7	4.6	3.8	4.1	3	2.3	2.4	2	2.3	2.4	2
Jammu & Kashmir	NA	NA	NA	NA	NA	NA	1.9	2	1.3	1.7	1.9	1.2
Jharkhand	NA	NA	NA	NA	NA	NA	NA	NA	NA	2.8	3	2.1
Karnataka	4.2	4.5	3.4	3	3.2	2.5	1.9	2	1.7	1.8	1.9	1.7
Kerala	4	4.1	3.6	1.7	1.7	1.7	1.8	1.9	1.8	1.9	1.9	1.8
Madhya Pradesh	5.7	6	4.5	4.4	4.7	3.1	3	3.2	2	2.8	3.1	2.1
Maharashtra	4.3	4.6	3.8	2.9	3.3	2.5	1.8	1.9	1.6	1.8	1.9	1.7
Odisha	4.7	4.8	4.2	3.2	3.3	2.4	2.1	2.2	1.5	2.1	2.2	1.5
Punjab	5.2	5.5	4.2	3.1	3.2	2.7	1.7	1.7	1.6	1.7	1.7	1.6
Rajasthan	NA	NA	NA	4.5	4.8	3.5	2.9	3.1	2.3	2.8	2.9	2.3
Tamil Nadu	3.8	4.3	3.1	2.2	2.3	2	1.7	1.7	1.7	1.7	1.7	1.7
Uttar Pradesh	6.5	6.8	4.8	5.2	5.5	4	3.3	3.4	2.5	3.2	3.4	2.5
West Bengal	NA	NA	NA	3	3.5	2	1.7	1.8	1.2	1.6	1.7	1.2

Source: SRS India.

socioeconomic categories reveals significant differentials by religion, caste, maternal education and occupation of household heads, age of brides and per capita monthly incomes or household expenditure. For example, ASFRs and TFRs of different religious groups by broad regions of the country, that is, northern, central, east, northeast, west and southern regions (classification of regions given in Table 7.5b), were computed from the data on births in the preceding three years available for each woman covered in the NFHS-1, 2 and 3 done during 1991–92, 1997–98 and 2005–06. The religious categories covered are four, that is, Hindus, Muslims, Christians and others that include Sikhs, Buddhists, Jains, Parsees, and others presented. The rates are presented in Table 7.5a.

Rates of fertility by age and total fertility had to be computed in these survey datasets by regions, aggregating the data available at the state level in view of the smallness of the sample sizes by religion at the state level. The groupings of states in different regions are given in Table 7.5b. It can be observed from the table that at the all India level, TFR of Muslims are the highest during the period 1991–2006 though it had also declined during this period. Muslim TFR in 1992–93 was 5.09, compared to 3.92 for Hindus and all India average of 4.05; and by 1998–99, Muslim TFR had declined to 3.59, compared to the level of 2.74 reached by the Hindus and all India average of 2.85. The same decreased further to 3.40 by 2005–06, while Hindu TFR came down to 2.59 with the all India average at 2.68. The gap between Muslim and Hindu TFR was 1.17 in 1992–93 survey, which came down to 0.85 in the 1998–99 survey and 0.81 in the 2005–06 survey. The estimates of TFR in these three surveys are based on the births that occurred to the women included in the sample during the preceding three-year period. Comparing such differentials by other characteristics reveals that when overall fertility levels decline, differentials tend to narrow, as in the case of Kerala that has practically no socioeconomic differentials in fertility.

However, one of the thorny problems in Indian fertility is that even in the context of declining total fertility, relatively high fertility in adolescent ages 15–19 seem to persist because of continuing prevalence of child marriages in different parts of the country.

Table 7.5a:
Total fertility rates by religious categories in different regions according to NFHS-1, 2 and 3

	NFHS-1 (1992–93)					NFHS-2 (1998–99)					NFHS-3 (2005–06)				
	Hindu	Muslim	Christian	Others	Total	Hindu	Muslim	Christian	Others	Total	Hindu	Muslim	Christian	Others	Total
India	3.92	5.09	3.92	3.72	4.05	2.74	3.59	3.02	2.62	2.85	2.59	3.40	2.34	2.21	2.68
North	4.06	5.18	3.89	3.88	4.08	3.08	4.14	3.28	2.78	3.15	2.59	3.47	1.08	1.90	2.64
Central	4.87	5.80	2.94	3.88	4.98	3.43	4.59	2.58	2.81	3.56	3.46	4.14	2.46	1.83	3.53
East	3.73	5.36	3.99	3.23	3.97	2.65	3.56	2.58	2.01	2.78	2.79	3.77	3.77	3.98	2.98
Northeast	4.23	5.79	4.81	5.52	4.71	2.50	2.97	4.55	3.62	2.91	2.01	3.65	3.51	3.06	2.57
West	3.59	4.75	3.54	3.48	3.71	2.57	3.50	2.93	2.43	2.66	2.13	2.80	1.29	2.25	2.21
South	3.21	3.86	3.48	2.02	3.30	2.12	2.63	2.66	2.35	2.21	1.87	2.17	1.83	1.18	1.90

Source: NFHS-1, 2 and 3.

Table 7.5b:
Classification of Indian states by region

North	Central	East	Northeast	West	South
Delhi	Chhattisgarh	Bihar	Arunachal Pradesh	Goa	Andhra Pradesh
Haryana	Madhya Pradesh	Jharkhand	Assam	Gujarat	Karnataka
Himachal Pradesh	Uttar Pradesh	Odisha	Manipur	Maharashtra	Kerala
Jammu & Kashmir		West Bengal	Meghalaya		Tamil Nadu
Punjab			Mizoram		
Rajasthan			Nagaland		
Uttaranchal			Sikkim		
			Tripura		

Source: Computed by author.

Table 7.6 gives the ASFRs in the age group 15–19 for women in the years 1971, 1991, 2011 and 2013, the most recent year for which the data are available from the SRS. It can be seen that at all India level, in 2013, there are 2.8 births per 100 women in the age group of 15–19, 3.2 in rural and 1.7 in urban areas. There are variations in this regard by states, highest being West Bengal at 5.4 per 100 women in 2013, 6.2 in the rural areas and 2.7 in the urban areas. It is 4 or more in Assam, Bihar Chhattisgarh and Jharkhand and less than 1 in Delhi, Goa, Jammu and Kashmir and Punjab. There has been a significant decline in adolescent fertility over the years, except in West Bengal where the declining trend is slow. A recent comprehensive study on Child marriages in India by Padmavathi Srinivasan and others (2015) indicates the wide prevalence of child marriages in selected parts of the country, especially in Tamil Nadu, Andhra Pradesh and even in the context of overall low fertility as much as in Bihar and Rajasthan with higher fertility levels. A map of India given by the author indicating the intensity of levels of child marriages in the country at the district level has been given as Figure 6.1. There appears to be strong cultural roots in getting their girls married at a very young age in some communities and as a consequence, exposing them to fertility at young ages when their body systems are yet to be fully developed. This is a serious problem that requires attention.

Table 7.6:
Births to young mothers

	1971			1991			2011			2013		
	Total	Rural	Urban	Total	Rural	Urban	Total	Rural	Urban	Total	Rural	Urban
India	100.8	110.6	64.9	76.1	84.5	46.1	30.7	35.3	16.5	28.1	31.7	16.5
Andhra Pradesh	140.1	148.9	100.5	121.5	133.0	80.0	38.8	46.0	21.2	27.0	31.1	16.9
Arunachal Pradesh				58.5	59.9	42.7	33.4	41.1	8.9	33.1	39.2	14.7
Assam	126.5	132.6	57.9	60.1	61.8	36.6	45.8	49.1	22.1	48.2	51.5	22.1
Bihar				78.5	82.2	45.7	33.0	34.0	24.2	35.5	36.9	21.7
Chhattisgarh							39.8	46.4	11.3	37.5	41.9	18.1
Delhi				5.6	3.1	10.8	9.2	15.3	8.2	9.2	6.9	9.6
Goa							6.5	4.2	7.7	9.1	3.7	12.1
Gujarat	72.3	75.3	63.9	39.5	41.0	35.7	23.4	27.1	16.9	21.7	25.7	14.5
Haryana	73.2	78.3	51.6	81.1	91.2	42.0	17.0	19.5	10.8	14.4	15.5	11.7
Jammu & Kashmir							5.7	6.1	3.6	4.1	4.7	1.2
Jharkhand							37.8	42.3	16.4	43.3	46.6	24.8
Karnataka	100.9	114.6	65.3	76.7	85.4	54.1	35.8	43.1	21.6	31.8	34.7	26.1
Kerala	51.8	49.1	66.9	25.5	25.7	24.7	20.3	21.9	15.1	17.9	19.0	14.6

Madhya Pradesh	166.8	181.4	97.4	124.6	137.9	68.0	32.5	37.1	14.9	31.2	35.7	14.0
Maharashtra	79.0	81.0	75.0	80.0	99.3	41.2	28.6	38.8	13.6	27.3	34.7	15.3
Odisha	118.4	118.8	113.0	62.0	64.7	36.4	29.8	31.6	18.2	30.6	32.4	17.9
Punjab	29.9	31.0	25.5	23.3	25.2	17.5	10.4	12.0	7.4	5.5	4.1	8.2
Rajasthan	N.A.	N.A.	N.A.	86.3	90.7	65.0	32.7	36.2	19.6	21.5	23.4	13.9
Tamil Nadu	70.7	85.2	43.2	45.3	47.8	40.6	19.4	20.1	18.5	21.1	22.0	19.8
Uttar Pradesh	98.8	126.7	61.8	72.2	80.6	38.4	26.1	28.9	13.1	20.5	22.0	13.1
West Bengal				83.5	95.6	46.5	55.4	63.5	27.8	54.0	61.8	26.6

Source: SRS India.

Unmet Need for Family Planning

In spite of strong program of family planning in vogue in the country for over five decades, there is still a high level of unmet need for contraception for both the purposes of spacing and for limitation of births.

Table 7.7 gives the percentages of currently married women in the reproductive ages (15–49) who have expressed an unmet need for spacing and limitation of births but not using contraception for various reasons (data collected from NFHS-1, 2 and 3 and from NFHS-4 for available states). From this table, it can be seen that at the national level the total unmet need for contraception, combining both for spacing and limitation, was 19.5 percent (per 100 currently married women in reproductive ages) in 1992–93; 15.6 in 1998–99 and 12.8 in 2005–06 as per NFHS-3. The need for spacing and limitation is roughly half–half from 1992–93 to 2005–06. The highest unmet need in 2005–06 was expressed in the state of Meghalaya at 35 percent, 11.8 for limiting and 23.2 for spacing. The next was in Nagaland, 26.1 percent with 16.1 for limiting and 10 for spacing. There appears to be some inconsistencies in the data as reported for Gujarat between NFHS-3 and NFHS-4. The percentage of couples expressing an unmet need for limitation was 3.7 in 2005–06, but it was reported as 10.3 in 2015–16. For all the other states, there is a consistency between NFHS-3 and NFHS-4 data on unmet need. This table provides a rough guideline as to the nature of family planning services to be provided in different parts of the country and generally, the northeastern states seem to need immediate attention.

Table 7.7:
Unmet need of couple as reflected in NFHS-1, 2 and 3

	NFHS-1 (1992–93)			NFHS-2 (1998–99)			NFHS-3 (2005–06)			NFHS-4 (2015–16)		
	Limiting	Spacing	Total Unmet	Limiting	Spacing	Total Unmet	Limiting	Spacing	Total Unmet	Limiting	Spacing	Total Unmet
India	8.5	11	19.5	7.5	8.3	15.8	6.6	6.2	12.8	NA	NA	NA
Andhra Pradesh	4.1	6.3	10.4	2.5	5.2	7.7	1.7	3	4.7	1.6	3.1	4.7
Arunachal Pradesh	7.4	12.9	20.4	9.3	17.2	26.5	10.6	8.3	18.8	NA	NA	NA
Assam	10.7	11	21.7	10	7	17	7.1	3.5	10.5	8.4	5.8	14.2
Bihar	NA	NA	NA	12.5	13.1	25.7	12.1	10.7	22.8	11.8	9.4	21.2
Chhattisgarh	NA	NA	NA	5.6	8	13.5	4.8	5.3	10.1	5.8	5.3	11.1
Delhi	7.9	7.6	15.4	7.5	5.9	13.4	4.5	3.3	7.8	NA	NA	NA
Goa	7.9	7.8	15.7	9.8	7.3	17.1	5.7	7.4	13.1	9.2	8.3	17.5
Gujarat	5.5	7.6	13.1	3.7	4.8	8.5	3.7	4.3	8	10.3	6.7	17
Haryana	7.6	8.8	16.4	4.7	2.9	7.6	5.2	3.1	8.3	5.5	3.8	9.3
Himachal Pradesh	5.6	9.2	14.9	4.9	3.6	8.6	4.9	2.4	7.2	NA	NA	NA
Jammu & Kashmir	NA	NA	NA	12.6	7.4	20	8.7	5.8	14.5	NA	NA	NA
Jharkhand	NA	NA	NA	9.9	11.1	21	11.9	11.3	23.1	NA	NA	NA
Karnataka	6.4	11.8	18.2	3.2	8.3	11.5	3.6	6	9.6	4.4	6	10.4

(Table 7.7 continued)

(Table 7.7 continued)

	NFHS-1 (1992–93)			NFHS-2 (1998–99)			NFHS-3 (2005–06)			NFHS-4 (2015–16)		
	Limiting	Spacing	Total Unmet	Limiting	Spacing	Total Unmet	Limiting	Spacing	Total Unmet	Limiting	Spacing	Total Unmet
Kerala	4.5	7.2	11.7	4.9	6.9	11.7	2.9	6	8.9	NA	NA	NA
Madhya Pradesh	NA	NA	NA	7.9	9.2	17.1	5.9	5.4	11.3	6.4	5.7	12.1
Maharashtra	6.8	7.3	14.1	4.9	8.1	13	3.9	5.4	9.4	5.4	4.3	9.7
Manipur	10	11.7	21.7	10	13.6	23.6	7.4	5	12.4	NA	NA	NA
Meghalaya	4.6	20.6	25.1	12.1	23.4	35.5	11.8	23.2	35	NA	NA	NA
Mizoram	2.8	9.2	11.9	3.7	11.7	15.5	5	12.3	17.3	NA	NA	NA
Nagaland	13.8	12.9	26.7	11.9	18.3	30.2	16.1	10	26.1	NA	NA	NA
Odisha	9.7	12.7	22.4	6.8	8.7	15.5	8.1	6.8	14.9	8.9	4.7	13.6
Punjab	6.5	6.5	13	4.5	2.8	7.3	4.7	2.6	7.3	3.8	2.4	6.2
Rajasthan	9	10.8	19.8	8.9	8.7	17.6	7.3	7.3	14.6	6.6	5.7	12.3
Sikkim	NA	NA	NA	13.2	9.9	23.1	11.2	5.6	16.9	NA	NA	NA
Tamil Nadu	6.7	7.8	14.6	6.4	6.6	13	4.5	4	8.5	5.3	4.8	10.1
Tripura	8.2	5.3	13.5	9.6	8.1	17.7	6.5	3.8	10.3	NA	NA	NA
Uttar Pradesh	NA	NA	NA	13.6	11.8	25.4	12.1	9.1	21.2	NA	NA	NA
Uttarakhand	NA	NA	NA	10.5	10.5	21	6.5	4.4	10.8	NA	NA	NA
West Bengal	8	9.4	17.4	5.5	6.3	11.8	4	4	8	4.5	3	7.5

Source: NFHS-1, 2, 3 and 4.

Mortality Declines

Crude Death Rates

Table 7.8 provides data on CDR for the years 1971–73, 1991–93 and 20011–13 of the major states of India for the rural, urban and combined areas. The data is taken from the SRS. CDR values have steadily declined in both the 20-year periods from 12.9 to 9.7 in the first and from 9.7 to 7.0 in the second. CDRs are higher in the rural areas than the urban areas in all the three periods. However, the rural–urban gap has narrowed down with mortality declines. In 2011–13, the maximum rural–urban gap was in Assam at 3.3 (8.4–5.10) and the minimum was in Delhi at 0.4 (4.6–4.2). The low death rate in Delhi might be due to the high proportion of the population in the working ages (in-migrants) and in these ages, the age specific mortality rates are relatively low.

Infant Mortality Rates

Table 7.9 presents data on IMRs for different states for the years 1972, 1992 and 2012 (as three year-moving averages centered in these years) and for 2015, the latest year for which data is available for the rural, urban and combined areas of the 19 large states of the country. From this table, it can be seen that in all the years, including 2015, the rural IMR values are higher than the urban values. In the country as a whole, the lowest IMR value in 2015 was in Kerala at 12 infant deaths per 1,000 births and the highest was in Madhya Pradesh at 50. The rates in rural Kerala and rural Madhya Pradesh were 13 and 54 respectively. The southern states as a whole and Himachal Pradesh, West Bengal and Goa have significantly lower IMR values than the large states in the Hindi belt Bihar, Chhattisgarh, Jharkhand, Rajasthan and Uttar Pradesh. For the urban areas, it was 10 in Kerala and 34 in Madhya Pradesh in 2015. Surprisingly, the state of Odisha, which has significantly lower fertility levels, has high IMR value at 46 in 2015. Each state lags behind of Kerala by a certain number of years, and Odisha lags behind of Kerala by 37 years as discussed in Table 7.12.

Table 7.8:
Crude death rate

	1971–73			1991–93*			2011–13		
	Total	Rural	Urban	Total	Rural	Urban	Total	Rural	Urban
INDIA	15.9	17.4	9.9	9.7	10.7	6.6	7	7.6	5.6
Andhra Pradesh	15.8	17	10.3	9.2	10.1	6	7.4	8.4	5.1
Assam	17.3	18.1	9.7	10.7	11.1	6.9	7.9	8.3	5.6
Bihar	NA	NA	NA	10.5	11	5.9	6.6	6.8	5.5
Chhattisgarh	NA	NA	NA	NA	NA	NA	7.9	8.3	6
Delhi	7.8	12	7.3	5.7	7.7	5.6	4.2	4.6	4.2
Gujarat	15.7	17	12.1	8.6	9.1	7.6	6.6	7.3	5.6
Haryana	11.3	11.9	8.3	8.3	8.8	6.5	6.4	6.9	5.3
Jammu & Kashmir	10.3	11.5	6.2	NA	NA	NA	5.4	5.6	4.6
Jharkhand	NA	NA	NA	NA	NA	NA	6.8	7.2	5
Karnataka	12.4	14.2	7.9	8.5	9.5	5.9	7	8	5.3
Kerala	8.9	9.1	7.8	6.1	6.2	5.9	6.9	7.1	6.6
Madhya Pradesh	17.1	18.1	10.9	13.1	14.2	8.4	8.1	8.6	6.1
Maharashtra	12.9	14.5	9.3	7.8	9.2	5.5	6.3	7.2	5
Odisha	17.9	18.5	11	12.2	12.9	6.6	8.5	8.8	6.4
Punjab	11.7	12.4	9.1	8	8.7	5.9	6.7	7.5	5.5
Rajasthan	NA	NA	NA	9.9	10.6	6.8	6.6	6.9	5.7
Tamil Nadu	14.5	16.9	8.8	8.5	9.4	6.7	7.4	8.1	6.4
Uttar Pradesh	21.7	22.9	13.5	11.9	12.7	8.5	7.8	8.2	6
West Bengal	NA	NA	NA	8	8.8	5.9	6.3	6.2	6.6

Source: SRS India.

Table 7.9:
Infant mortality rate

	1971–73			1991–93*			2011–13			2015		
	Total	Rural	Urban	Total	Rural	Urban	Total	Rural	Urban	Total	Rural	Urban
India	134	144	85	78	85	50	42	46	28	37	41	25
Andhra Pradesh	109	119	64	69	75	48	41	46	30	37	41	26
Assam	137	141	84	79	81	51	55	57	33	47	50	25
Bihar	NA	NA	NA	71	73	45	43	44	34	42	42	44
Chhattisgarh	NA	NA	NA	NA	NA	NA	47	48	39	41	43	32
Delhi	NA	NA	NA	37	61	35	26	36	24	18	27	18
Gujarat	144	157	106	65	70	51	38	45	24	33	41	21
Haryana	90	93	69	70	74	53	43	46	33	36	39	30
Jammu & Kashmir	NA	NA	NA	NA	NA	NA	39	41	28	26	27	24
Jharkhand	NA	NA	NA	NA	NA	NA	37	38	27	32	35	22
Karnataka	93	101	63	72	83	43	33	36	25	28	30	23
Kerala	58	61	46	15	16	12	12	13	9	12	13	10
Madhya Pradesh	145	154	96	109	116	72	57	60	38	50	54	34
Maharashtra	107	117	84	56	66	37	25	30	17	21	26	14
Odisha	134	139	78	116	121	73	54	55	39	46	48	35
Punjab	112	120	79	55	60	40	28	30	24	23	24	20
Rajasthan	NA	NA	NA	84	89	56	49	54	31	43	48	27
Tamil Nadu	114	127	76	57	66	41	21	24	18	19	22	16
Uttar Pradesh	132	189	124	96	101	73	53	56	39	46	48	36
West Bengal	NA	NA	NA	65	70	39	32	33	26	26	27	24

Source: SRS India.

Table 7.10:
Under-five mortality rates (U5MR) by sex and residence, India and bigger states

India & Bigger States	Total						Rural						Urban					
	2008			2013			2008			2013			2008			2013		
	Total	Male	Female	Total	Male	Female	Total	Male	Female	Total	Male	Female	Total	Male	Female	Total	Male	Female
India	**69**	**64**	**73**	**49**	**47**	**53**	**76**	**71**	**81**	**55**	**51**	**59**	**43**	**41**	**46**	**29**	**28**	**30**
Andhra Pradesh	58	55	61	41	40	42	64	62	67	46	44	48	40	36	45	29	29	30
Assam	88	81	96	73	68	77	93	85	101	77	72	82	50	50	51	34	34	35
Bihar	75	69	82	54	51	58	77	70	84	56	52	60	56	52	59	37	38	36
Chhattisgarh	71	65	78	53	47	59	74	68	80	56	49	62	56	49	64	38	38	39
Delhi	40	38	43	26	25	28	40	39	40	40	41	40	41	38	44	24	22	26
Gujarat	60	58	63	45	44	46	72	70	76	53	53	53	38	38	39	28	25	32
Haryana	65	60	71	45	42	49	70	66	75	49	45	55	50	43	59	34	34	35
Himachal Pradesh	50	37	64	41	37	45	50	37	65	41	38	45	39	38	41	32	28	38
Jammu & Kashmir	55	55	55	40	40	39	58	57	58	42	42	41	41	41	42	29	30	28
Jharkhand	65	58	72	48	45	51	69	61	77	51	48	55	44	41	46	27	26	29
Karnataka	55	54	56	35	33	36	62	61	64	38	37	39	40	40	40	28	25	30
Kerala	14	12	15	12	11	14	14	13	15	13	12	15	12	8	16	9	7	10

	92	90	93	69	65	74	98	95	101	75	70	81	62	65	59	40	40	40
Madhya Pradesh	92	90	93	69	65	74	98	95	101	75	70	81	62	65	59	40	40	40
Maharashtra	41	39	42	26	26	27	49	48	51	32	31	32	28	26	29	18	17	19
Odisha	89	87	91	66	65	68	93	91	95	70	68	71	59	56	63	39	37	41
Punjab	49	45	55	31	26	36	55	48	63	35	29	41	39	38	41	24	21	26
Rajasthan	80	72	88	57	50	65	88	80	97	63	55	71	49	44	55	32	29	36
Tamil Nadu	36	36	36	23	22	24	39	38	40	26	26	27	31	33	30	17	16	19
Uttar Pradesh	91	83	100	64	60	70	97	89	106	68	62	75	63	57	71	44	45	43
West Bengal	42	42	42	35	34	35	45	45	44	37	36	38	32	30	35	26	25	27

Source: SRS India.

Table 7.11:
Malnourished children under three years from NFHS-1, 2 and 3

Children Under 3 Years Who Are	NFHS-1 (1992–93)			NFHS-2 (1998–99)			NFHS-3 (2005–06)		
	Stunted	Underweight	Wasted	Stunted	Underweight	Wasted	Stunted	Underweight	Wasted
India	NA	51.5	NA	51	42.7	19.7	44.9	40.4	22.9
Andhra Pradesh	NA	42.9	NA	47.2	34.2	11	38.4	29.8	14.9
Arunachal Pradesh	54	32.1	15.5	30.3	21.5	10.3	37	29.7	17
Assam	56.4	44.1	14	54	35.3	19	41.1	35.8	16.7
Bihar	NA	NA	NA	58.4	52.2	25.4	50.1	54.9	32.6
Chhattisgarh	NA	NA	NA	60.8	53.2	24.8	52.6	47.8	24.1
Delhi	46.9	36.2	15.9	43.2	29.9	15.7	43.2	24.9	17.2
Goa	34.9	29.3	17.5	21.7	21.3	16.5	25.9	21.3	12.8
Gujarat	50.1	42.7	23.9	52	41.6	20.3	49.2	41.1	19.7
Haryana	50.5	31	7.8	55.6	29.9	7.8	43.3	38.2	22.4
Himachal Pradesh	NA	38.4	NA	48.8	36.5	17.9	34.3	31.1	19.9
Jammu and Kashmir	NA	NA	NA	44.6	29.2	14.8	33.1	24	18.1
Jharkhand	NA	NA	NA	54.1	51.5	28	47.2	54.6	35.8
Karnataka	47.6	46.4	24.2	41.9	38.6	25.1	42.4	33.3	18.9

Kerala	32.8	22.1	13.7	28	21.7	13	26.5	21.2	15.6
Madhya Pradesh	NA	NA	NA	55.1	50.8	25.2	46.5	57.9	39.5
Maharashtra	47	47.3	27.6	47.1	44.8	23.6	44	32.7	17.2
Manipur	32	19.1	9.9	38.5	20.1	9.7	29	19.5	10.8
Meghalaya	52.6	36.9	18.9	48.8	28.6	14.9	47.7	42.9	31.8
Mizoram	41	17.2	5.2	41.3	19.8	13.3	35.1	14.2	9.7
Nagaland	32.7	18.7	12.2	38.7	18.8	13.6	34.1	23.7	15.8
Odisha	50.8	50	28.2	49.1	50.3	29.7	43.9	39.5	23.7
Punjab	45.2	39.9	20.8	45.2	24.7	8.1	34.7	23.6	10.2
Rajasthan	45.5	41.8	23.8	59	46.7	16.2	40.1	36.8	22.5
Sikkim	NA	NA	NA	35.7	15.5	6.5	31.8	17.3	12.8
Tamil Nadu	NA	40.7	NA	35.2	31.5	22.5	31.1	25.9	22.9
Tripura	52.3	42.1	20.6	44.6	37.3	18	34.1	35.2	24
Uttar Pradesh	NA	NA	NA	60.7	48.1	16.9	52.4	41.6	19.5
Uttarakhand	NA	NA	NA	52.5	36.3	9	39.6	31.7	18.2
West Bengal	NA	53.2	NA	50.4	45.3	17.3	41.8	37.6	19.2

Source: NFHS-1, 2 and 3.

Table 7.12:
Maternal mortality ratio between 1997–98 to 2011–13

India & Bigger States	Period						
	1997–98	*1999–2001*	*2001–03*	*2004–06*	*2007–09*	*2010–12*	*2011–13*
INDIA TOTAL	**398**	**327**	**301**	**254**	**212**	**178**	**167**
Assam	568	398	490	480	390	328	300
Bihar/Jharkhand	531	400	371	312	261	219	208
Madhya Pradesh/Chhattisgarh	441	407	379	335	269	230	221
Odisha	346	424	358	303	258	235	222
Rajasthan	508	501	445	388	318	255	244
Uttar Pradesh/Uttaranchal	606	539	517	440	359	292	285
EAG AND ASSAM SUBTOTAL	**520**	**461**	**438**	**375**	**308**	**257**	**246**
Andhra Pradesh	197	220	195	154	134	110	92
Karnataka	245	266	228	213	178	144	133
Kerala	150	149	110	95	81	66	61
Tamil Nadu	131	167	134	111	97	90	79
SOUTH SUBTOTAL	**187**	**206**	**173**	**149**	**127**	**105**	**93**
Gujarat	46	202	172	160	148	122	112
Haryana	136	176	162	186	153	146	127
Maharashtra	166	169	149	130	104	87	68
Punjab	280	177	178	192	172	155	141
West Bengal	303	218	194	141	145	117	113
Other		276	235	206	160	136	126
OTHER SUBTOTAL	**184**	**229**	**199**	**174**	**149**	**127**	**115**

Source: SRS India.
Note: EAG: Empowered Action Group.

Under-Five Mortality

Table 7.10 presents data on under-five mortality rates, or probability of a child dying before the age of five, for the years 2008 and 2013 for males and females and rural and urban areas separately. For India as a whole in 2008, it was 68 per 1,000 live births, 64 for males and 73 for females. In 2013, after five years, this rate came down to 49, but the male–female differential has persisted, with 47 for males and 53 for female, although the gap has somewhat narrowed. In the rural areas, the gap was of 10 points in 2008 that down to 8 by 2013. In the urban areas, the gap was of 5 in 2008 that to 2 by 2013. Thus urbanization and reduction of overall mortality levels seem to narrow down the gender gap in under-five mortality. The gap was highest at 17 points in Uttar Pradesh rural areas in 2008 that reduced to 13 points by 2013. At all levels of under-five mortality, a residue of gap between male and female mortality persists, the latter being higher contrary to the Western experience where under-five mortality of boys is higher than girls, indicating a strong gender bias among the parents. Given the same nurture and health care for children of both the sexes, a girl child tends to have slightly lower child mortality than a male child.

Malnutrition among Children

NFHS collected data on the height and weight of children below 3 years of age and from this data, we can compute percentage of children stunted in terms of below 2 SD (standard deviation) of the World Health Organization (WHO) standard height for age, the percentage underweight in terms of below 2 SD below the weight for age and wasted in terms of height for weight. The percentages of children in these three categories are given in Table 7.11 for different states.

At the all India level, the percentage of children underweight in 1992–93 was 51.5, which came down to 42.7 in 1998–99 and further to 40.4 in 20015–06. The declines over 13-year period were only marginal. In 2005–06, Kerala had the lowest percentage of malnourished children in all the three categories at 26.5, 21.2 and 15.6 respectively. Even in Punjab, which is an agricultural surplus production state, the rates of stunting and underweight (34.7 and 23.6) among children are higher than Kerala. In Bihar, Chhattisgarh and Uttar Pradesh, it is pathetic to see that more than half the children below 3 years of age are stunted, and close to half are underweight.

Maternal Mortality Ratio

MMR—the number of deaths within 42 days after delivery per 100,000 live births—is a powerful indicator of the health care provided to women and is a component of any gender equity index. This is one indicator that sharply distinguishes the developed from the developing countries. Traditionally, India had a very high MMR value of 600–700 maternal deaths per 100,000 live births and in rural areas, even now, any safe delivery for a pregnant woman is considered a second birth for her. With the introduction of institutional deliveries as the preferred place of delivery for all pregnant women in the country since the early 1990s and increased availability of hospital beds for delivery, MMR in India has recently declined considerably. Table 7.12 gives MMR values that have been estimated by the SRS through visits to deaths of women in the reproductive ages in the sample blocks and enquiries through a detailed questionnaire whether the death of the woman took place within 6 weeks of delivery and can be considered a maternal death.

MMR has been computed on the basis of such verbal autopsies of all deaths to women in the reproductive ages in sample areas covered under the SRS. The rates are provided for the periods 1997–98, 2004–06 and 2011–15 for the major states. It can be seen that in the country as a whole, MMR values have declined from 398 in 1997–98 to 254 in 2004–06 and to 167 in 2011–13, that is, about 36 percent decline in 15 years. This is a good indicator of Janani Suraksha Yojana program or the Safe Delivery Program encouraging institutional deliveries to pregnant woman. Among all the states during 2011–13, southern states have low MMR values—61 in Kerala, 70 in Tamil Nadu and 133 in Karnataka. The Empowered Action Group states, with special attention at the center, still have high MMR values, that is, above 200, and the highest is in Bihar at 300. In all these states, there are considerable declines in MMR values since 1997–98.

Lags in Fertility and Mortality

Kerala has experienced the transition to low fertility and mortality rates almost two decades before the other states. We carried out a lag analysis of the number of years each state lags behind of Kerala in its 2013 value. It is computed based on the time difference between the years at which Kerala experienced the value experienced by the states in 2013. The lags have been computed for the demographic parameters of TFR, CBR, IMR, e0, e15, e45 and e60 values (expectations of life at birth, ages 15, 45 and

60) to study how the fertility, mortality and life expectancy at different ages in different states have been moving in relation to Kerala. Kerala is the dream baby for demographers within India. The lag values and the actual values on these parameters in 2013 are given in Table 7.13a.

We wanted to find out how India compares with the conditions in the United Kingdom from which it got independence in 1947. Values for the United Kingdom were taken from the World Bank country data and the human mortality database (mortality.org). The time lags of Indian parameter for 2013 were 42, 66, 66, 65, 61, 45 and 40 years from those of the United Kingdom in terms of TFR, CBR, IMR, e0, e15, e45 and e60. This means that India in 2013 lags behind of United Kingdom by 42 years on TFR, 65 years on CBR, 66 years on IMR and so on. These figures are given in the first panel of Table 7.13a.

This is a terrible and humbling finding with regards to India's development over the past six decades. On most of the mortality variables, we lag, as a country, behind of United Kingdom by almost six decades.

Instead of comparing all India figures with UK figures, when we compare the figures of each state with Kerala and Kerala with UK figures, we find a different picture. Kerala values on these seven parameters in 2013 taken from the SRS, and the lag in years from the UK values are given in Table 7.13b.

TFR of Kerala in 2013 was 1.8 and the United Kingdom had this value 38 years earlier in 1975. Kerala had an IMR of 12 in 2013 and the United Kingdom had this value 34 years earlier in 1979. This is not a bad picture. An interesting finding is that as we move to older ages the lags in the expectations of life of Kerala and the United Kingdom narrows down. For example, the expectation of life at 65 in Kerala was 19.9 years in 2013 and the United Kingdom had same value 21 years earlier in 1992, but the lag in terms of expectation of life at birth was 30 years that the United Kingdom had Kerala value in 1983.

If we compare the states of India with Kerala, we would find that in most of the variables all the states in the north lag behind of Kerala by almost three decades. For example, on these seven parameters, Uttar Pradesh lags behind of Kerala by 37, 37, 37, 35, 35, 35 and 30 years. Tamil Nadu lags behind of Kerala by 19, 10, 24, 24, 24, 23 and 23 years. The lags between Kerala and other states is the least in terms of TFR and CBR values and largest in terms of mortality indicators. Even on the mortality indicators, we find the gaps in the expectations of life at 65(e65) is the least and highest on e0, implying that there is a greater homogeneity in morality at older ages.

Table 7.13a:

India's lag in years behind the UK on TFR, CBR, IMR and life expectancy at different ages

		TFR	CBR	IMR	e0	e15	e45	e60
India	Values	2.3	21.4	40	67.5	57.1	29.9	17.9
	Years lag	42	66	66	65	61	45	40

Lags of Other Indian States Behind Kerala on TFR, CBR, IMR and Life Expectancy at Different Ages

		TFR	CBR	IMR	e0	e15	e45	e60
Andhra Pradesh	Values	1.8	17.4	39	67.9	56.4	29.7	18.0
	Years lag	22	19	33	30	30	30	23
Assam	Values	2.3	22.4	54	63.3	54.1	27.5	16.4
	Years lag	27	27	38	35	40	40	30
Bihar	Values	3.4	27.6	42	67.7	57.1	29.8	17.3
	Years lag	37	37	35	30	30	30	30
Gujarat	Values	2.3	20.8	36	68.2	57.7	30.4	18.4
	Years lag	27	26	32	30	24	23	22
Haryana	Values	2.2	21.3	41	68.2	57.6	30.7	19.0
	Years lag	26	26	34	30	24	16	21
Himachal Pradesh	Values	1.7	16	35	71.0	59.7	32.1	19.7
	Years lag	19	10	32	22	19	8	18
Jammu & Kashmir	Values	1.9	17.5	37	72.0	61.1	32.9	20.4
	Years lag	23	16	32	22	Yet to reach	Yet to reach	Yet to reach
Karnataka	Values	1.9	18.3	31	68.5	56.8	29.8	17.9
	Years lag	23	22	28	25	30	24	24
Kerala	Years lag	1.8	14.7	12	74.8	60.9	32.6	19.9
Madhya Pradesh	Values	2.9	26.3	54	63.8	55.3	28.4	16.4
	Years lag	35	33	37	35	40+	35	30
Maharashtra	Values	1.8	16.5	24	71.3	58.6	31.1	18.7
	Years lag	22	10	25	16	22	22	22
Odisha	Values	2.1	19.6	51	64.8	55.8	29.0	17.2
	Years lag	26	23	37	35	35	30	30
Punjab	Values	1.7	15.7	26	71.1	59.2	32.1	20.1
	Years lag	19	10	25	16	21	5	Yet to reach

		TFR	*CBR*	*IMR*	*e0*	*e15*	*e45*	*e60*
Rajasthan	Values	2.8	25.6	47	67.5	58.4	31.1	18.9
	Years lag	32	31	36	30	22	11	22
Tamil Nadu	Values	1.7	15.6	21	70.2	57.4	30.1	18.1
	Years lag	19	10	24	24	24	23	23
Uttar Pradesh	Values	3.1	27.2	50	63.8	55.2	28.4	16.8
	Years lag	37	37	37	35	35	35	30
West Bengal	Values	1.6	16	31	69.9	58.0	30.2	17.7
	Years lag	Yet to reach	10	28	24	24	24	24

Source: SRS India and the Human Mortality Database.

Table 7.13b:
Lags of Kerala with the United Kingdom on demographic parameters

		TFR	*CBR*	*IMR*	*e0*	*e15*	*e45*	*e60*
Kerala	Values	1.8	14.7	12	74.8	60.9	32.6	19.9
	Years Lag	38	41	34	30	26	23	21

Sex Ratio

India shares a distinctive feature of the South Asian and Chinese populations with regard to the sex ratio, with a centuries-old deficit of females to males—the opposite in the case of non-Asian countries. In India, the deficit of females is largely attributed to women's lower status in the society that has contributed to their higher mortality in all ages up to 45. Of more serious concern to the country is that the sex ratio, defined as the number of females per 1,000 males, has been declining almost consistently over the decades, except for a small improvement in 1981. The sex ratio, computed to be 972 in the 1901 census, declined steadily to 930 by 1971, rose marginally to 934 by 1981, but again declined to 927 in 1991 and rose a little to 933 by 2001 and 940 by 2011. Such fluctuations may be more indicative of the quality of census data in the counting of number of women in the censuses than actual sex ratios.

Table 7.14 provides the usually derived and discussed three types of sex ratios in India, that is, the population sex ratio (PSR) or the number of females per 1,000 males, child sex ratio (CSR) or the number of female children per 1,000 male children in the age group of 0–6 or below 7 and

Table 7.14:
Sex ratios of population of India and bigger states for 2001 and 2011

	Sex Ratio at Birth[1]			Population Sex Ratio[2]		Child Sex Ratio[2] (0–6)	
	2001	*2006*	*2011*	*2001*	*2011*	*2001*	*2011*
India*	**892**	**901**	**908**	**933**	**940**	**927**	**919**
Andhra Pradesh	945	915	914	978	992	961	939
Assam	945	939	922	932	954	965	962
Bihar	870	909	909	921	916	942	935
Chhattisgarh		969	979	990	991	975	969
Delhi		871	884	821	866	868	871
Gujarat	844	891	909	921	918	883	890
Haryana	804	843	857	861	877	819	834
Himachal Pradesh	826	931	939	970	974	896	909
Jammu & Kashmir		854	895	900	883	941	862
Jharkhand		927	918	941	947	965	948
Karnataka	952	926	950	964	968	946	948
Kerala	911	958	966	1058	1084	960	964
Madhya Pradesh	920	913	921	920	930	932	918
Maharashtra	899	871	896	922	925	913	894
Odisha	944	933	948	972	978	953	941
Punjab	775	837	863	874	893	798	846
Rajasthan	890	865	893	922	926	909	888
Tamil Nadu	926	944	928	986	995	942	943
Uttar Pradesh	864	881	874	898	908	916	902
West Bengal	949	936	944	934	947	960	956

Sources: *Includes all States/UTs; [1]SRS; [2]Census.
Note: Figures relate to mid point for the periods 1998–2000 to 2011–13.

the sex ratio at birth (SRB) being the number of male births to 100 female children born in an year. These are provided for the latest two censuses 2001 and 2011 for PSR and CSR and for SRB, the data for the same years is obtained from the SRS. These sex ratios have different significance to the study of gender equity. PSR indicates the overall mortality conditions of females in comparison to males in the population and includes the effects of CSR and SRB. CSR reflects the relative nurture and health care given to female children compared to male children but includes the effects of SRB. SRB, the third indicator, is specific to gender-specific abortions or female feticide in the country. Table 7.14 reveals that while PSR has increased from 933 to 940 (from 2001 to 2011) and the sex ratio has also increased from 892 to 904, CSR has declined during this period from 927 to 919. On the other hand, SRB has increased between the two censuses from 933 to 940. This indicates that the programs to prevent prenatal detection of the sex of the child and selective female feticides have been successful, but the quality of care of the female child after birth is not good until the age of 7. After the age of 7 when the child is able to find its own food and is partly able to take care of herself, the relative rise in female mortality levels declined.

In many states, especially the large Hindi-speaking ones, decline in PSR was substantial between 1981 and 2011. For example, in Bihar, it fell from 946 to 921 in 2001 and further to 916 in 2011. In Uttar Pradesh, from an already quite low figure of 885, it increased somewhat to 908 by 2011. Surprisingly, even Maharashtra, considered one of the most pro-gressive states in the country with better status for women, recorded a sex ratio of 934 in 1991 that declined to 922 in 2001 and with a negligible increase to 925 in 2011. Only Kerala has had a favorable female sex ratio throughout this century (1,036 females per 1,000 males in 1991 that increased to 1,084 in 2011). Moreover, this is the only state that has surplus of females in the population, as is found in developed countries of the West. This is followed by Himachal Pradesh with a sex ratio of 976, remaining practically unchanged in 2011 at 974. Thus, the Indian population, except for Kerala, has had a deficit of females to males throughout the known history. Women's lower status in Indian society contributes to their low age at marriage, lower literacy and relatively higher fertility and mortality levels during the reproductive ages.

One possible explanation for the factors that contributed to women's lower status and the discriminatory treatment meted out to the girl child in the old civilizations, such as China, the Middle East and India, comes from the prevailing understanding or perceptions of people of the differential survival capabilities of the sexes. From centuries of observa-tions on the mortality of male versus female, these civilizations may have realized that, given equal nutrition and care at every age from conception onward, the male is the biologically the weaker sex and needs relatively better treatment and attention for equalizing the chances of survival. One expects this to happen at the family level where the relatively weaker child gets better nutrition and attention than the others do. To have a balanced sex ratio in the population, similar mechanisms seem to have operated at the societal level with regard to male children under patriarchy. However, over the centuries, the additional care required for the male child became institutionalized by him having an intrinsic social and religious value not possessed by the female child. Preferential nutrition practices might have then become institutionalized. Without such an explanation, it is difficult to understand how the sex ratio in many of these countries became more unfavorable to females in recent decades than what it was in earlier periods.

Quality of Data

I. Census Data on Age and Sex

Age Reporting Biases   In the censuses, data on the age of individuals in the completed years was routinely collected and in the 2011 census, data was also collected on the actual date of birth. When information on age is not reported by a respondent, it is customary to assume that for each sex, their age–marital status distributions would be the same as for those for whom the data is available. In the 2001 census in Kerala, we found that for 26,454 persons, the age data was not available and in 2011 census, such information was lacking for 34,486 persons. With the increase in the literacy and educational levels, this is puzzling. However even for those whose age data was not available, information on their sex and marital status was available. Hence, these persons were distributed within each marital status category for males and females, as per the age distributions of those for whom the information was available.

In developing countries, there are also unconscious prejudices and biases for numbers ending with certain digits, particularly those ending with 0 and 5. Even educated people when asked about their age may state it close to the nearest digit ending with 5 or 0. This type of bias is also called "heaping" or "digit preference" and is very common in the age data of developing countries. In developing countries, the order of preference of numbers in terms of digit preference has been found to be 0, 5, 2, 4, 6, and 8, and the least preferred are the other odd numbers. Although there is a universal bias of reporting of numbers ending with 5 or 0, the extent of preference varies between the developed and developing countries. In the category of biases, there is also another type of bias wherein culturally oriented, systematic over-reporting or under-reporting of ages have been noticed—widows and older persons in India tend to over-report their ages. These types of biases tend to push the population totals up or down to higher or younger ages. Graphs of single year age data for the 2001 and 2011 censuses are given in Figures 7.1 and 7.2. These line graphs of the age data clearly shows the peaks in ages ending with digits 0 and 5 and troughs in the adjacent two digits 1, 9, 6 and 4.

Demographers have developed a number of indexes and scores to study the extent of digit preferences. Some of the indexes are Whipple's index that measures the extent of preference to digits ending with 0 and 5, or to all specified digits as preferences or aversions (Myers index), differential reporting for the two sexes (sex ratio scores), crossover across age groups (age ratio scores) and a United Nations Joint score that combines the age and sex ratio scores. These index values compute for India, Rajasthan and Kerala, based on the recently published 2011 census single year age data (see Table 7.15). From this table, it can be seen that even the age data in the 2011 census for Kerala state, which is considered to have the most educated population in India, is poor in quality, loaded

Figure 7.1:
Single year age returns in Kerala: Males and females, 2001

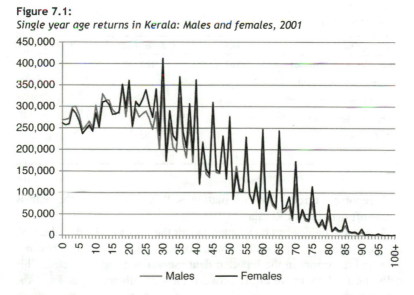

Source: Census of India, Registrar General of India (2001).

Figure 7.2:
Single year age returns in Kerala: Males and females, 2011

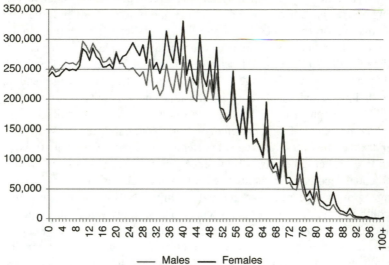

Source: Census of India, Registrar General of India (2011).

Table 7.15:
Errors in age-sex data in 2011 census

Index of Quality	India	Rajasthan	Kerala
Whipples index (female) (Accuracy level < 105)	167	167	121
Myers Index (female) (Accuracy level = 0)	26.4	29.7	10.6
UN Joint Score (<20)	20.5	24.8	21.8

with reporting errors. The consolation is Rajasthan where the data is worse off than that of Kerala.

These techniques can be adapted to suit the errors in the distributions by other characteristics such as years of schooling, working days in a year and the errors in the reported data ascertained and corrected. This calls for a collaborative effort between the disciplinary experts and the demographers.

Age Not Stated in the Census: Table 7.16 gives data on the number of persons per 100,000 populations for whom age was not recorded in the censuses of 1991, 2001 and 2011 by states and by the educational level of the respondents. The table makes an interesting and instructive reading. In 1991 for the country as a whole, 560 out of 100,000 persons' age was not recorded. In 2001 census, it was 266 and 371 in 2011. One expects that with increased years of experience with census taking, the proportion of age not stated would go down; this is not so. One would also expect that this proportion of age not stated should go down by the educational qualification of the individuals; this is not so either. For persons with "graduate or above level qualification," it was 413 in the 2011 census compared to only 356 among the illiterates. The highest rate of "age not stated" is in the category of "literates without educational level" where it is between 1,000 and 2,000, and it was very high in the state of Goa in 2001 at 21,288. In the most educated state of Kerala, it was 243 in 1991, 83 in 2001 and 103 in 2011 and among those with graduate and higher qualifications in Kerala, it was 217, 38 and 84. The level of age not stated in this highly educated category varied from a high of 1,154 in Andhra Pradesh to a low 41 in Tripura. One plausible explanation that has to be considered in explaining this anomalous situation with our similar finding in the earlier section of prevalence of high levels of digit preferences even in reported ages (for digits ending with 0 and 5) is that information on the ages of the individuals in the censuses are not carefully enquired and recorded by the investigators, but they report the ages as they deem it fit or appropriate for each individual. The age distributions we get are largely based on the perceptions by the census takers. The biases and omissions may be from the census enumerators more than from the respondents.

HIV/AIDs Data: Till 2006, the estimates of prevalence of HIV+ cases in India were based on data collected from blood tests for selected surveillance centers (i.e., HIV sentinel surveillance or HSS), antenatal clinics for mothers and children and high risk groups, such as female sex workers, gay males, transport workers and others. Based on several assumptions on the distributions of populations in these groups these estimates from different groups were merged and estimates of prevalence of HIV+ at the states level was worked out by NACO. Estimates in India were based on HSS data and several assumptions. During 1998–2002, these estimates got further addition of twenty percent into them to

Table 7.16

Age not stated by educational qualification for India and states for 1991, 2001 and 2011

	Total Population			Illiterate			Literate Without Educational Level			Higher Secondary/ Intermediate/ Pre-University/Senior Secondary			Graduate & Above		
	1991	2001	2011	1991	2001	2011	1991	2001	2011	1991	2001	2011	1991	2001	2011
India (Excluding J&K)	560	266	371	158	287	356	6,904	2,558	1,910	409	170	317	539	225	413
Andaman & Nicobar Islands (Ut)	588	640	97	8	683	86	14,023	6,450	847	135	350	110	560	208	83
Andhra Pradesh	305	175	912	40	181	740	11,818	1,662	4,298	123	134	990	158	172	1194
Arunachal Pradesh	583	101	109	333	109	93	17,959	1,359	1,390	472	75	88	934	100	157
Assam	374	109	60	25	124	60	15,965	1,273	360	235	82	56	668	109	83
Bihar	984	214	388	214	198	347	10,163	2,441	2,223	854	103	381	1,060	126	453
Chandigarh (UT)	879	144	33	48	202	35	20,377	2,288	658	169	96	20	162	85	25
Chhattisgarh	NA	135	90	NA	155	80	NA	595	784	NA	88	83	NA	102	114
Dadra & Nagar Haveli (UT)	267	47	108	25	45	110	14,118	1,140	397	57	10	74	165	76	120
Daman & Diu	214	45	146	25	57	109	2,740	2,483	1,724	0	49	76	52	0	94
Delhi	459	153	99	30	192	114	20,418	4,067	452	211	90	77	249	108	77
Goa	277	520	144	29	389	139	13,752	21,288	567	83	111	115	98	143	91
Gujarat	508	93	395	178	126	337	8,594	2,731	1,334	286	46	397	279	62	406
Haryana	49	381	124	11	619	128	4,009	3,154	725	45	143	104	74	182	117
Himachal Pradesh	330	242	148	88	503	161	7,858	1,944	713	256	77	153	314	83	139

State/UT														
Jammu & Kashmir	NA	451	121	NA	523	95	NA	2,226	2,379	NA	284	88	NA	351	90
Jharkhand	NA	124	354	NA	103	283	NA	3,183	1,758	NA	76	469	NA	87	586
Karnataka	543	98	75	62	121	62	9,718	1,493	427	277	53	63	334	61	82
Kerala	243	83	103	38	213	126	1,013	1,705	618	190	37	74	217	38	84
Lakshadweep (UT)	219	87	178	12	63	260	573	1,367	879	0	0	98	1,314	0	174
Madhya Pradesh	922	264	114	598	306	106	6,903	972	586	986	183	118	1,191	219	162
Maharashtra	397	122	363	46	173	329	11,282	1,801	1,495	158	57	307	245	65	365
Manipur	1,063	209	272	92	223	234	5,895	1,398	1,808	1,061	151	230	432	166	236
Meghalaya	1,033	136	195	278	155	171	14,286	1,061	1,192	823	82	286	1,017	68	138
Mizoram	1,180	87	58	402	138	38	33,173	654	1,433	898	51	41	693	83	60
Nagaland	1,332	238	74	310	269	72	7,512	2,981	489	938	143	42	1,459	170	49
Odisha	501	169	284	100	189	275	6,978	2,207	1,895	411	105	302	1,601	126	323
Pondicherry (UT)	297	83	88	10	87	104	7,392	2,418	679	120	50	68	176	42	52
Punjab	486	385	150	1	581	150	15,888	3,543	1,011	286	203	120	268	233	112
Rajasthan	310	509	393	10	532	377	8,350	1,985	1,503	248	392	401	499	486	386
Sikkim	1,284	358	193	571	382	182	7,513	1,536	698	956	221	169	1,772	132	129
Tamil Nadu	328	687	93	89	628	81	1,984	1,999	762	147	651	60	171	1,283	80
Tripura	227	150	44	31	176	44	4,633	1,391	242	158	153	37	344	122	41
Uttar Pradesh	701	443	812	179	402	745	5,206	5,607	3,924	537	267	726	907	325	969
Uttaranchal	NA	209	165	NA	181	137	NA	6,877	1,550	NA	87	161	NA	117	191
West Bengal	586	139	123	161	155	96	6,403	2,165	1,613	445	97	118	444	106	170

Source: Census of India.

compensate certain high risk populations with relatively high prevalence which were not included in estimation process. In 2003, however, it was replaced by identifying the FSW as a separate group and applying to them the rates applicable based on survey data. The States which did not have such sites, the HIV prevalence of the STD sentinel sites were applied. Further, in order to give due representation to child population, we estimated separately vertical transmission among children and added to the pool of HIV infections. It was done by applying the general fertility rate (GFR) to the women infected with HIV and then multiply by the percentage infected, i.e., 0.3 (which is as the worst case scenario that 30 percent children are born infected to infected mothers) to get the number of children born infected. The estimates for HIV infected people for different years.

This complicated estimation procedure lead to estimates on the number of persons in India living with HIV+ status in different years (see Table 7.17).

In 2005 India was cited globally as the country with the second largest country with HIV/AIDs cases in the world with 5.216 million cases next only to South Africa. Then came the data from the NFHS-3 conducted during 2005–06 that provided data at the state level estimates of HIV prevalence which was based on actual blood testing of a sample of population across the country. This estimate was of 2.6 million HIV+ cases in 2005, just half of the cases estimated from a number of subgroups of population and merging them before this year. It was said that before the publication of NFHS-3 results on HIV+ cases estimation, there were many people living "off HIV/AIDs than with HIV/AIDS." There were a number of NGOs working on HIV/AIDs that and were beneficiaries of international donors such as Melinda and Bill Gates Foundation and others. It was in their interest to show a high prevalence to attract donor funds from within and outside the country. This collapsed with the publication of NFHS-3 results which was based on a cross-national blood testing for HIV/AIDs.

Table 7.17:
Estimates of HIV people, 1998–2005

Year	1998	1999	2000	2001	2002	2003	2004
No. in Millions	3.5	3.7	3.86	3.97	4.58	5.11	5.13

Source: Census of India.

From 2005, the sentinel surveillance was extended to all districts. The community-based HIV prevalence measured by NFHS-3 in 2006 provided opportunity to replace many of the earlier assumptions with evidence-based information and improve the HIV estimate closer to reality.

> State-wise adult HIV prevalence among different risk groups observed from HSS 2006 was adjusted for site level variations using a random effects model and for the previous four years the same was back calculated using trend equations derived from a mixed effects logistic regression model based on consistent sites prevalence. (Pandey et al. 2009)

The adjusted HIV prevalence among the general population was calibrated to the estimates from NFHS-3. Overall point estimates of adult HIV prevalence in each state for 2002–06 were derived from the UNAIDS Workbook and projected for the period 1985–2010. The results were put into spectrum to derive estimates of the number of people living with HIV in all ages and other epidemic impacts. The revised national adult HIV prevalence was 0.36 percent from the earlier 0.7 percent. Further, more recent analysis showed that the prevalence rate of HIV/AIDs is declining in the country since 2006; however, the total number of cases is between 2.3 to 2.1 million. Thus, we have a peculiar situation that not only the earlier level figures of HIV prevalence was halved based on NFHS-3 figures but also the earlier rising trends in HIV prevalence were reversed after 2006. This is a great stigma as serious as HIV/AIDs in our national's statistics.

The authors conclude,

> The improvement in the 2006 estimates of the HIV burden in India is attributable to the expanded sentinel surveillance and representative data from the population-based survey in 2006, combined with an improved analysis. Despite the downward revision, India continues to face a formidable challenge to provide prevention, treatment and care to those in need The estimated number of people living with HIV in India maintains a steady declining trend from 23.2 lac in 2006 to 21 lac in 2011.
>
> … The estimated number of people living with HIV was 2.47 million (range 2.0–3.1 million) in 2006. The national adult HIV prevalence remains stable around 0.4 per cent between 2002 and 2006. The States with the highest estimated prevalence were Manipur, Nagaland and Andhra Pradesh. The States with the highest burden were Andhra Pradesh, Maharashtra, Karnataka and Tamil Nadu. (Pandey et al. 2009)

Quality of Civil Registration System (CRS) in India

In a series of landmark papers on civil registration of births and deaths recently published in the May issue of *The Lancet* (Counting of Births and Deaths, Vol. 386, May 15, 2015). It has been argued effectively in the papers that a comprehensive and reliable system of registration of births is absolutely essential for planning, monitoring and evaluation of the health and development programs in any country in the coming decades, as recommended in the post-2015 sustainable development goals (SDGs) set by the United Nations. No alternative systems, such as sample surveys or studies, surveillance systems and indirect mathematical models, can fill this need and replace such a CRS. The alternative such as SRS in India can provide reliable estimates of fertility and mortality at state and even district levels but will not be useful for the planning and monitoring of health programs at the local level. The authors (AbouZahr et al. 2015) also assert that such as a civil system for vital statistics can be established within a span of 5–10 years with the use of ICT and policy commitments from the government.

Following the United Nations recommendations in the 1960s, in India, CRS is defined by the Indian Registrar General (1964) as a "unified process of continuous, permanent and compulsory recording of the vital events and characteristics thereof, as per legal requirements in the country". In India, CRS covers registration of births and deaths only. In most of the countries, especially in the developed world, and in the last few years in many developing countries as well, it provides the best source of information on the vital rates at all levels, national and sub-national, and a legal basis for the nationality and citizenry of the country and hereditary and property rights. A certificate of birth and death from an appropriate registration authority is accepted as evidence in a court of law. Registration of the birth of a child in its place of birth is a considered a fundamental and basic right of the child, according to UNICEF. The importance of complete and accurate registration of births with all their required essential characteristics including the cause of death cannot be overstated.

CRS in India requires compulsory registration of every birth and death in the country—within 21 days of its occurrence—though this duration varies somewhat from state to system. It was established as a national system by the 1969 act of parliament called the Registration of Births and Deaths Act, 1969. As required by the act, most of the states have ratified the act in their state legislatures since, according to the division of powers between states and the center in the Constitution, registration of births and deaths fall within the purview of the state governments. In spite of the fact that the act is in vogue for over 46 years, the registration of births and deaths is still far from complete either in coverage or in the accuracy of the characteristics of the births and deaths registered. Even according to the assessment made by the Registrar General of India, who is the authority to implement the birth and death act, only 82 percent of the births and 69 percent of the deaths were registered in the country as a whole in 2010, and this estimate was based on a comparison of the estimate of the birth rate ascertained by CRS with those obtained from the SRS. The SRS in itself is a sample survey subject to a sampling error. The registration efficiency varied widely among the different states, large and small, with the southern states recording more than 90 percent of births and 80 percent of deaths while the large Hindi-speaking states of the north have done very poorly, with Bihar registering 47 percent of the births and only 17 percent of the deaths in 2010; Chhattisgarh registering 52 percent and 60 percent; Jharkhand 56 percent and 49 percent; Madhya Pradesh 82 percent and 55 percent and Uttar Pradesh 60 percent and 61 percent. Among the large Hindi-speaking states, Rajasthan has shown better registration with 92 percent of births 82 percent of deaths registered in 2010. The above is an observation on the deficiencies in the registration coverage. If we take into account the accuracy of the characteristics of the events registered, the errors are appalling. However, there is some silver lining: Conditions are improving in the recent years, even from the perspective of people themselves, as reported by them on the extent to which they have registered the birth of their children.

Table 7.18 provides the percentages of births of children under 5-years of age in sample households surveyed during 2005–06 under NFHS-3 and during 2015–16 under NFHS-4 whose births were reported as registered by the parents. Since the fact sheets at the state level for NFHS-4 has been released only for 15states where the survey has been completed by the end of 2015, the data is given only for these 15 states to have an idea of the improvements in birth registration in the recent years, between 2000–05 and 2010–15.

From Table 7.18, it can be seen that there are significant improvements in birth registrations, as reported, by the parents in all the states. Even in the rural areas of Bihar, that has shown consistently high levels of under registration of births, the improvements are dramatic, from 4.7 percent to 64.5 percent. All the other 14 states have shown birth registration over 80 percent.

Table 7.18:
Children (living) under age 5 years whose birth was registered (%)

	NFHS-4			NFHS-3		
	Rural	*Urban*	*Total*	*Rural*	*Urban*	*Total*
Andhra Pradesh	90.1	79.9	82.7	35.6	49.4	40.3
Andaman	97.2	98.4	97.9	NA	NA	NA
Bihar	64.5	60.3	60.7	4.7	13.7	5.8
Goa	98.9	99	98.9	93.9	95.3	94.7
Haryana	94	94.3	94.2	70.5	75.5	71.7
Karnataka	95	94.9	94.9	49.8	72.3	58.3
Madhya Pradesh	92.2	78.4	81.9	27.5	37.3	29.7
Meghalaya	89.2	78.4	79.8	38.8	66	43.3
Pondicherry	99.2	98.7	99	NA	NA	NA
Sikkim	98.6	98.4	98.5	84.2	93.3	85.7
Tamil Nadu	98.5	98.2	98.3	81.9	90.3	85.8
Telangana	89.9	76.5	82.9	NA	NA	NA
Tripura	96.8	89.9	91.6	72.8	84.3	74.4
Uttarakhand	81.8	74.2	76.7	32.4	56.1	38.4
West Bengal	97.3	96.7	96.9	73.2	85.4	75.8

Source: NFHS-3 and 4.

Challenges for Governance in Dealing with Population Issues

Good governance is crucial for success of any program including health and family planning programs and complete and accurate registration of births and deaths. Sound and well-meaning policies can fail with bad implementation and governance. This is one of the important areas that need immediate attention. In common parlance, the term "governance" connotes the process by which an organization, especially a government, formulates its policies, enacts appropriate laws, implements the related programs, evaluates and modifies them when necessary, changes the laws and programs if needed and becomes accountable to the stake holders/ citizens and gets its mandate to govern. On a wider scope, governance refers to "all processes of governing, whether undertaken by a government, market or network, whether over a family, tribe, formal or informal organization or territory and whether through laws, norms, power or language" (Bevir 2012). The term *governance* is distinguished from *government* which is a formal body invested with the authority to make decisions in a given political system. Governance is the process while government is the structure. In the case of a government, the governance process includes the functions of all the actors involved in influencing the decision-making process—citizens, political parties, media, election process, elected leaders, form of government etc.—and is mainly concerned with the processes of the elected government and the bureaucracy that implements the laws and regulations. In India, it refers to the processes of the constitutionally set up three tiers of government—central government, various state governments and local bodies (the panchayats in the rural areas and the Nagar Palikas in the urban areas). Srinivasan and Selvan (2015) offer a good review of studies on governance in India.

In India, a number of attempts have been made in the past to study governance and the government and make them efficient. Many articles and books have been published on the topic (Godbole 2014; Laxmikanth 2011). Prime Minister Sri Narendra Modi has repeatedly emphasized on "minimum government and maximum governance," underlining the need to improve the efficiency and effectiveness of the government departments. "This should include technological changes such as mobile governance, e-governance, solid waste management, waste water management etc. There is a need for extensive brainstorming on these issues" (Modi 2014). Attempts have already started on e-governance and paperless government. However, only a few systematic studies have been made to quantitatively evaluate various dimensions of governance and to monitor them over time to study the progress in governance. This is urgently needed in India, especially with regard to health, family welfare and human development programs. At the international level, the World Governance Institute (WGI), set up under the auspices of the World Bank, has attempted to measure the effectiveness of governments in six dimensions, compiled data on various indicators used in each dimension and publishes an annual report providing the World Governance Index for each country. The same, also how India fairs internationally, will be discussed in Chapter 8. We will focus on national-level studies on governance in the next section.

There were two studies in India to assess the level of governance at the state level quantitatively. The first was by Virmani Sahu and Tanwar (2006) who computed an index of quality of governance at the state level, based on selected output variables classified under "public goods," "quasi-public goods" and "government monopolized goods." The list of output variables selected by the authors in each category is given in Table 7.19.

The second study by Mundle et al. (2012) constructed an index of governance at the national and state levels for 17 large states and constructed the indicators under three pillars of democracy—the executive, judiciary and the legislative. The executive pillar is considered in four dimensions—delivery of infrastructure services, delivery of social services, fiscal performance and maintenance of law and order. The "judicial pillar" was measured by the speed of delivery of legal services and the legislature pillar by the quality of the legislature. Thus, there were six dimensions and the indicators included in these dimensions are given in Table 7.20 (Srinivasan and Selvan 2015).

We attempted to check whether the governance index at the state level computed by Mundle et al. in 2012 correlated with the development indicators such as HDI at the state level and state domestic product (SDP) and the percentage of population having mobile phones. The data is given in Table 7.21.

We have used the percentage of mobile phones in the population because the rapid and unprecedented changes in communication technology during the past three decades have revolutionized humankind in many ways. The continuing widespread use of mobile phones, personal computers and penetration of internet services have brought scientific knowledge and made market information about goods and services easily accessible to common man. In addition, making transactions that were very difficult and inaccessible to many in earlier years have now become easily accessible. Online ticketing services for bus, railroad and air have contributed toward wider use of these facilities in India and to some extent, buying and selling of goods online have reduced time and costs of trading which is also a reason of these services being widely used. They have drastically reduced the dependence of the people on the government in their day-to-day life. The information on prices of various agricultural products in different places can immediately be known to farmers and traders throughout the country, and there is automatic stabilization of prices of many products and prevention of hoarding of these products. Efficiency in terms of balancing between demand and supply through price regulation of various goods and services have been facilitated by the computer technology and the widespread use of cellphones. While some years back there was corruption in the sale of train, bus and air tickets, these have considerably been reduced in India because of the penetration of computer technology and mobile phones. Many of the

Table 7.19:
Governance indicators

Public Goods		Quasi-Public Goods			Government-Monopolized Goods
Law and Order	*Roads*	*Education*	*Irrigation*	*Post*	*Public Health*

Law and Order	*Roads*	*Education*	*Irrigation*	*Post*	*Public Health*	*Government-Monopolized Goods*
1. Police personnel per thousand persons 2. Crime reported per thousand persons 3. Ratio of property recovered to stolen cases	1. Surfaced road length in km per thousand sq km of Area 2. Unsurfaced road length in km per thousand sq km of area	1. No. of schools per thousand persons 2. Teacher–pupil ratio 3. No. of enrolments per thousand persons 4. Literacy rates (%)	1. Net irrigated area by government canals per net owned area	1. No. of post offices per thousand persons 2. Postal articles handled 3. No of inland money orders issued	1. Life expectancy at birth (years) 2. Infant mortality rate (per thousand live births)	1. Per capita electricity consumption 2. No. of hospitals and dispensaries per thousand persons 3. Railway route length per thousand sq km of area 4. Telephone lines per thousand persons

Source: Virmani A. et al. (2006).

Table 7.20:
Governance performance index

Dimensions	Infrastructure Service Delivery	Social Service Delivery	Fiscal Performance	Law and Order	Judicial Service Delivery	Quality of Legislature
Indicators	Water supply and sanitation • Households with safe drinking water (%) • Households with improved sanitation (%) • Per capita power consumption • Road length per sq. km	Health • Infant mortality rate • Maternal mortality rate • Life expectancy at birth Education • Literacy rate • Gross enrolment rate • Average years of schooling	• Development expenditure as percentage of total expenditure • Own revenue GSDP ratio	• Rate of violent crimes • Complaints registered against police per person • Police strength per lakh population	• Trials completed in 1–3 years as % of total trials in all courts	• Proportion of MLAs with serious criminal charges pending (%) • Proportion of women MLAs (%)

Source: Mundle et al. (2012).

issues of governance have been automatically resolved by the technological changes. Thus, technology has become an important factor influencing governance, per capita income and human development. We tested
the impact of technology on governance as measured by Mundle et al.
(2012), with variables as income and HDI, circa 2011 given in Table 7.21,
using a path model (Figure 7.1).

First, we computed the bivariate correlation coefficients among the
four variables at the state levels (Table 7.22).

On the given correlation confidents, we superimposed a path model
(Figure 7.3), and the path coefficients were calculated and given in the
model.

In the path model, "technology" (x1) was measured by the percent of
household using mobile phone as given in the latest 2011 census; the
"governance index" (x2) was taken from the study by Mundale et al.
(2012), reviewed above (the index based on principal component
analysis); "state per capita domestic product" (x3) was taken from the
published records and HDI (x4) as reported by the Planning commission
for 2011. All the above four factors in the model change with time.
Technology has a direct impact on HDI and indirect impacts on HDI
through governance, SDP and governance and SDP. The estimated
values of these effects using the path model are given below. These are

Table 7.21:
*Indicators of governance in selected dimensions and HDI values for two periods
at the state level in India*

State	Governance Index by S. Mundle et al.	SDP (Rs.)	Percentage of Mobile Phones	HDI
	2011	2011–12	2011	2011–12
Andhra Pradesh	0.606	56,817	54.93	0.309
Assam	−0.478	30,786	43.45	0.138
Bihar	−0.78	11,558	51.6	0.158
Chhattisgarh	−0.053	44,826	27.19	0.18
Gujarat	0.49	63,961	58.59	0.477
Haryana	0.792	55,214	66.92	0.493
Himachal Pradesh	–	–	–	–
Jharkhand	−1.123	22,780	44.1	0.222

(Table 7.21 continued)

(Table 7.21 continued)

State	Governance Index by S. Mundle et al. 2011	SDP (Rs.) 2011–12	Percentage of Mobile Phones 2011	HDI 2011–12
Karnataka	0.073	37,464	56.53	0.42
Kerala	0.167	46,511	46.77	0.911
Madhya Pradesh	−0.191	19,736	40.59	0.186
Maharashtra	0.218	57,458	53.71	0.629
Odisha	−0.277	24,098	35.63	0.261
Punjab	0.911	43,539	62.27	0.538
Rajasthan	0.194	34,189	62.49	0.324
Tamil Nadu	0.407	46,823	62.09	0.633
Uttar Pradesh	−0.331	23,132	61.2	0.122
West Bengal	−0.627	45,346	42.94	0.483
Correlation Coefficient	0.530	0.641	0.331	−

Sources: (a) HDI Source: National Institute of Public Finance and Policy (2012); (b) SDP data from Planning Commission; (c) percent with mobile phones from 2011 Census data.

based on the standardized regression coefficients (path coefficients) calculated from the bivariate correlations given in Table 7.22.

From Table 7.21 and the path coefficients, we can see that the percentage of households having mobile phones is significantly and positively correlated with the index of governance. The index of governance is also positively and significantly correlated with state per capita domestic product and HDI. With the help of above-mentioned path model of causation, we can estimate the path coefficients using the following regression equations.

Using small letters to denote normalized variables (deducting the mean from the variable and dividing by the standard deviation), we have the following equations from the above path model.

$$x4 = b14 \times x1 + b24 \times x2 + b34 \times x3 \tag{1}$$

$$x3 = b13 \times x1 + b23 \times x2 \tag{2}$$

$$x2 = b12 \times x2 \tag{3}$$

Table 7.22:
Correlations of governance, mobile phones, HDI and GSDP per capita

	Governance Index Circa 2011	HDI 2011–12	Percentage of Household using Mobile 2011	GSDP Per Capita 2011
Governance Index c. 2011	1	0.530*	0.564*	0.728**
HDI	0.530*	1	0.331	0.641**
Percentage of Household using mobile phones	0.564*	0.331	1	0.314
GSDP per capita	0.728**	0.641**	0.314	1

Note: * = statistically significant at 5 percent level; ** = statistically significant at 1 percent level.

Figure 7.3:
Path model

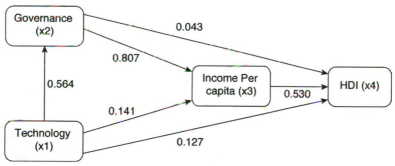

Using the above equations, we can estimate the direct and indirect effects of technology as represented by percentage of households having mobile phones on human development as represented by HDI, which is as follows:

Direct effect of technology on HDI ($b14$) = 0.127

Indirect Effects:

1. Through governance ($b12 \times b24$) $\Rightarrow 0.564 \times 0.043 = 0.024$
2. Through income ($b13 \times b34$) $\Rightarrow -0.141 \times 0.570 = -0.080$
3. Through governance and income ($b12 \times b23 \times b34$) $\Rightarrow 0.564 \times 0.807 \times 0.570 = 0.259$
   Total Indirect Effects $= 0.203$
   Total Effects, direct plus indirect $\Rightarrow 0.127 + 0.203 = 0.330$

Thus, we see that the indirect effects of technology on development are roughly twice the direct effects and almost two thirds of the total effects. This fact needs to be explored further by taking other proxies for technology and indices of governance and development. Technology is going to make sweeping changes in governance, income and development of the population as a whole, irrespective of the political system and fractionalization of the society on the basis of language and religion. This is an important point that needs to be addressed by future studies on governance (Mukherjee et al. 2014).

8

India in Comparison

Comparative Demography

In the previous chapter, we studied the trends and differentials in selected demographic and developmental variables at the state level and the challenges they pose to the population issues in the country. In this chapter, we will explore how India, as a country, compares with selected other countries of the world at the international level in selected variables. The countries with which we compare India are five relatively most populous developed countries, France, Germany, Russian Federation, the United States of America and the United Kingdom, and four large developing countries, Bangladesh, Brazil, China and Indonesia. Thus for 10 counties, 5 developed and 5 developing (including India), we present and analyze the data in this chapter.

Development and demography are interlinked human processes; changes in one contribute to changes in the other. However, both are influenced by the policies and programs for development that are taken up at the national and subnational levels and the quality of governance with the explicit purposes of accelerating development and demographic processes. There are no absolute standards to measure demographic processes and developmental changes. They are both relative to other populations of countries or regions and the indicators we use to measure progress. Development is a relative factor, and it is measured in relative terms how, for example, India compares with other countries and what indicators we use. One can always choose a variable, such as stability of the institution of marriage, (discussed in Chapter 7) in which India ranks very high in comparison with all other developed countries. But on the whole, in most of the internationally used developmental variables, India has been doing poorly. However, a light at the end of the tunnel has been seen in the recent years.

Table 8.1 presents data at two points of time, 1992 and 2014, on the population size, density, annual growth rates for rural, urban and combined populations, and TFR, IMR and life expectancy at birth. These are the common demographic variables that we use. The data is selected from the publication by the World Bank and the World Development Indicators (2016). Hence, the population size and growth rate figures for India may differ from the census figures for the country presented in the earlier chapters but, since comparisons are made with other countries, we chose to use international figures for India as well. India ranks second in the population size among the 10 countries both in 1992 and in 2014, next to China. In terms of annual growth rates of population in 1992, only India and Bangladesh had growth rates of 2 percent or more while all the four developed countries except the United States of America had less than 1 percent growth rate. The United States of America had a population growth rate of 1.39 percent in 1992 and China had 1.23 percent, less than

Table 8.1:
Demographic Indicators

	Population		Population Density (People Per Sq. Km of Land Area)		Annual Growth Rates	
	1992	*2014*	*1992*	*2014*	*1992*	*2014*
France	58,851,216	66,217,509	107.5	120.9	0.50	0.44
Germany	80,624,598	80,970,732	230.9	232.3	0.76	−1.42
Russian Federation	148,689,000	143,819,569	9.1	8.8	0.04	0.22
United Kingdom	57,580,402	64,559,135	238.0	266.9	0.27	0.67
United States	256,514,000	318,857,056	28.0	34.9	1.39	0.74
Bangladesh	110,987,459	159,077,513	852.6	1,222.1	2.26	1.21
Brazil	155,379,009	206,077,898	18.6	24.7	1.60	0.89
China	1,164,970,000	1,364,270,000	124.1	145.3	1.23	0.51
India	906,461,358	1,295,291,543	304.9	435.7	2.00	1.23
Indonesia	187,762,097	254,454,778	103.6	140.5	1.69	1.26

	Rural Population Growth (Annual %)		Urban Population Growth (Annual %)	
	1992	*2014*	*1992*	*2014*
France	−0.17	−0.68	0.729	0.74
Germany	0.42	−2.24	0.88	−1.15
Russian Federation	0.06	−0.06	0.038	0.32
United Kingdom	0.00	−0.75	0.347	0.98
United States	−0.25	−0.16	1.909	0.95
Bangladesh	1.81	0.07	3.985	3.52
Brazil	−1.42	−0.89	2.602	1.19
China	0.00	−2.18	4.425	2.82
India	1.72	0.68	2.796	2.38
Indonesia	0.08	−0.32	5.080	2.69

	TFR		IMR		Life Expectancy at Birth	
	1992	*2014*	*1992*	*2014*	*1992*	*2014*
France	1.74	1.99	6.7	3.6	77.1	82.4
Germany	1.29	1.39	6.2	3.2	75.8	80.8
Russian Federation	1.55	1.70	22	8.5	66.9	70.4
United Kingdom	1.79	1.83	7	3.7	76.4	81.1
United States	2.04	1.86	8.8	5.7	75.6	78.9
Bangladesh	4.14	2.17	92.1	32.1	59.7	71.6
Brazil	2.64	1.79	46.8	14.4	66.2	74.4
China	2.11	1.56	41.2	9.8	69.3	75.8
India	3.87	2.42	83.9	39.3	58.9	68.0
Indonesia	2.93	2.46	57.4	23.6	64.0	68.9

Source: World Development Indicators, World Bank, 2016.

the United States of America. The higher growth rate in the United States of America, compared to the other developed countries, is due to the higher fertility of the migrant population in the United States of America and their relative population size has been increasing over time. In 2014, the growth rates of all the 10 countries have declined significantly, and it was negative (population decreasing) in Germany at an astounding –1.42 percent. Only India, Indonesia and Bangladesh had growth rates over 1 percent. When we consider rural populations, the annual growth rates have declined drastically in all the 10 countries, developed and developing. India recorded a decline from 2.00 to 1.23, Bangladesh from 2.26 to 1.21, Indonesia from 1.69 to 1.26, and in all other 7 countries, the growth rates are less than 1 or negative. In rural populations, the declines are more remarkable: in India, from 1.72 to 0.68; in Bangladesh, from 1.81 to 0.07; and in all other countries, there is negative growth in the rural populations in the rural areas. The absolute population sizes in the rural areas of these countries have actually declined. The maximum decline in the rate of growth of rural populations is in Germany (–2.24 percent) followed by China (–2.18 percent). Only in Bangladesh, India and Indonesia the rural population had a positive growth rate in 2014.

Thus fertility levels have been falling even in the developed countries from their already low levels in 1992, and death rates are getting higher than the birth rates. Germany had an overall negative growth rate of 1.43 percent in 2014, –2.24 percent in the rural areas and 1.15 percent in the urban areas. Only India, Indonesia and Bangladesh are having more than 1 percent growth rates in their rural populations. Germany had 0.42 percent growth rate in its rural population in 1992 and –2.14 percent in 2014. On the other hand, China had zero growth rates in its rural population in 1992 and a negative growth rate of –2.23 percent in 2014. The world as a whole is becoming urbanized at a rapid rate with absolute population sizes in rural areas shrinking continuously.

In terms of fertility changes measured in TFR, as expected, the developing countries had significantly higher fertility than the developed countries both in 1992 and in 2014. In 1992, among the five developing countries, TFR ranged from a low of 2.11 in China to 4.15 in Bangladesh with India at 3.88; and among the five developed countries, it ranged from a low of 1.29 in Germany to a high of 2.05 in the United States of America. After 22 years, in 2014, the fertility of all the developing countries declined, with a low of 1.56 in China to a high of 2.46 in Indonesia and India at 2.43; and in the developed countries except the United States of America, there was a marginal rise in the fertility levels. Germany's TFR increased from 1.29 to 1.39, France from 1.74 to 1.99, the United Kingdom from 1.79 to 1.83, and the Russian Federation from 1.55 to 1.77. There appears to be a global homogenization of fertility, sweeping across both the developing and developed countries, probably around a TFR value of 2 births per woman. The recent higher fertility of the migrant population in the developed world seems to more than compensate the declining fertility levels in their native populations. The political implications of this shift are yet to be realized.

In terms of IMR, there are sharp declines in the rates in both the developed and developing countries between 1992 and 2014. In 1992, in the developing countries, IMR ranged from a high of 92 in Bangladesh to a low of 41 in China with India at 84; and in 2014, it ranged from a low of 10 in China to a high of 39 in India. In the five developed countries, it ranged from a low of 6 in Germany to a high of 22 in Russia in 1992 and from a low of 3 in Germany to a high of 9 in Russia in 2014. As in fertility levels, there appears to be a rapid convergence of IMR values both in the developed and in the developing countries to levels below 10. In developing countries such as India, the national average masks the enormous diversities that exist among the states as discussed in the last chapter.

In terms of life expectancy at birth, there still exist considerable variations between the developed and developing countries. In 2014, among the five developing countries, it ranged from 68.0 in India to a high of 75.8 in China while in the developed countries it ranged from a low of 70.4 in Russia to a high of 82.4 in France. The life expectancy of 70.4 in Russia makes it appear more as a part of the developing world than of the developed world.

The demographic parameters start impinging on development mainly through the changes in the dependency ratios of the population caused by declines in fertility and mortality and to some extent migration. Table 8.2 provides data on CBR, CDR and young-age dependency ratio (YDR) and old-age dependency ratio (ODR) with the working population defined as those in age group 15–64, unlike within India it is considered as in the age group 15–59, for the years 1992 and 2014. Since these ratios are determined largely by earlier birth and death rates, we will discuss them first.

In 1992 in the developed world, CBRs ranged from a low of 10 in Germany to a high of 16 in the United States of America, and it dropped to 9 in Germany and 13 in the United States of America in 2014. CBRs in all the developed countries are continuing to decline; however, their TFR values showed a marginal increase, mainly because of the changes in the age distributions of their populations. Among the five developing

Table 8.2:
Comparison on the basis of demographic and health parameters

	Age Dependency Ratio (% of Working-age Population)		Age Dependency Ratio, Old (% of Working-age Population)		Age Dependency Ratio, Young (% of Working-age Population)		Birth Rate, Crude (per 1,000 People)		Death Rate, Crude (per 1,000 People)		Mortality Rate, Under-5 (per 1,000)	
	1992	2014	1992	2014	1992	2014	1992	2014	1992	2014	1992	2014
France	51.9	59.2	22.1	29.7	29.8	29.5	13.1	12.4	9.2	8.4	8	4
Germany	45.4	51.6	22.0	31.9	23.4	19.7	10.0	8.6	11.0	10.8	8	4
Russian Federation	50.7	42.0	16.7	18.8	34.1	23.2	10.7	13.3	12.2	13.1	26	10
United Kingdom	53.9	54.3	24.4	27.0	29.4	27.3	13.6	12.0	11.0	8.8	8	4
United States	52.4	50.3	19.2	21.6	33.2	28.6	15.8	12.5	8.5	8.1	11	7
Bangladesh	81.0	53.7	5.8	7.6	75.1	46.1	33.5	19.8	9.5	5.4	132	40
Brazil	62.7	45.1	6.9	11.0	55.8	34.1	23.0	14.7	6.9	6.1	55	16
China	51.9	35.8	8.4	12.5	43.5	23.4	18.3	12.4	6.6	7.2	52	11
India	70.8	53.1	6.7	8.4	64.1	44.7	30.3	20.0	10.3	7.3	119	50
Indonesia	64.7	49.5	6.5	7.6	58.2	41.8	24.6	20.0	7.7	7.2	77	28

Source: World Development Indicators, World Bank, 2016.

countries, CBR ranged from a low of 18 in China to 33 in Bangladesh with India at 30 in 1992 and the lowest was again in China at 12 and highest at 20 uniformly in Bangladesh, India and Indonesia in 2014. Thus, CBRs in the developing countries are declining at an accelerated pace in the last 20 years.

On CDRs in the developed world, the range was from a low of 9 in the United States of America to a high of 12 in Russia in 1992. In 2014, there were only marginal declines in CDR values in these countries from a low of 8 in the United States of America to a high of 13 in Russia. CDRs in the developed world can be expected to rise in the coming years, even in the context of a small rise in the expectation of life at birth, because of the continued aging of their populations. With simultaneous forces of increase life expectancy and decline in fertility, the birth rates will fall and death rates can rise because of aging populations and this could lead to negative population growth rates as in Germany.

Among the five developing countries, CDR ranged from a low of 6.6 in China to 10.3 in India in 1992 and has dropped to about 7 in all the five countries by 2014. The changes in the age structures in the developing countries are conducive to a rise in their birth rates and a decline in their death rates contributes to even a rise in their growth rates. Thus, the proportion of the population in the developed world can be expected to shrink further in the coming years because of the age distribution of population working in the opposite directions in the developed and the developing worlds.

In 1992, the YDR (percentage of children below 15 to those aged 15–64) among the developed countries ranged from a low of 23 in Germany and a high of 34 in Russia and by 2014, there was decline in this ratio in all the countries from a low of 20 in Germany to a high of 29 in the United States of America. On the other hand, in the five developing countries, the YDR values in 1992 ranged from a low of 44 in China to a high of 75 in Bangladesh, with India at 64. This has declined in all the five countries by 2014 because of strong family planning programs in these countries, from a low of 23 in China to a high of 46 in Bangladesh, with India at 44. The ODR increased in all the countries: the maximum in Germany from 22 to 32 and just from 7 to 8 in India, 7 to 11 in Brazil and from 8 to 13 in China. While the developed world has to grapple with the enormous number of old people (almost one third of the populations as now in Germany), the bulk of the working population has to come from the developing countries such as India, Indonesia, China and Brazil. This large and growing labor supply in the developing countries can be taken full advantage of by both the developed and developing countries for global economic development.

Sex Ratios

The sex ratios in a population give a graphic picture of the gender biases that exist in the population. At birth, as stated earlier, in any human population without any biases of care and nutrition during pregnancies, there are 1,050–70 male births to 1,000 female births and any excess of male births beyond 1,070 per 1,000 female births is indicative of selective interferences during pregnancy to abort the female fetus. Similarly, in the population as a whole, without any bias of nutrition and health care provided to male and female children, the females tend to live longer than men do, and PSRs are less than 100 men per 100 women.

Table 8.3 presents data on the PSR and SRB as the number of males per 1,000 females in the 10 selected countries for the periods 1990–95 and 2010–15. The table reveals where India stands in relation to the five

Table 8.3:
Sex ratios (males per 1,000 females) in different countries

	Sex Ratio at Birth		Population Sex Ratio	
	1990–95	*2010–15*	*1990–95*	*2010–15*
France	1,052	1,052	940	938
Germany	1,058	1,058	938	963
Russian Federation	1,068	1,060	879	857
United Kingdom	1,051	1,051	946	971
United States of America	1,049	1,049	954	969
Bangladesh	1,048	1,048	1,074	1,026
Brazil	1,050	1,050	985	968
China	1,120	1,160	1,067	1,075
India	1,090	1,108	1,077	1,071
Indonesia	1,050	1,050	1,001	1,012

Source: UN Population Prospects Medium Variant.

developed countries and the other four developing countries. India's SRB, males per 1,000 female births is the second highest next to China, 1,090 males per 1,000 females in 1990–95, which increased to 1108 in 2010–15. China had 1,120 and 1,160 in these two periods. In all the five developed countries, this ratio varied from 1,048 to 1,068 during 1990–95 and from 1,049 to 1,060 during 2010–16. As stated earlier, the range of SRB is biologically determined between 1,050 and 1,070, and India and China clearly falls out of this range indicating selective abortion of female fetuses in these two countries. In China, with its one-child policy and Chinese culture being patriarchal favoring a male child, there would have been millions of abortions of female fetuses conceived as the first pregnancy. In India, the preference for a male child has its roots in the culture and religion. The developing countries of Brazil, Bangladesh and Indonesia do not appear to have this problem of female feticide. The PSR, number of males per 1,000 females, reflects the overall gender bias in the populations. In India and China, there were 1,077 and 1,067 males per 1,000 females in 1990–95 while in the developed countries, it ranged from 879 in Russia to a high of 954 in the United States of America, and a similar picture emerges even in 2010–15. In a population that has no female feticide and girls are given equal nurture and health care, they tend to live longer than men. PSRs reflect this very phenomenon in the United States of America, the United Kingdom, France and Germany where these ratios vary from 940 to 970. In Russia, the acute deficit of males is due to their higher mortality attributable to deaths in wars and increased alcoholism.

Human Development

Development of a country or a region can be defined, following the United Nations, as the enlargement of opportunities to all its citizens by the state to realize the maximum potential of its citizens in their lifetime through good health and longevity, good education and productive employment and a minimum income to achieve the above for themselves and their family. For the first time in 1990, the HDI, developed by the United Nation, facilitated a cross-national comparison of the countries on the basis of a single composite index. It is a statistical tool used to measure a country's overall achievement in its social and economic dimensions. It was first developed by a Pakistani economist, Professor Mahbub ul Haq, who created the index combining four major indicators—life expectancy for health, gross enrolment ratio that includes enrolment of children in primary, middle and secondary levels or mean of years of schooling for education and gross national income per capita—to measure standard of living in terms of purchasing power parity in US$. Every year, the UNDP ranks countries on the basis of HDI and reports them in their annual report. HDI is one of the best tools to keep track of the level of development of a country, as it combines all major social and economic indicators that are responsible for economic development. It also helps the governments to prioritize the areas of development where there is a serious shortfall.

Table 8.4 provides data on HDI values and their three component variables for the years 2005 and 2014 for the 10 countries. In the year 2005, among the five developed countries, HDI values, on a 0–1 scale, ranged from 0.80 in Russia to a high of 0.95 in the other four countries. Among the five developing countries, the range was from 0.55 in Bangladesh and 0.62 in India to 0.78 in China. On the first of the three components of HDI, that is, life expectancy at birth, variations between the developed and developing countries was quite low, from 63.1 in Bangladesh and 63.7 in India to a high of 80.2 in France. The life expectancy of Russia was only 65 years, lower than that of Brazil, China and Indonesia. On the second component, that is educational enrolment, among the developed countries, variations ranged from 88 percent in Germany to 97 in France while in the developing countries, it ranged from 56 in Bangladesh and 63.7 in India to 88 in Brazil. On the third component of per capita income (in terms of purchasing power parity US$), among the developed countries, the range was from 10,845 in Russia to a high of 41,890 in the United States of America, On the other hand, in the developing countries, the range was from 2,053 in Bangladesh and 3,452 in India to a high 8,402 in Brazil. Thus, the level of income variability of the developed countries is much larger than among the developing countries.

In the year 2014, France, Russia, the United States of America and the United Kingdom had registered declines in their HDI values, probably because of the difference in the measurement of the educational component of HDI. In 2014, it was measured by the two factors of average years of schooling and expected years of schooling, the latter based on the current enrolment rates. Because of the possibility of such a change, there was a fall in the HDI values of the developed countries; the maximum fall was in France from 0.95 in 2005 to 0.89 in 2015. Similarly, all the five developing countries had also experienced a decline in their HDI values:

Table 8.4:
HDI values and its components

	HDI Value 2005	Life Expectancy at Birth 2005	Combined Gross Enrolment Ratio (Pri. Sec. and Ter.) 2005	GDP Per Capita (PPP US$) 2005	HDI Value 2014	Life Expectancy at Birth 2014	Expected Years of Schooling 2014	Mean Years of Schooling 2014	Gross National Income (GNI) Per Capita 2014
France	0.952	80.2	96.5	30,386	0.888	82.2	16.0	11.1	38,056
Germany	0.935	79.1	88	29,461	0.916	80.9	16.5	13.1	43,919
Russia	0.802	65	88.9	10,845	0.798	70.1	14.7	12.0	22,352
United States	0.951	77.9	93.3	41,890	0.915	79.1	16.5	12.9	52,947
United Kingdom	0.946	79	93	33,238	0.907	80.7	16.2	13.1	39,267
Bangladesh	0.547	63.1	56	2,053	0.570	71.6	10.0	5.1	3,191
Brazil	0.8	71.7	87.5	8,402	0.755	74.5	15.2	7.7	15,175
China	0.777	72.5	69.1	6,757	0.727	75.8	13.1	7.5	12,547
Indonesia	0.728	69.7	68.2	3,843	0.684	68.9	13.0	7.6	9,788
India	0.619	63.7	63.8	3,452	0.609	68.0	11.7	5.4	5,497

Source: World Development Indicators, World Bank, 2016.

India from 0.62 to 0.61 and Brazil from 0.8 to 0.76. On life expectancy, all the 10 countries have experienced substantial gains, India from 63.7 to 68.0 and Russia from 60.5 to 70.1. Table 8.4 reveals that in the developing countries, there was a greater homogeneity in the human longevity and expected school enrolment ratios in the recent years, and the gap between the developed and developing countries may narrow down in the future. The largest gap was on the scale of per capita income in 2014, ranging from $3,191 in Bangladesh and $5,497 in India to a high of $52,947 in the United States of America. Almost all the poor countries are equally poor, but the rich countries vary quite a bit in their prosperity levels.

Gender Equity

Inequalities between males and females in education, employment, income and access to basic health facilities are present all over the world, but they are more acute in developing countries than in developed countries. In all social, educational, health, employment and political opportunities, men seem to have an edge over women. The United Nations has computed a Gender Inequality Index (GII) that is based on four components, that is, MMR, adolescent fertility rate of female births to young women in the age group of 15–19, percent representation of women in parliament and the gap between males and females in the proportion with at least primary education.

Table 8.5 gives GII values and the four components that make it for the years 2008 and 2014 for the 10 countries. The higher the GII value greater is the gender inequality in the country. On this index, there was no significant difference between the developed countries, ranging from 0.26 in France to a 0.44 in Russia in 2008, and from 0.09 in France to 0.28 in the United States of America in 2014. Thus, gender inequality has decreased significantly in the developed countries between 2008 and 2014. Among the developing countries, in 2008, it was quite high, ranging from 0.40 in China to a high of 0.75 in India. Some improvement has been observed in 2014, with the index ranging from 0.19 in China to a high 0.56 in India. Among all the 10 countries, India had the maximum GII both in 2008 and in 2014. This problem needs to be attended on a priority basis if India has to join the comity of developed nations. We cannot hope to develop with half of our population being backward. On all the four components that make up the GII, India's performance is

Table 8.5:
Gender inequality for 2008 and latest

	Gender Inequality Index	Maternal Mortality Ratio	Adolescent Fertility Rate	Female Share of Seats in Parliament	Population with At least Secondary Education (% ages 25 and Older)		Gender Inequality Index	Maternal Mortality Ratio	Adolescent Fertility Rate	Female Share of Seats in Parliament	Population with At least Secondary Education (% ages 25 and Older)	
					Female	*Male*					*Female*	*Male*
	2008	*2003–08*	*1990–2008*	*2008*	*2010*	*2010*	*2014*	*2013*	*2010–15*	*2014*	*2005–14*	
France	0.26	8	6.9	19.6	79.6	84.6	0.088	12	5.7	25.7	78.0	83.2
Germany	0.24	4	7.7	31.1	91.3	92.8	0.041	7	3.8	36.9	96.3	97.0
Russian Federation	0.442	28	25.1	11.5	90.6	71.3	0.276	24	25.7	14.5	89.6	92.5
United States	0.355	8	24.1	19.6	68.8	67.8	0.280	28	31.0	19.4	95.1	94.8
United Kingdom	0.4	11	35.9	17	95.3	94.5	0.177	8	25.8	23.5	99.8	99.9
Bangladesh	0.734	570	71.6	6.3	30.8	39.3	0.503	170	80.6	20.0	34.1	41.3
Brazil	0.631	110	75.6	9.4	48.8	46.3	0.457	69	70.8	9.6	54.6	52.4
China	0.405	45	9.7	21.3	54.8	70.4	0.191	32	8.6	23.6	58.7	71.9
Indonesia	0.68	420	39.8	11.6	24.2	31.1	0.494	190	48.3	17.1	39.9	49.2
India	0.748	450	68.1	9.2	26.6	50.4	0.563	190	32.8	12.2	27.0	56.6

Sources: World Development Indicators, World Bank, 2016.

very poor by international standards. By comparison with the developed countries, India is lagging behind substantially. China is far ahead of India in this regard.

Institutional Facilities in Health and Energy

Table 8.6 provides data on the basic health facilities available in the 10 countries in terms of doctors and hospital beds per 1,000 population, improved access to sanitation faculties in the rural, urban and combined populations, and the percent of population practicing open defecation, population with improved source of water supply in the rural, urban and combined areas and per capita energy use (kg of oil equivalent) and per capita electric power consumption for the latest available year on or after 2011. The Table 8.6 shows the sharp differences that exist between the developed and developing countries, and how far India lags behind even among the five developing countries. Availability of hospital beds per 1,000 populations in 2011 among the developed countries ranged from 2.9 in the United States of America to 8.2 in Germany while in the developed countries, it ranged from not available in Indonesia to 0.7 in India to 3.0 in Brazil. In terms of physicians per 1,000 populations, the data ranged from 2.4 in the United States of America to 4.3 in Russia. On the other hand, among the developed countries, it ranges from 0.1 in Indonesia, 0.3 in Bangladesh and 0.7 in India to 1.8 in Brazil. The paucity of physicians and hospitals per 1,000 population in India compared to the other developing countries and developed countries deserves serious attention.

Sanitary latrines for the safe disposal of human excreta are one of the essentials of any modern society. Traditionally in India, especially in villages, people used to defecate in their own agricultural fields with the assumption that the excreta would serve as a fertilizer for the soil. This custom of open defecation has been a part of Indian history which is yet to be broken in rural areas. The proportion of population practicing open defecation in the developed and developing countries is quite revealing. It is practically zero in the developed world except in Russia (probably in Asian region of the Russian Federation), where it is 1 percent. In 2014, among the five developing countries, it was staggeringly high at 44.6 percent in India, which means roughly half of the rural population still defecates in the open. The percentage is 20.5 in Indonesia and less than 2 in Bangladesh and Brazil. This is one of the most serious concerns in

Table 8.6:
Facilities in developed and developing countries

Country Name	Hospital Beds (Per 1,000 People)		Physicians (Per 1,000 People)		People Practicing Open Defecation (% of Population)		Improved Sanitation Facilities (% of Population with Access)		Improved Sanitation Facilities, Rural (% of Rural Population with Access)		Improved Sanitation Facilities, Urban (% of Urban Population with Access)		Improved Water Source (% of Population with Access)		Improved Water Source, Rural (% of Rural Population with Access)		Improved Water Source, Urban (% of Urban Population with Access)		Energy Use (Kg of Oil Equivalent Per Capita)		Electric Power Consumption (kWh Per Capita)	
	1991	2011	1991	2010	1992	2014	1992	2014	1992	2014	1992	2014	1992	2014	1992	2014	1992	2014	1992	2013	1992	2013
France	9.6	6.4	3.1	3.4	0	0	98.7	98.7	98.9	98.9	98.6	98.6	100	100	100	100	100	100	3,954.0	3,842.6	6,475.8	7,379.2
Germany	10.1	8.2	2.8	3.7	0	0	99.2	99.2	98.9	99	99.3	99.3	100	100	100	100	100	100	4,191.0	3,867.6	6,445.9	7,019.0
Russian Federation	12.7		4.0	4.3	1	1	72.7	72.2	58.3	58.7	77.9	77	93.7	96.9	82.4	91.2	97.9	98.9	5,351.2	5,093.1	6,107.5	6,539.2
United Kingdom	5.6	2.9	1.6	2.7	0	0	99.2	99.2	99.6	99.6	99.1	99.1	100	100	100	100	100	100	3,684.7	2,977.7	5,452.4	5,407.3
United States	4.8	2.9	1.9	2.4	0	0	99.6	100	98.7	100	99.8	100	98.5	99.2	94.4	98.2	99.7	99.4	7,677.4	6,914.3	12,015.0	12,985.4
Bangladesh	0.3	0.6	0.2	0.3	30.9	1.2	36.7	59.6	33.9	60.8	47.6	57.2	69.7	86.2	66.6	86.1	81.5	86.3	119.4	215.5	58.8	293.0
Brazil		2.3	1.0	1.8	15.1	2.1	68.3	82.7	32.7	51.5	79.9	88	89.6	98.1	69.3	87	96.2	100	929.0	1,437.8	1,483.3	2,529.3
China	2.6	3.8	1.5	1.5	6.3	0.7	49.8	75.4	42.1	62.8	69.3	85.9	69.8	94.8	59	91.5	97.1	97.5	752.6	2,226.3	604.7	3,762.1
India	0.8	0.7	1.3	0.7	73.7	44.6	17.8	39.5	6.6	28.5	49.9	62.6	72.6	94.1	66.6	92.6	89.6	97.1	365.4	606.1	305.4	765.0
Indonesia	0.7		0.1	0.1	38.2	20.6	37.5	60.6	25.7	47.5	62	72.3	71.2	86.8	62.2	75.7	89.8	94	574.3	850.2	194.3	787.7

Sources: World Development Indicators, World Bank, 2016.

India's development, and it is sad that years of implementation of rural sanitation programs seem to have gone in vain. We can only hope that the newly launched Swachh Bharat program by the new government will turn the tide. Improved sanitation facilities are available to almost 100 percent of the population in the developed countries except Russia, where it is only 77 percent. In the developing countries, it is lowest in India at 39.5 percent, 28.5 in the rural and 62.6 in the urban areas. Thus, the provision of hygienic sanitary facilities in every household of the country, in both rural and urban areas, is the top priority item of India's development agenda. Success in this endeavor is crucial for India to be accepted in the group of developed nations.

Availability of and access to safe water for drinking and for daily use (for bathing, toileting and cooking etc.) has become a major issue in India's development agenda. In 2014, the percentage of population with access to improved source of water was 94.1 percent, 92.6 in the rural areas and 97.1 in the urban areas. It should be close to 100 percent in any modern society. The energy use per capita in terms of kilograms of oil equivalent was quite low in India at 606 compared to 2,226 in China, 1,437 in Brazil and 6,914 in the United States of America. Increasing the availability of electricity, and providing the population with enough resources to pay for the increased use, is another major developmental issue.

Institution of Marriage

It has been discussed in detail in Chapter 7 how the institution of marriage is breaking down in the Western countries in terms of a high proportion of young men and women cohabiting together in live-in arrangements without formal marriage and having children outside marriage as single mothers. It was also pointed out that this proportion of births to single mothers has risen sharply in the recent years and, in some countries as the United Kingdom and France, about 50 percent of the births occur to single mothers. Even among the married women, the percentage of divorces has risen sharply. The three parameters namely, proportion of women remaining single in the age group 30–34 (PS), proportion of women divorced or separated among ever-married women in the age group 30–34 (DS) and percent of births to single mothers out of all births (BS) seem to define the strength or otherwise of the institution of marriage. It was also pointed out that the relative stability of the institution of marriage in India is mainly due to the overarching influence of religion and caste in the choice of partners in marriage and the high economic and social costs of any breakdown of marriage for any married couple. It was also pointed out, after a detailed analysis of marriage data, that the institution of marriage is relatively more stable in India. While modernization and development tends to break the institution of marriage in the Western countries, it only increases the age at marriage of women in India. However, by the age of 35, in the age group 30–34, most women get married. In addition, the proportion of divorce and separation in this age group is quite low, and the number of births to single women is practically insignificant. Table 8.7 presents data on these three variables for the 10 countries at two points of time, circa 1990 and circa 2010.

It can be seen from Table 8.7 that the percentage of single women in India in 1990 was 1.8 which increased only to 1.9 by 2010. In all the developing countries, except Brazil, the proportion of single women in the age group of 30–34 was less than 3 percent in 2010, while it was as high as 51.1 percent in Brazil. In terms of all the three parameters, PS, DS and BS, Brazil seems to be a significant outlier from the other four developing countries. In terms of births outside marriage, it tops the list among the 10 countries at 66 percent, higher than France (55 percent).

Table 8.7:
Marital stability of developed and developing countries—Circa 2010

	Circa 1990			Circa 2010		
Country	*PS*	*DS*	*BS*	*PS*	*DS*	*BS*
France	14.4	9.1	33.2	48.7	9.2	55
Germany	17	9.8	14.9	46.8	12	33.3
Russian Federation	7	11.5	NA	14.7	16.3	24.9
United Kingdom	18.2	12.6	30.8	47.8	11.1	46.9
United States	18.2	19.8	30.1	26.3	24.3	41
Bangladesh	1.1	5.2	0	1.2	2.7	0
Brazil	15.2	8.3	NA	51.1	8.1	66
China	0.6	0.9	0.5	5.4	1.8	0.5
India	1.8	3.1	0.5	1.9	1.8	0.5
Indonesia	4.5	6.2	1	6	3.2	1

Sources: UN World Marriage Prospects (2012) and Eurostat (2013).

India, China, Indonesia and Bangladesh seem to have a relatively higher stability of the institution of marriage than Brazil.

Assessing the Quality of Civil Registration System in India

In a series of landmark papers published in the May 2015 issue of *The Lancet* (Vol. 386, May 15, 2015), the civil registration of births and deaths in various countries of the world have been studied from the points of view of the registration systems prevailing in the countries, their data quality and its assessment through an index called the vital statistics performance index (VSPI). It has been argued effectively by the authors that a comprehensive and reliable system of registration of births and deaths is essential for planning, monitoring, and evaluation of the health and development programs in any country in the coming decades, as recommended in the post-2015 SDGs set by the United Nations. No alternative systems, sample surveys or studies, such as the SRS in India, surveillance systems and indirect mathematical models can fill this need and replace such a CRS. The alternatives, such as the SRS in India can provide reliable estimates of fertility and mortality at state and even district levels, but they will not be useful for planning and monitoring health and family welfare programs at the local level. For such a purpose, we need accurate information not only on the number of births and deaths that take place in a village, region, state and the country but also on the place of birth, type of delivery, weight of the baby at birth, genetic deficiencies, if any, at the births and importantly on the cause of death as accurately as possible, which should be based on International Classification of Diseases (ICD) not verbal autopsy as is done on a selection of deaths in the SRS in India. Table 8.8 shows the specific aspects on which a good vital statistics registration system scores over other systems.

The authors also assert that such a civil system for vital statistics can be established within a span of 5–10 years with the use of ICT and policy commitments from the government. It is absolutely essential that India launches such a system without any further delay. From Table 8.8, it can be seen that the SRS as it exists in India today has limited scope both in the analysis of data on births and child and adult mortality from the point of view of planning and monitoring of health and family welfare programs

Table 8.8:
Relative efficiency of different methods of collection of data on vital events

	CRS	Demographic Surveillance Sites	SRS	Population Censuses	National
Births					
National	Yes	No	Yes	Perhaps*	Yes
Subnational	Yes	Limited to specific sites	Limited†	Perhaps*	Limited†
Socioeconomic Differentials	Limited‡	Limited to study population	Limited†	Perhaps*	Yes
Continuous Trends	Yes	Limited to study population	Yes	Partly, if intercensal projections available and reliable	Partly, if surveys are conducted regularly
Child Mortality					
National	Yes	No	Yes	Yes§	Yes§§
Subnational	Yes	Limited to specific sites	Limited†	Yes§	Limited†
Socioeconomic Differentials	Limited‡	Limited to study population	Limited†	Yes§	Yes
Continuous Trends	Yes	Limited to study population	Yes	Partly, if intercensal projections available and reliable	Partly, if surveys conducted regularly, but problem of wide CIs
Adult Mortality					
National	Yes	No	Yes	Perhaps*¶	Weak
Subnational	Yes	Limited to specific sites	Limited†	Perhaps*¶	Weak, but might be possible with new techniques

(Table 8.8 continued)

(Table 8.8 continued)

	CRS	Demographic Surveillance Sites	SRS	Population Censuses	National
Socioeconomic Differentials	Limited‡	Limited to study population	Limited†	Perhaps*¶	Weak, but might be possible with new techniques
Continuous Trends	Yes	Limited to study population	Yes	No	No
Cause of Death					
National	Yes, ICD‖	No	Yes VA**	Perhaps VA††‡‡	Yes**
Subnational	Yes	Yes VA** limited to study population	Limited†	Perhaps VA	Maybe VA, but sample sizes generally too small for stable estimates
Socioeconomic Differentials	Limited‡	Limited to study population	Limited†	Unlikely	Possibly, using VA
Continuous Trends	Yes	Limited to study population	Yes	Unlikely	Possibly if surveys with VA conducted regularly but sample size problem

Source: Carla AbouZahr et al. (2015).

Notes: ICD = International Classification of Diseases; VA = verbal autopsy; adapted from Hill and colleagues.26; *With assessment and possible adjustment: methods do not always work; †for high-level administrative areas (e.g., regions and provinces) only; ‡possible if registration records can be linked to socioeconomic data; §for a recent period by indirect estimates; ¶for an intercensal period; ‖medical certification by ICD rules generates individual- and population-based causes of death; **Use of VA generates population cause-specific fractions onl; ††if VA applied in post-censal follow-up study; ‡‡only for maternal mortality and road traffic accidents; §§where mortality is high.

and assessing the current status. The location of the vital events is crucial in any health program.

In the above study, the data quality of the civil registration is based on an analysis of the data on deaths compiled from CRS in different countries under the database of deaths (DBD) maintained by the WHO from 1980 to 2012. This database is unique in human history wherein all the deaths taking place in different years from 1980 that have reliable information on place of death, age and sex of the deceased and cause of death (under the ICD definitions) are available. Based on this dataset, the authors developed VSPI for quinquennial periods, from 1980 to 2012, based on six components connected with deaths registered in a country: (a) completeness of death reporting, (b) quality of death reporting, (c) level of cause-specific detail, (d) internal consistency, (e) quality of age and sex reporting and (f) data availability or timeliness. Each of these components captures different aspect of data accuracy and utility. The data on each component is first standardized on a 0–1 scale and combined to have a composite index of VSPI, which again ranges from 0 to 1; countries having scores near 0 are having very poor performance on death registration in coverage and accuracy and those having VSPI near 1 are having excellent registration systems. VSPI values were estimated for 148 countries and for the period 2009–12. India, in 2012, ranks 122 among the 148 countries and very close to bottom of the ladder. As expected, all the developed countries of the West—Japan, Australia, New Zealand—have VSPI values above 0.7. Among the developing countries, Philippines and South Korea have relatively good systems.

Table 8.9 provides VSPI values for the 10 countries. It is interesting to note that in India while the coverage of death registration has improved since 1980 as indicated earlier, the quality of the characteristics of the deaths registered, including the cause of death, has declined. The VSPI value has declined from 20.5 percent during 1980–84 to 3.8 percent during 2009–12.

On the other hand, China has improved its mortality reporting system very rapidly in 6 years, 2006 to 2012, raising its VSPI values from 7.3 percent to 28.6 percent. In contrast, all the five developed countries had a VSPI score of over 70 percent during 2010–12, ranging from a low of 71.1 in Russia to 91.3 in the United Kingdom. All the five developing countries are way below 30 percent except Brazil which is quite above at 68.8 percent.

In a recent article (Bulletin of WHO, 2015/94 pp.10–21), Mamta Gupta (2015) has analyzed the death registration data in a sample of

Table 8.9:
Five-year annual average vital statistics performance index (VSPI) scores, by country or territory, 1980–2012

	1980–84	1985–89	1990–94	1995–99	2000–04	2005–09	2010–12
France	83	83.9	84.8	84.6	84.7	86.4	72.0*
Germany	86.5	86.9	87.8	88.5	88.9	89.5	89.8
Russia	54.5	55.4†	65.4†	70.1†	70.4	70.6	71.1
UK	90.2	90.9	90.9	90.1	90.4	90.8	91.3
USA	90.8	90.2	90.1	89.5	90.3	91	75.4*
Bangladesh	0	0	0	0.0†	0	0	0
Brazil	65.8	65.5	67.6	71.5	75.3	79.9	68.8*
China	0	0	0.2	0.5	0.7†	7.3†	28.6
India	20.5	13.7	14.5	8.2	4.9	4.6*	3.8*
Indonesia	NA	NA	NA	NA	NA	NA	NA

Sources: CSR Lancet article (2015); Lene Mikkelsen et al. (2015).
Notes: *All-causes only (at least 1 year in current period); †Index computed without garbage (at least 1 year in current period).

areas in Punjab and at the district level in 2011 from the points of view of coverage and quality of cause of death data reported by qualified medical personnel and concluded as follows:

Although we found the legal framework and system design to be appropriate, data collection was based on complex inter-sectoral collaborations at state and local level and the collected data were found to be of poor quality. The registration data were inadequate for a robust estimate of mortality at national level. A medically certified cause of death was only recorded for 965,992 (16.8%) of the 5,735,082 deaths registered. The data recorded by India's civil registration and vital statistics system in 2011 were incomplete. If improved, the system could be used to reliably estimate mortality. We recommend improving political support and inter sectoral coordination, capacity building, computerization and state-level initiatives to ensure that every death is registered and those reliable causes of death are recorded—at least within an adequate sample of registration units within each state.

Governance

In the aforementioned context, the quality of governance plays a significant role in the improvement of not only the CRS but also in the planning, implementation, management and evaluation of any development programs in the country. In the next few paragraphs taken from Srinivasan and Selvan (2015), we will review the quality of governance in India as a whole as assessed by the World Governance Institute, a body set up by the World Bank.

Coincidently, governance has become one of the hotly debated topics in India during the past one year. This follows the party that came to power with an overwhelming majority at the center in May 2014, having governance as one of its major election slogans: "less government better governance" (or "minimum government, maximum governance"). The international interest on "governance" per se arose in the early 1990s when the World Bank and multilateral donor agencies felt that the developmental assistance they extended to many African countries during the previous two decades did not have the desired impact on development of these countries, and their grants and loans literally went down a bottomless pit. Their main finding for this failure of developmental assistance having no desired impact on development in these countries was due to their governments' lack of "proper" and "effective" governance.

The same criticism can now be levelled against many of the backward states in India that have received huge funding from the center under the Plan funds during the past 50 years but have failed to record commensurate improvements in various dimensions of development. For example, even in 2012, IMRs (deaths of infants below one year of age to 1,000 live births) have varied widely across the states, from high levels of 56 in Madhya Pradesh and 55 in Assam to low levels of 12 in Kerala and 10 in Goa. The levels of female literacy rates in 2011 have varied from 53 percent in Bihar and 52 in Rajasthan to 89 in Mizoram and 92 in Kerala. With such variations existing across the states and a major factor underlying these differences being the quality of governance at the state level, it is imperative that studies on governance have attracted a good deal of attention. Further, the rapid developments in the field of information technology have offered a unique and unprecedented opportunity for India to improve its governance very rapidly, closer to levels comparable with developed countries.

Definitional Differences and Towards Acceptable Definition for India

In modern times and in a democracy, the term "governance" connotes the process by which an organization, especially a government, formulates its policies, enacts appropriate laws, implements the related programs, evaluates and modifies them when necessary, changes the laws and programs if needed and becomes accountable to the stakeholders/citizens and gets their mandate to govern. At a broader level, governance refers to "all processes of governing, whether undertaken by a government, market or network, whether over a family, tribe, formal or informal organization or territory and whether through laws, norms, power or language" (Bevir 2012). It relates to "the processes of interaction and decision-making among the actors involved in a collective problem that lead to the creation, reinforcement, or reproduction of social norms and institutions" (Hufty 2011). Thus, the term governance can be used for all the organizations, formal or informal, and not just restricted to the government.

Although governance is applicable to any institution or body, corporate, NGOs, among others, the worldwide interest began to focus on the governance by the government or what was called the "statist" view.

In 1990s, the topic of governance gained international currency when the World Bank commissioned the World Governance Institute to develop indicators of governance and to apply them uniformly across all the countries of the world and rank them. The World Bank Group working on governance indicators defined governance as

> consisting of the traditions and institutions by which authority in a country is exercised. This includes the process by which governments are selected, monitored and replaced; the capacity of the government to effectively formulate and implement sound policies; and the respect of citizens and the state for the institutions that govern economic and social interactions among them. (World Bank 1997)

Good governance is considered as a key and essential ingredient of social and economic development, especially in developing countries. Governance can be broadly defined to encompass the following:

1. It is politically circumscribed.
2. It is multi-dimensional and the indicators selected in each dimension may change over time.

3. It is a process by which the governments realize the goals set for themselves, effectively and efficiently within the time specified.
4. It takes into account the common good and development of the society as a whole without generating gross inequities and without violence and corruption.

The term "effectiveness," mentioned in point 3 previously, denotes if the set goals are realized or not, and the term efficiency connotes the cost at which they are realized and within the time limits set for the goals.

During the late 1980s and early 1990s, a committee was set up by the World Bank to formulate dimensions and indicators of governance and assess all the countries annually on the basis of these indicators. The World Governance Indicators (WGI) were formulated by this committee and tested out in some countries. Since 1996, the data on these indicators has been published for over 200 countries regularly and been one of the criteria on which international assistance was provided (Kaufmann, Kraay and Mastruzzi 2007 and 2010). The WGI reporting on three broad dimensions of governance for 215 countries annually during 1996–2013 included:

1. The process by which governments are selected held accountable, monitored and replaced;
2. The capacity of governments to manage resources efficiently, and to formulate, implement and enforce sound policies and regulations; and
3. The respect for the institutions that govern economic and social interactions among them.

Each of these three dimensions was measured in two "functional areas" (FAs) as follows:

1. Voice and accountability (VA) for dimension 1.
2. Political stability and absence of violence (PV) for dimension 1.
3. Government effectiveness (GE) for dimension 2.
4. Regulatory quality (RQ) for dimension 2.
5. Rule of law (RL) for dimension 3.
6. Control of corruption (CC) dimension 3.

The data related to each of these "functional areas" was compiled over a number of related variables for which information was available or was collected from one or more of the following sources:

Data compiled by various international bodies on government functioning such as the World Bank, Asian Development Bank, African Development

Bank and the IMF. Some of this information has been found to be confidential, shared only with the WGI group.

1. Opinions or perceptions on related variables by selected corporate bodies.
2. Perceptions by NGOs.
3. Data compiled from selected sample surveys.

The variables were first converted into appropriate indicators, normalized and standardized, and then merged with appropriate weights to have an index for each functional area. The WGI gives governance ratings for 212 countries and is based on some 310 variables, derived from 33 different agencies—public, private and NGOs—totaling some 10,000 plus data points. The 310 variables are aggregated for six governance dimensions: voice and accountability, political stability and absence of violence, government effectiveness, and regulatory quality, rule of law and control of corruption. For each of these functional areas, the individual indicators are aggregated into a combined index in terms of estimated governance performance score ranging between –2.5 and +2.5, and percentile rankings of countries are given on the basis of these scores. This model attaches weights to individual variables, which reflect the precision of the respective data sources. Thus, it is a four-step process: (a) identify the variables relevant to each functional area; (b) collect data on these variables from secondary or primary sources; (c) convert the variables into indicators and (d) combine them into a composite index. The WGI has gone one step further and computed and ranked the countries on the basis of percentile scores. This has contributed to the criticism of the countries on the basis of the governance scores. Table 8.10 provides estimated values of governance indicators for each of the six dimensions for the years 1996 and 2014 for the 10 countries under our study.

From Table 8.10, it can be seen that in all the six dimensions of governance, India has scored poorly, at 38.9, 45.2, 13.6, 34.6, 54.3 and 61.1, in percentile ranking. Only in the areas of voice and accountability and rule of law, India has over 50 percent score because of its democratic system. Among the developed countries, the Russian Federation scored more poorly than India and other developing countries in 2014. The collapse of the Soviet Union in 1988 has disrupted many of the systems that prevailed earlier in Soviet Union. The dimension of "government effectiveness"—where India's score has declined from 53.7 to 45.2 during 1996 and 2014—is the crucial factor in the improvement of CRS and for the effective implementation of public health programs, which needs to be improved.

Table 8.10:
Governance indicators percentile ranking

	Control of Corruption		Government Effectiveness		Political Stability and Absence of Violence/ Terrorism		Regulatory Quality		Rule of Law		Voice and Accountability	
	1996	2014	1996	2014	1996	2014	1995	2014	1996	2014	1996	2014
France	85.9	88	88.8	88.9	73.6	59.2	78.9	82.2	91.9	88.5	88.9	89.2
Germany	94.6	94.7	93.7	94.7	92.8	79.1	91.2	94.2	93.8	93.3	90.4	96.1
Russian Federation	15.6	19.7	32.7	51.4	12	18.4	39.2	36.5	23.4	26.4	40.9	20.2
United Kingdom	96.1	92.8	95.1	92.8	76.9	60.7	99.5	97.1	94.7	94.2	88.5	92.1
United States	91.7	89.4	92.2	89.9	75.5	67	96.1	88.5	92.3	89.9	90.9	79.8
Bangladesh	27.3	18.8	24.4	21.6	25	18	16.2	18.3	18.7	26	47.6	32.5
Brazil	56.1	44.2	50.7	47.1	38	45.1	65.2	50.5	41.6	55.3	53.8	60.6
China	43.9	47.1	46.8	66.3	41.3	29.6	47.5	45.2	36.4	42.8	12	5.4
India	40	38.9	53.7	45.2	19.2	13.6	32.4	34.6	59.3	54.3	62	61.1
Indonesia	30.7	34.1	37.1	54.8	13	31.1	57.4	49	39.7	41.8	23.6	53.2

Source: World Development Indicators, World Bank, 2016.

9

Wobbling International and Academic Concerns on Population

As briefly discussed in Chapter 2, the international concerns on population issues have been largely based on Malthusian fears of over population, that is, population growth out-stripping means of subsistence leading to wars and famines and newer epidemics, especially in the developing countries. Neo-Malthusian Leagues, that encouraged curtailment of fertility levels through adoption of artificial methods of contraception (in this respect they differed from Malthus, since Malthus did not accept the use of artificial methods of contraception considering them vice and hence use of the term Neo-Malthusianism), were set up in England and India in 1920s to discuss and promote contraception. The spurt in population growth was accelerated by a delinking of declines in death rates from their social and economic development from the beginning of the fifth decade of the last century, at end of the Second World War. Earlier in 1796 when Malthus wrote his magnum opus, *Essays on the Principles of Population*, he was more concerned with the increasing population growth rates in the European populations; in most of these countries, there were historically unprecedented rates of population growth. These were mitigated by large-scale migrations to Americas and Australia, beginning the eighteenth century.

In the less developed countries, such an option of large-scale migrations out of the country was not available. In many countries after their independence in the 1940s and 1950s, their annual growth rates, exceeded 2.5 percent, historically unprecedented, causing a fear of their populations doubling every 28 years. These high growth rates were due to rapid declines in death rates with constant or even rising fertility levels. They created the collective fears at the governmental and public level but more so in the more developed world—fears of the massive population sizes of China and India without concomitant improvements in their economic conditions, dragging the world into famines, wars and epidemics, reminiscent of the dark ages. The declines in the death rates in the more developed countries were slow and mostly related to their economic development and discoveries in public health, medicines, causes of death, and so on. On the other hand, in the less developed countries, these discoveries, especially of antibiotics and vaccines, were readily available with assistance from international and bilateral donors. This contributed to a rapid control of epidemics such as plague, cholera, small pox and other acute illnesses. The decline in mortality that the Western world achieved in a century were achieved by these developing countries in 25 years, without any equivalent improvements in their economic conditions. Many developing countries, such as, India, Pakistan, Bangladesh, Korea, Indonesia and Brazil, decreased their mortality levels, death rates to lower levels without any significant increase in their economic conditions. CDRs in these countries declined to the levels that were achieved by the developed societies when their economic conditions were quite advanced.

From the Tables (9.1 and 9.2), it can be seen that the annual rate of growth of population during 1950–55, before the large-scale interventions in fertility levels through national programs of family planning in the developing countries, was 2.03 percent in less developed regions (Asia excluding Japan, Africa and South America) and 1.19 percent in the more developed regions of the world (Europe, North America, Japan, Australia and New Zealand) with a growth rate gap of 0.84 percent. Six decades later (during 2010–15), after all the intense family planning activities and rapid reductions in fertility in the developing countries, the growth rate in the less developed region has come down to 1.36 percent. However, the growth rate in the more developed region has also declined to 0.29 percent, and the gap in the growth rate has actually increased from 1950 to 2015 by 1.07 percent. The fertility levels in many developed countries have fallen well below the replacement levels and continue to decline and attempts to increase their fertility by giving incentives to women to have children have had limited success. A comparison of the trends in the birth death and growth rates of population in the 60-year period between the five of the larger developed countries and five of the less developed countries is given in Table 9.2.

Table 9.1:
Population in thousands and average annual rate of population change (percentage)

	1950	1950–55	1970	1970–75	1990	1990–95	2010	2010–15	2020	2020–25
France	41,880	0.77	50,844	0.84	56,943	0.45	62,961	0.45	65,720	0.36
Germany	69,789	0.43	78,367	0.08	78,958	0.66	80,435	0.06	80,392	−0.11
Russian Federation	102,799	1.6	130,126	0.56	147,569	0.10	143,158	0.04	142,898	−0.24
United Kingdom	50,616	0.2	55,611	0.20	57,110	0.28	62,717	0.63	66,700	0.54
United States of America	157,813	1.58	209,486	0.89	252,848	1.04	309,876	0.75	333,546	0.68
Bangladesh	37,895	2.12	65,049	1.82	105,983	2.22	151,617	1.20	170,467	0.98
Brazil	53,975	2.98	95,982	2.44	150,393	1.58	198,614	0.91	215,997	0.64
China	544,113	1.91	808,511	2.27	1,154,606	1.23	1,340,969	0.52	1,402,848	0.17
India	**376,325**	**1.68**	**553,943**	**2.31**	**870,602**	**1.97**	**1,230,985**	**1.26**	**1,388,859**	**1.02**
Indonesia	69,543	2.12	114,835	2.59	181,437	1.64	241,613	1.28	27,1857	0.91
Less Developed Regions	1,712,161	2.03	2,674,806	2.39	4,165,205	1.84	5,696,349	1.36	6,49,1797	1.12
More Developed Regions	812,989	1.19	1,007,682	0.77	1,144,463	0.44	1,233,376	0.29	1,266,360	0.17
World	**2,525,149**	**1.77**	**3,682,488**	**1.96**	**5,309,668**	**1.54**	**6,929,725**	**1.18**	**7,758,157**	**0.97**

Source: World Development Indicators 2016.

Table 9.2:
Birth and death rates of population of 10 selected countries since 1950

	1950–55		1970–75		1990–95		2010–15		2020–25	
	CBR	CDR	CBR	CDR	CBR	CDR	CBR	CDR	CBR	CDR
France	19.1	12.8	16.0	10.8	12.7	9.3	12.4	8.9	11.6	9.2
Germany	15.6	11.1	11.4	12.4	9.9	11.3	8.3	10.8	8.7	11.6
Russian Federation	26.9	11.0	15.4	9.4	10.9	13.3	12.7	13.9	11.3	14.4
United Kingdom	15.1	11.8	13.5	11.9	13.3	11.2	12.6	9.2	12	9.1
United States of America	24.4	9.6	15.6	9.4	15.6	8.7	12.6	8.2	12.5	8.6
Bangladesh	46.2	24.8	46.8	19.8	33.0	9.3	20.4	5.5	16.9	5.2
Brazil	44.2	15.6	33.9	9.5	22.7	6.9	15.1	6.1	12.9	6.6
China	42.2	23.1	32.2	9.3	19.0	6.6	12.4	7.0	9.8	7.9
India	**43.6**	**26.8**	**38.4**	**16.1**	**30.0**	**10.2**	**20.4**	**7.4**	**17.8**	**7.3**
Indonesia	42.7	21.4	38.3	12.2	24.4	7.6	20.5	7.2	17.1	7.5
Less Developed Regions	43.6	23.2	37.2	12.9	27.7	8.8	21.4	7.4	18.8	7.3
More Developed Regions	22.4	10.6	16.0	9.6	12.4	10.0	11.1	10.0	10.5	10.6
World	**36.9**	**19.2**	**31.6**	**12.0**	**24.5**	**9.1**	**19.6**	**7.8**	**17.5**	**7.9**

Source: World Development Indicators 2016.
Note: CBR—Crude birth rate (births per 1,000 population); CDR—Crude death rate (deaths per 1,000 population).

Among the developed countries, the United States of America has the highest fertility levels mostly because it has a higher proportion of migrant population with higher fertility levels. The fear psychosis of Malthusian calamities was compounded in the developed world and it continues to haunt them even today of the increasing proportions of the populations in the less developed world. The aging populations of the Western world compared to the burgeoning youthful populations of the less developed world were considered as a major destabilizing force in global peace and stability. In this context, the concerns were shifted from the Western world scholars to the United Nations and other multilateral institutions. We will review the various international efforts made through the auspices of the United Nations and NGOs to understand and advance the causes of national programs of family planning in developing countries.

Wobbling International Concerns by the United Nations

In this context, the First World Population Conference was organized by the United Nations in Rome in 1954 to exchange mainly scientific information on population variables, their determinants and the consequences. This was eminently an academic conference and was motivated to generate fuller information and data on the demographic situation of the developing countries. One of the major recommendations of this conference is for the United Nations to take a leading role in collection, compilation and publication of population-related data at the country level for all the member countries on a yearly basis and to set up regional training centers in demography that would help to address population issues at the national and local levels by regionally trained demographers as specialists in demographic analysis. The annual publication by the United Nations, the *Demographic Year Books*, since the mid-1950s, was a great achievement in the history of human population studies. The setting up of the regional demographic training and research centers in Bombay, Cairo and Chile, was the second major outcome of this conference. Unlike the succeeding conferences by the United Nations, it did not involve itself in the making of demographic goals and national policies and programs to reach these goals.

The second World Population Conference was organized in 1965 by the International Union for the Scientific Study of Population (IUSSP) jointly with the United Nations in Belgrade, Yugoslavia, and most of the participants were experts in the population field. The focus of this international meeting was on the analysis of fertility as part of a policy for the development planning. This conference was held at a time when expert studies on the population aspects of development coincided with the start-up of population programs subsidized by the USAID.

The third conference by the United Nations was organized in 1974 at Bucharest. The industrialized nations were keen on promoting global family planning programs for the less developed countries. The United States of America had even talked about global targets for reducing CBRs of less developed countries by 10 points in 10 years. The less developed countries reacted sharply to this proposal by declaring the sovereign right of each country to solve the population problem as it deemed fit. India lashed out with the famous slogan, "development is the best contraceptive," and China's head of delegation declared, "Population is not a problem under socialism." However, after heated debates, an acceptable and well-moderated World Population Plan of Action (WPPA) was drafted reiterating the sovereign right of each nation to resolve its population problem as it deemed fit. At the end of the conference, the industrialized nations felt they had placed an undue emphasis on family planning programs for the developing countries but what happened within the developing countries after Bucharest was puzzling.

China intensified its birth control campaign with "one-child family" and reduced its birth rate dramatically by over 10 points in ten years—a historically unprecedented pace. India also intensified its family planning program in 1975; in June 1976, an NPP was formulated for the first time in the country and about 6 million sterilizations were done from June 1976 to December 1976 during the national emergency (see Chapter 2). Unlike China, the family planning program in India, after 1977, had to be implemented within a democratic framework, partly because due to the overzealous approach to the program during the emergency period, there was a political backlash in the 1977 elections and the program suffered a serious setback. If the pace of the program of 1976 had continued even for a few years more, India's birth rate would have tumbled down as well, as in China. What the developing countries did within their own countries on family planning was diametrically opposite of what they declared internationally in the Bucharest Conference.

The point is why the stance taken by these two most populous countries at the international conference was at variance with what they did subsequently at home. For their motivations and success in the implementation of family planning programs, India and China were even given the UN Population Awards in 1983. In developing countries, there is a subtle dislike for the developed countries preaching them about family planning not out of love or the well-being of their populations but out of a fear that increasing populations under poverty and misery will directly and indirectly impinge on their economic prosperity and command over world resources. When the developing countries really felt by themselves that high population growth rates are really hurting their developmental efforts, they acted and acted fast. On the basis of such experiences, one expected that at the next World Population Conference held in Mexico in 1984, the industrialized countries particularly the United States of America, which is a major donor country in this field, would strongly support state-run family planning programs. However, it was a surprise that not only did they underplay the importance of population as an issue but indicated that developing countries were not going overboard on their family planning programs as a demographic overreaction. In its statement at Mexico, every developing country underscored the success it had achieved in the implementation of WPPA, integrating development and population policies and reinforcing the validity of the WPPA to guide the destiny of its population in future years.

It is true that the acceleration of the annual rate of growth of the population of the world as a whole has slowed down since Bucharest, from about 2.03 percent in 1974 to 1.67 percent in 1984, mainly because of the huge reduction in the fertility levels of China because of its one-child policy. There appeared to be some euphoria about it that the hump of the global population problem had been crossed somewhere in the late 1970s. However, this sharp decline in the growth rate is mainly due to the remarkable achievement of China's firm population policy which reduced its growth rate by about 50 percent, from about 2.0 percent in 1973 to 1.1 percent in 1983. If we exclude China, the rate of growth in the rest of the world has declined from 2.1 percent to only 1.9 percent during the same period. The decline is not at all impressive in a number of large countries including ours (though it has been in some small countries and some Indian states).

During this period, 1974 to 1994, the world's population increased from 3,980 to 4,750 million, adding a total of about 770 million people in the world. In other words, another India has been added to the world population since Bucharest. About 90 percent of this increase has occurred in developing countries. By the year 2000, the population of the globe was expected to further increase to 6,100 million. The absolute number of people added below the poverty line and the ranks of the unemployed and malnourished are increasing year after year. The gap between the developed and developing countries is also widening at an alarming pace.

In this context, it was surprising that the chief of the US delegation to Mexico, James Buckley, observed, "More people do not necessarily mean less growth." and went on to emphasize that population was a neutral issue, that its growth was a problem in those countries where government policies had disputed economic incentives, rewards and achievements. The free market system of economy was advocated as an ideal for rapid economic growth. China's dramatic success in reducing fertility in a controlled economic system was not taken note of and only their fertility declines in a few smaller countries under a free market economy, such as Singapore, Hong Kong and South Korea, were highlighted. There was an intrinsic dislike that the communist system in China had arrested the population growth rates in China beyond the wildest dreams of the capitalist system in the United States of America. It was the dislike for communist success in arresting population growth that seemed to offend the United States of America and failed to appreciate the contributions that it had made to the global population problem. Politics and population issues were at loggerheads.

There were also hectic discussions on the ethics of induced abortion as a method of family planning—ignoring the experience of Japan and East European countries in this regard. At Mexico, the United States of America played the tune that the developing countries had in Bucharest in 1974: playing down the role of official programs of family planning, repeating that development was accelerated in a free market system. On the other hand, the developing countries and countries under socialistic systems substantially played up their role, what the United States of America did at Bucharest, emphasizing the role of official family planning programs in reducing fertility levels. Thus, family planning was a play tool between capitalism and communism.

The role reversals were dramatic and breathtaking in the Mexico conference in 1984. In a way, Karl Marx and Thomas Malthus became the closest of allies at Mexico. One thing was clear: the stance that national governments were taking at home could be very different and at times even diametrically opposite to what they say in international forums and this has become an internationally accepted and respected form of dialogue, especially on population issues.

It should be realized, however, that many of the issues connected with the population problem are really intractable and consequently any recommendation at an international conference has to be general. For example, one of the major recommendations of WPPA made in Bucharest and reinforced at Mexico reads, "The Governments are urged to ensure that all couples and individuals have the basic right to decide freely and responsibly the number and spacing of their children...." Another recommendation reads, "Governments that have adopted or intend to adopt fertility policies are urged to set their own quantitative targets in this area." How can it be ensured that individual human rights to decide on the number of offspring and national goals of population growth go together? How and who are to decide the extent of responsibility in the field of reproduction? There are no acceptable answers for any even homogenous groups of people within a country. Policies and programs for population are necessarily to be interpreted and guided by the political system the country adopts and can change with the system. It is naive to believe that political system and population policies can be kept separate.

ICPD held in Cairo in 1994 under the auspices of the United Nations is considered as, officially, the third conference in the series. Beginning the late 1980s of the last century, women's groups were becoming active in Northern Europe and the United States of America and started asserting their rights, reproductive rights, freedom to choose when and how many children they should have and demanded that they should not be subjected to obey their governments polices to meet and accept the demographic targets. It was, in a way, the revolt of the women claiming their reproductive and women's rights. It is considered a milestone in the history of population and development. The result was an impressive and ambitious set of goals for improving sexual health and reproductive rights all over the world. These goals are postulated as an accepted set of recommendations by almost all the countries and known as the ICPD PoA. Even China, under the communist regime, supported the PoA. The focus of PoA is wider than sexual and reproductive health and, in essence, it is the global establishment of women's rights and women's health as global priority. It links the interrelationships between population, sustained economic growth, health, education, economic status and empowerment of women. Remarkably, it was the first time that the world leaders agreed to invest in people, not demographic targets. A total of 179 countries were committed to implement this by 2015. It was to be reviewed in 2014. Whereas earlier world conferences on population had focused on controlling population growth in developing countries, mainly through family planning, the Cairo conference enlarged the scope of policy discussions.

A mid-term evaluation of ICPD, done in 1999 (ICPD 5+), showed that the PoA has resulted in significant changes to health policies in many countries, in the sense like in India in many countries family planning program was considered a part and parcel of the RCH program. By 2004, evidence from the previous 10 years indicated that with adequate funding PoA could save more lives of women. The early 1990s thus marked a dramatic departure from conventional ideas about how governments should try to influence the size and well-being of the societies they govern, and brought a broad consensus among national governments about population policy. This new perspective shifted the emphasis of population policies away from slowing population growth to improving the lives of individuals, particularly women. The policies spawned by this consensus continue to evolve to the present day.

Governments now agree that population policies should address social development beyond family planning, especially the advancement of women, and that family planning should be provided as part of a broader package of reproductive health care. Underlying this new emphasis was a belief that enhancing individual health and rights would ultimately lower fertility and slow population growth.

The Cairo conference was thus far larger and more inclusive than earlier world population conferences. By placing the causes and effects of rapid population growth in the context of human development and social progress, governments and individuals of all political, religious and cultural backgrounds could support the recommendations. Although there were ideological and religious differences over issues such as definitions of reproductive health, adolescent sexuality and abortion, all but a few nations fully endorsed the final program.

The Cairo PoA defined reproductive health as "a state of complete physical, mental, and social well-being and not merely the absence of disease or infirmity, in all matters relating to the reproductive system." This definition goes beyond traditional notions of health care as preventing illness and death, and it promotes a more holistic vision of a healthy individual.

A review of ICPD programs implemented over a 10-year period, 1994–2004, indicated that here was an uneven progress across the countries and even on commitment to this concept. In many low-income countries, addressing such a wide range of health and social concerns requires greater resources and organizational capacity than are currently available. The funding from donor agencies to support these changes has fallen well below expectations. Under the Cairo guidelines, the donor/developing country breakdown would have translated to $5.7 billion and $11.3 billion, respectively, in 2000. In fact, the United Nations estimates that donor-funding levels in 2000 were less than half the required amount.

The shortfalls in estimated spending apply only to the estimated costs included in the Cairo PoA for providing family planning and basic elements of safe motherhood and for preventing sexually transmitted infections. They did not include the cost of meeting additional goals supported in principle in the Cairo document, including improving over-all health care systems, providing emergency care for childbirth compli-cations, closing the gap between girls' and boys' education, eliminating harmful practices against women, improving women's job opportunities, or the costs associated with the treatment of STIs, including HIV/AIDS. Given the enormous challenges faced in less developed countries and the limited resources devoted to population and reproductive health activities, even small progress toward the international community's goals is note-worthy. In fact, the five-year review of the ICPD documented a great deal of commitment and progress, perhaps, in part because of the wide-spread appeal of the concepts in the Cairo agreement and the activism of NGOs. Thus, larger goals advocated and supported by the developed countries were mere ideological goal posts and not supported by adequate additional funding.

In the twenty-first century, continued high population growth presents many of the same challenges to development as the rapid growth of the last century. However, governments' responses to growth (in parti-cular, their public stances) are dramatically different from what it was a decade ago: Policies aimed at population control are no longer accept-able in most of the countries and the panic buttons are no longer there.

It was obvious that national population goals cannot be pursued without some form of public scrutiny, either at home or abroad in democratic regimes. If individuals' perspectives and needs are disregarded, policies will likely meet with evasion or open resistance. Now that NGOs and citizen activists have taken on a prominent monitoring role in inter-national agreements, they are likely to continue to pressure governments to respect individual rights. Given (a) the growing body of evidence showing the links between women's status and population and develop-ment trends and (b) the growing influence of women's groups, it is hard to imagine that women's health and rights issues will disappear from population policy debates. Issues related to sexuality and childbearing are value-laden and complex, ensuring that policy debates will continue.

The Cairo conference stated that "in no case should abortion be promoted as a method of family planning," and that "in circumstances in which abortion is not against the law, such abortion should be safe." This consensus, however, has not held firm over time.

Debates also continue about the importance of controlling population growth, and if the entire Cairo agenda is feasible. It is because large numbers of young people are in or approaching their childbearing ages and the world population will continue to grow well into the twenty-first century. In some countries as Bangladesh and Egypt, surveys reveal that average family size has hardly declined in the second half of the 1990s. These findings were surprising given that the drop from 5 or 6 children to 3.5 children on average occurred rapidly between the 1970s and 1990s. It is possible that the two-child average is still a long way off, or will never be reached, in some societies. RCH approach may widen the gaps in growth rates between not just the developed and developing countries but also within the developing countries.

Wobbling Academic Concerns of Overpopulation

Considerable controversies have been created in the academic circles in the second half of the twentieth century. There were scholarly articles on the advantages of reduced fertility or number of children per woman to the family and economy of developing countries through higher savings per household and greater investments at the national level contributing to economic growth. While there were empirical investigations on the magnitude of such economic benefits, there were also studies at the other end on what would happen because of famines, pandemics and so on, contributing to millions dying if the growth rates are not curtailed immediately. The benefit pendulum of size and growth of population was swinging from one end to the other. The ghost of Malthus seems to reemerge with the newer global threats of global warming because of the emission of greenhouse gases, rise of nationalism against globalization in the developed countries and reemergence of religious dogmatism.

Studies on Demographic Dividends

The demographic transition in developing countries, including India, made significant changes not only in lengthening the life, reducing fertility levels, increasing and later reducing population growth rates but also altered the age structure of the population. When fertility levels fall, the ratio of economically dependent population, that is, children in the age group of 0–15 and older persons (65+), to the productive population of 15–64 declines, and this enables the diversion of household and public expenditures from consumption-related items to savings and investment, leading to accelerated economic growth. This will happen under any economic situation of the country. The first major empirical study on the effects of high dependency ratios on the savings and investments at the household and the governmental level was conducted by Coale and Hoover (1958) in their first classic study on the effects of population growth on the economic development in India and Mexico. They empirically, but more intuitively, proved in their study that reduction of fertility through national programs of family planning would contribute to overall economic development by increasing savings and investment at the household and national levels. Their study paved the way, by providing economic justification for the launch of the national programs of family planning in India and later in a number of other developing countries, including China, as a part of their developmental strategy. They did not use the term "demographic dividends," which came into use later in 1990s.

The necessity of more systematic studies on the effects of changes in the dependency ratios of an economy arose in the late 1980s and 1990s because of what was considered an economic miracle of the East Asian countries, especially China, Korea, Singapore and Taiwan, after they have experienced a rapid declines in their fertility and mortality levels earlier. Their economic dependency ratios declined faster, and the impacts of these on their high economic growth had to be disentangled and estimated leading to what is termed as "demographic bonus," "demographic dividend," "window of opportunity" and so on (Bloom and Williamson 1998). While Coale and Hoover justified the launch of national family planning programs in the developing countries in the 1950s as programs that would contribute to the economic development, the later authors measured the contribution of such programs to economic development because of reductions in dependency ratios. These terms are also used to connote the period of time when the dependency ratio in a population started to decline because of earlier declines in their fertility levels up until it started to rise again because of the rise in the proportion of older persons caused by continuing declines in fertility and increasing longevity. The second rise in the dependency ratios was because the pace of rise in the ODRs was more than to compensate for the declines in the YDRs. Usually this period of demographic bonus is dependent on the pace of decline in the fertility levels of a population. If the switch to small families is fast, the demographic bonus can give considerable push to development as it happened in China, beginning the early 1980s with the rapid declines in the fertility levels of the population because of its one-child policy.

Many studies have empirically shown that the sheer fact of reduction in the child dependency ratios in a population, just by reducing the consumption expenditures at the household level and at the national levels, contributed to 10–20 percent of the increase in the per capita incomes of the populations of East Asia and South Asia that have grown economically fast during the last three decades. However, it was not pointed out that all the East Asian countries that achieved this development miracle and rapid demographic transition were countries under authoritarian political systems, including Marxist communist regime of one-party rule in China. Since the leaders in these countries became aware of the economic benefits of reducing the dependency ratios in the population by rapid reductions in fertility levels, they implemented aggressive family planning programs such as the one-child policy in China from the early 1970s onwards; similar policies were also implemented in South Korea. Thus both the demographic transition and economic development were benefitted by the authoritarian systems, and reductions in dependency ratios and increase in per capita income were both pursued as policy goals; although, the former indirectly benefitted the latter. India, though a country that launched the official family planning program much earlier in the 1950s, could not achieve such an economic miracle as the East Asian Tigers because of its democratic political system.

If the period of "demographic bonus" were considered a "window of opportunity" and public investments during this period were made wisely in health care and secular education with emphasis on skill development of the population as happened in the East Asian countries, the contribution of this reduction in dependency ratios would be higher in India. The Republic of Korea, for example, increased net secondary school enrollment from 38 to 84 percent between 1970 and 1990 by increasing the expenditure per secondary pupil three times. India did not and possibly could not make such investments. It is estimated that even up to 40 percent of the growth of per capita income can be derived as demographic dividend as was in China and South Korea. During the 25-year period (1965–90), GDP per capita in East Asia grew annually by an average of 6.1 percent, and the changes in the age structure contributed an estimated 0.9 to 1.5 percentage points. Thus, only 25 percent of the per capita GDP increase can be attributed to the demographic dividends, but 75 percent came from a well-planned economic development program that did not seem possible in a democratic system as India. Changing demographic structures now present similar opportunities and challenges in the South Asian countries and there is evidence that they are also poised for similar growth in the coming decades, although not to the same level as East Asian Tigers (Bloom, Canning and Sevilla 2003). In India, the TFR has declined from 6.03 in 1951–61 to 2.4 in 2011. Although there is a positive impact of this decline in fertility on the increase in per capita GDP through declines in the dependency ratios in the population, the increase in per capita GDP does not match the pace of increase achieved by the East Asian Tigers. The political system has a strong role to play both in demographic transition and economic development, and this factor is not fully recognized by the international community and scholars who are only harping on family planning programs as the main engine of development. Developmental strategies have to go hand in hand with strategies for fertility and mortality decline; although they play a synergistic role, one cannot replace the other. International communities and agencies sometimes tend to over play one or the other, ignoring the effects of the political system under which both have to operate.

The Population Bomb and the Limits to Growth Studies

The Population Bomb

Two major studies in the 1960s and the early 1970 have focused urgent attention on population and development issues in order to avoid large-scale catastrophes. The first is *The Population Bomb*, a best-selling book written by a Stanford University Professor, Paul R. Ehrlich, and his wife, Anne Ehrlich, in 1968. It warned of the impending mass starvation and deaths of humans in the 1970s and 1980s owing to overpopulation, especially in India, as well as other major societal upheavals, and advocated immediate action to limit population growth, some of them in the extremes. Fears of a "population explosion" were already widespread in the 1950s and 1960s, but the book and its authors brought the idea to an even wider audience by calling it a Bomb. The book ran into many editions and the early editions began with the statement,

> The battle to feed all of humanity is over. In the 1970s hundreds of millions of people will starve to death in spite of any crash programs embarked upon now. At this late date nothing can prevent a substantial increase in the world death rate. (Ehrlich, 1968)

Much of the book is describes the state of the environment and the global food security situation, which is suggested to be increasingly dire. Ehrlich argued that as the existing population was not being fed adequately and was growing rapidly, it was unreasonable to expect sufficient improvements in food production to feed everyone in a growing population. He further argued that the growing population placed escalating strains on all aspects of the natural world. His recommendations were draconian and Orwellian. "What needs to be done?" he asked. He further suggests, "We must rapidly bring the world population under control, reducing the growth rate to zero or making it negative. Conscious regulation of human numbers must be achieved. Simultaneously we must, at least temporarily, greatly increase our food production." Ehrlich described a number of ideas on how these goals might be reached. He believed that the United States should take a leading role in population control, both because it was already consuming much more than the rest of the world and, therefore, had a moral duty to reduce its impact, and because it would have to lead international efforts owing to its prominence in the world. In order to avoid charges of hypocrisy or racism, it would have to take the lead in population reduction efforts. Ehrlich floated the horrendous idea of adding "*temporary* sterilants" to the water supply or staple foods. However, he rejects the idea as unpractical owing to "criminal inadequacy of biomedical research in this area." He suggested a tax scheme in which additional children would add to a family's tax burden at increasing rates for more children and luxury taxes on childcare goods. He suggested incentives for men who agree to permanent sterilization before they have two children and a variety of other monetary incentives as well, for countries such as India. He proposed a powerful department of population and environment which "should be set up with the power to take whatever steps are necessary to establish a reasonable population size in the United States and to put an end to the steady deterioration of our environment." The department should support research into population control, such as better contraceptives, mass sterilizing agents and prenatal sex discernment (mostly because families often continue to have children until a male is born). Ehrlich suggested that if they could choose a male child, this would reduce the birth rate. Legislation should be enacted guaranteeing the right to an abortion, and sex education should be expanded. The methods suggested by him are draconian to the core.

The book has been criticized since its publication for its alarmist tone and, in recent decades, for its inaccurate predictions. India became a food exporting country in the 1980s and 1990s, and instead of increase in death rate as he has predicted, it declined. With all his alarmist predictions going wrong even in 2009, the Ehrlichs stood by the basic ideas in the book, stating that "perhaps the most serious flaw in *The Bomb* was that it was much too optimistic about the future" and believed that it achieved their goals since "it alerted people to the importance of environmental issues and brought human numbers into the debate on the human future."

An exactly opposite view was expressed by Julian Simon (1981), who in his book, *The Ultimate Resource*, argued that it was in times of high population growth and serious challenges to human survival that great discoveries were made that contributed to increased human welfare and development. He cites all the major technological and agricultural innovations at the times of high population growth rates and argued that population is the ultimate asset and should be allowed to regulate itself without any external or government interventions. The book argues how population growth ultimately creates more resources. The basic argument underlying Simmons thesis is that as resources become scarcer, the price rises, creating an incentive to innovate and adapt. It suggests that the more a society has to invent and innovate, *ceteris paribus*, the more easily the society will raise its living standards and lower resource scarcity.

Thus, academic opinion on the effects of population growth on development seems to be divided among scholars.

The Limits to Growth

Simultaneously in Europe, a global think tank called the Club of Rome was started in 1968 in the Accademia dei Lincei, Rome, by an Italian philanthropist, Aurelio Peccei, to study scientifically the global issues of human wellbeing, including development, utilization of nonrenewable resources, global warming and humanitarian problems. The Club of Rome describes itself as "a group of world citizens, sharing a common concern for the future of humanity." Researchers working out of the Massachusetts Institute of Technology, for the project, including husband-and-wife team of Donella and Dennis Meadows, built a computer model called World 3 to track the world's economy and environment, which was a cutting edge model on system dynamics.

The Club raised considerable public attention in 1972 with its report *The Limits to Growth* (Meadows et al. 1972) in the context of the earlier publication, *The Population Bomb* by Ehrlich (1968). The second study is more scientific and predictive on the basis of actual data, levels and trends and forecasting the future trends in five major areas of human activities in the planet, that is, industrialization, population, food, use of nonrenewable and renewable resources and pollution. A complex computer model was developed and using real data until 1970, they developed a range of scenarios up to 2100, depending on whether humanity took serious action on environmental and resource issues. If that didn't happen, the model predicted an "overshoot and collapse" in the economy, environment and population before 2070. This was called the "business-as-usual" scenario (Meadows et al. 1972). This was predicted to happen if we continue with the existing trends of activities in each of the five dimensions.

It predicted that death rates would rise before 2070 and millions would die in the developing countries if the pace of economic growth through exploitation of nonrenewable natural resources and the high population growth in the developing world are not controlled. The 1973 oil crisis increased public concern about this problem. The catastrophe scenario was similar to the findings of *The Population Bomb* but postponed by almost a century and was based on a complex forecasting model. Hence, the findings were taken more seriously by scholars and leaders.

However, immediately after *The Limits to Growth* was published, Eduard Pestel and Mihajlo Mesarovic of Case Western Reserve University worked on a far more elaborate model, separately for 10 world regions of the world, involving 200,000 equations. This research had the complete support of the Club and the final publication, *Mankind at the Turning Point*, was accepted as the official second report to the Club of Rome in 1974. In addition to providing a more refined regional breakdown, Pestel and Mesarovic had succeeded in integrating social as well as technical data. The second report revised the predictions of the original *The Limits to Growth* and gave a more optimistic prognosis for the future of the environment, noting that many of the factors were within human control and therefore, the environmental and economic catastrophes were preventable or avoidable.

In 1991, the Club published *The First Global Revolution* as a follow up of the first one. It analyzed the problems facing humanity, calling these collectively or in essence the "problematique." It noted that, historically, social or political unity has commonly been motivated by common enemies.

> The need for enemies seems to be a common historical factor. Some states have striven to overcome domestic failure and internal contradictions by blaming external enemies. The ploy of finding a scapegoat is as old as mankind itself—when things become too difficult at home, divert attention to adventure abroad. Bring the divided nation together to face an outside enemy, either a real one, or else one invented for the purpose. With the disappearance of the traditional enemy, the temptation is to use religious or ethnic minorities as scapegoats, especially those whose differences from the majority are disturbing. (King and Schneider 1991)

> Every state has been so used to classifying its neighbours as friend or foe, that the sudden absence of traditional adversaries has left governments and public opinion with a great void to fill. New enemies have to be identified, new strategies imagined, and new weapons devised. In searching for a common enemy against whom we can unite, we came up with the idea that pollution, the threat of global warming, water shortages, famine and the like, would fit the bill. In their totality and their interactions these phenomena do constitute a common threat which must be confronted by everyone together. But in designating these dangers as the enemy, we fall into the trap, which we have already warned readers about, namely mistaking symptoms for causes. All these dangers are caused by human intervention in natural processes, and it is only through changed attitudes and behaviour that they can be overcome. The real enemy then is humanity itself. (King and Schneider 1991)

The increasing identities of nationality overriding internationalism, religiosity overriding secular thinking, barriers to trade overriding free trade and more stringent restrictions on immigrations can be added to the list of barriers to growth. The present conflicts between religious and racial groups emerging in both the developed and developing countries prove this point.

If human beings of all countries begin to take as their collective human enemy, the problems of environmental degradation, global warming and the huge disparities in income and wealth, then the battle for human survival will be won collectively. In 2001, the Club of Rome established a think tank called *tt30*, comprising around 30 men and women aged 25–35 to identify and solve problems in the world from a younger generation's perspective. Every report of the Club of Rome swings from extremes of pessimism to optimism on the fate of mankind.

Another study by Graham Turner of the Commonwealth Scientific and Industrial Research Organisation (CSIRO), Australia, in 2012 found that "40 years of historical data compare favourably with key features of a business-as-usual scenario called the 'standard run' scenario, which results in collapse of the global system midway through the 21st century."

The message of this book that still holds today: The earth's interlocking of resources—the global system of nature in which we all live which, probably, cannot support present rates of economic and population growth much beyond the year 2100, if that long, even with advanced technology. However, without basic changes in the human values across the globe, catastrophes cannot be avoided by technology alone. Thus, we see that the international and academic concerns about human population size and growth of the developing countries in the developed world were essentially Malthusian in orientation, which was based on the relatively higher growth rates of the population of the developing countries leading to their higher numbers and influence on the human race. The term "means of subsistence," raised by Malthus mainly as limiting population growth in 1799 to indicate food supply, now connotes a wider range of goods and services that affect the environment such as global warming and pollution, strong national, religious and racial identities and rabid exploitation of nonrenewable resources, posing collective threats of gradual and even sudden collapse of the population. This can be a slide back in the living standards of the people in the developed countries. It is not love of human beings, per se, that made the international organizations to study, analyze and conclude on various population issues of the developing countries but an innate fear that their dominant role hitherto enjoyed by them in the world may be shaken in the future.

10

The Way Forward

The fundamental issues in India's population remain almost essentially the same as they were at the time of independence in 1947: its large size, large number of unwanted births still occurring, easily avoidable deaths mostly among children, preventing very early marriages especially marriages in childhood, employment generation and eradication of poverty, ensuring that the various benefits aimed at the poor or those below the poverty line reach them and none else and improving gender equity. We had these concerns seven decades ago, and we still have them, though not with the same intensity and to the same extent but even now despite the wherewithal to handle them efficiently. These should all have been mostly resolved to a much greater extent some decades earlier, because we had these objectives mentioned in almost every Five-Year Plan. China, Korea, Malaysia, Taiwan and Thailand, all of which launched their developmental and population programs much later than India, under different political ideologies, have done better—reduced infant and maternal mortality rates, achieved lower fertility levels and achieved better income levels and human development. Where have we gone wrong, and is it too late for us to catch up with them? These questions constantly nag me, and I want to put forth a few suggestions in which these challenges, within the country, have to be resolved or attended to without any further delay, if we have to do the catching up with the East Asian Tigers.

First, we have to realize that while focusing on bigger issues, we failed to attend to basic things with regard to human welfare. To list the major failings: we did not properly register our births and deaths, get the ages of individuals correctly, not even count all the individuals in the country correctly in the censuses, as the huge differences between our census figures and UN estimates reveal (see Chapter 8). We should have launched a massive program for the registration of births and deaths in the country immediately after our independence, as China and other Asian Countries did; however, we thought that, statistically, having indirect or sample estimates of birth and death rates at the state level would suffice. The SRS, as a dual recording system, was started in 1966 as a pilot project in Gujarat and was extended to the whole country by 1968 by implementing it in samples of blocks in rural and urban areas. When the SRS was planned, it was specifically stated in the original plan that the system will be in vogue for 10 years, until 1977, when it will no longer be needed, since by then the civil registration system would be fully developed and the SRS would not be needed. Alas, still in 2017, even after 40 years, we have the SRS with new samples drawn from the 2011 census, and we are still talking of getting reliable estimates of birth and death rates even at the district levels from the SRS. The SRS is a good case study to prove the point that if any program is started by the government as a temporary measure, it can find its way to become a permanent fixture, preventing higher benefits. It has been found that with every new sample after each census, there is a discontinuity in the estimates, but we are still carrying on with this method. We equate the ability to estimate birth and death rates from the SRS to having a good civil registration system. It is true, as is also internationally recognized, that we have excellent statisticians but poor statistics.

As is shown in Chapters 7 and 8 from *The Lancet* study, any system other than the civil registration system is not good for any developmental purposes, and I hope we realize the significance and urgency of having complete and accurate registration of births and deaths, including the cause of death, as an important ingredient of attending to various population issues.

The second immediate problem is to get the correct ages of individuals. The newly introduced Aadhaar Card (Unique Identity Number or UID) for each national of the country, if done properly, would serve this purpose. We should not mess it up, as we have adeptly done with so many good systems. Our census enumerators have, it seems, started assigning their own estimates of ages for the citizens of this country, as seen from the enormous number of persons having ages with digits ending in 0 and 5, and age not even stated in the 2011 census in the well-educated state of Kerala (Chapter 7). I think the era of population censuses is coming to an end with the details of each individual available in the Aadhaar Cards and mobile networks, and the government should utilize the modern technology to the maximum to achieve this goal within a time limit. These massive census-taking operations should become part of history, as early as possible. The problem of updating the Aadhaar Card by linking it with the civil registration system to create new cards for new individuals (through birth or immigration) and discontinuation of some of the Aadhaar Cards because of death and emigration should also be developed as quickly as possible.

Third, I think many of the developmental and demographic problems of India can be traced to wrong planning for development with which we started after independence in 1947, with the First Five-Year Plan launched in 1951. It is not too late to realize this and adopt a suitable approach. We followed the Soviet model of development based on "input–output" analysis (the famous Tinbergen School), which is appropriate for a centrally controlled economy that the Soviet Union was at the time. They had seven-year plans, and we started with five-year plans. The whole economy of the Soviet Union failed in the 1980s, with the final collapse of the system in 1984 and breakup of the component units into different countries, but we bravely continued with this system tongue-in-cheek until 2014. For example, we started a number of Indian Institutes of Technology (IITs), six of them to start with, to train top-class engineering graduates. Pandit Nehru had said, "These are the temples of modern India," while inaugurating the Bhakra Nangal Dam (the first large hydroelectric dam constructed in independent India), in 1954, to describe the scientific research institutes, steel plants, power plants and large dams being launched in India after independence to jumpstart scientific and industrial progress. These projects were part of his vision for the development of modern India with a combination of heavy industries and scientific research institutes. Most of the large public sector units (PSUs) and scientific institutions such as the IITs were created by him as part of his vision of modern India.

Most of the graduates from these institutes could not get appropriate jobs in India and migrated to the United States of America and Europe. The following pyramids of developmental situations in India and the developed world symbolize who can fit in where in the pyramids from one country to the other.

Instead of starting IITs or in addition to them, we should have launched a massive program of good primary education, as China and Korea did, with a network of good schools and teacher training schools opened throughout the length and breadth of the country. Education of a large number of people—millions of illiterate population—should start from

Figure 10.1:
Pull of talents by the developed from developing countries

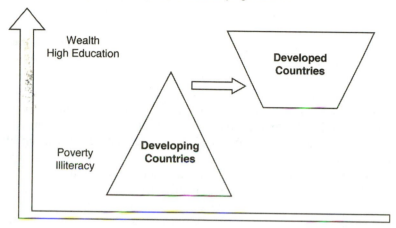

below and built upwards. Instead, our programs had a top-down approach following the Soviet model. This is true not only for our educational planning but for all other developmental planning. The state of Tamil Nadu showed the way in the early 1970s with its mid-day meal scheme to attract and retain children in the schools; however, this was adopted by the center only after two decades.

The next major problem, fourth, is the continued prevalence of child marriages in significant number, in many parts of the country, in spite of the fact that the age at marriage has considerably gone up during the past three decades. Even in states such as Tamil Nadu and Kerala, which have achieved a relatively high age at marriage for girls, there are pockets in the state where child marriages are still prevalent. These societies should be identified and special behavioral campaigns launched to inform them of the hazards to health and survival of their daughters in getting them married early (see Chapter 6). The custom of arranged marriages, which is deeply rooted in the Indian culture and followed by almost all the religious groups within the country, cannot be changed through any national policies and programs, though child marriages should be prevented by law.

The next major problem, fifth, in our development and program strat-egy is to have allowed the slowing down of our family planning efforts under the guise of integration of family planning programs with many other programs or in the holier approach of decentralization of services. Of course, the earlier mistakes of mass sterilizations done during the

Emergency in 1975–77 should never be repeated, and camp approaches should be discarded. The program need not be implemented in any aggressive, target–oriented, or dictatorial manner but in a humane and empathetic manner to meet the felt needs for spacing and limitation of births by couples. Estimates from surveys reveal that even in 2015, millions of unwanted births—either wrongly timed or unwanted by the parents themselves—took place in the country. Most of them occur in poorer and socio-economically backward segments of the society because of their ignorance and unavailability of good quality, affordable contraceptive services. NFHS-3 estimates reveal that there are still around 50 million couples with unmet needs for family planning—either for spacing of births or for limitation (see Chapter 8). It is a pity we still have this large number of people with unmet needs in a country that was the first in the world to start an official program of family planning, in as early as 1952, and showed the way for other developing countries to follow. Most of the Asian and Latin American countries drew their inspirations for national programs of family planning from India, started such programs much later and have already achieved replacement levels of fertility a decade ago. Where have we gone wrong? It is good to ponder and act wisely and steadily.

Of course, there were unexpected triggers for sudden change of policies and program strategies. Just as destiny or situations play unexpected roles in triggering change of directions in one's life, so also at the country level, unexpected situations play a trigger for change of direction. Our family planning program would not have been launched in 1952 but for the strong recommendations made in the reports of the Bengal Famine Enquiry Committee and the Bhore Committee on Health in 1945–46 (see Chapter 1). It was destiny, acting through the Bengal Famine, which drove our government to formulate a national program of family planning, with male vasectomy as the preferred method. Otherwise, we were strict Gandhians who believed in abstention from sex as the only method of birth control. Similarly, the national Emergency declared by Indira Gandhi in 1975 was mainly to protect her position as prime minister after the Allahabad High Court decision declaring her election to the Lok Sabha null and void. But this Emergency period witnessed the launch of compulsory sterilization programs by her son Sanjay Gandhi and the subsequent public backlash to the program. Instead of working against poverty, we started sterilizing the poor. The Emergency was not intended for any aggressive family planning program but led into it. Can we still call it destiny?

Similarly, when the program was steadily improving to meet the unmet needs of couples for spacing and limitation, came the ICPD and the women's movement that diluted many programs by combining and integrating them under the rubric of RCH, and thus, many programs suffered a setback (see Chapter 4). Family Planning (FP) became Family Welfare (FP plus MCH), then turned into RCH, then rechristened as Reproductive and Maternal and Newborn Child Health (RMNCH) and most recently as RMNCH+A, adding adolescent health as a special focus area. If we did not do one job well, can we hope to do the same job better if it is integrated in a plethora of programs and is decentralized in order to achieve greater efficiency and effectiveness? Integration and decentralization of programs are eye-catching slogans, but are they effective and efficient in the field we are considering? The analysis of data given in Chapter 4 proves otherwise. Thus, at the macro level, there were situations beyond the control of family planners or health administrators that influenced the directions and strategies of their programs. Family planning has become a dirty term to be abhorred by program strategists and administrators because it was implemented badly in the past. However, it need not be so.

At the cost of repetition, I reiterate that the term "family planning" was initially coined to connote "to have babies by choice and not by chance" by Margaret Sanger in her pioneering social work promoting the use of contraceptives in the slum population of Harlem, New York, in the early twentieth century. It has become the universal term to denote the use of contraceptives to limit or space births by couples. They were popularized by women's groups throughout the world as "liberating women from the wheels of child-bearing" and preventing backstreet abortions. It was in the All India Women's Conference in 1935, held in Trivandrum (now Thiruvananthapuram), that it was resolved to advocate the use of modern methods of contraception in India as a part of women's right to have babies by choice and not by chance. Family planning clinics came to be accepted as a part of efforts to save mothers from unwanted fertility. Protection of mother's health and life was the sine qua non of family planning. Thus, the roots of family planning lie in the empowerment of women and protection of their health. The program was started in India with this objective. However, since 1994, it is because of global women's movement that family planning has become a dirty term to be abhorred. I do not know the reason or the logic behind it. It was considered a part of reproductive and child health, women's rights and women's health, and these are supposed to subsume family planning. In this war of letters, simple and effective family planning programs, as originally envisioned by Margaret Sanger and others, have been lost. We have to restore the credibility of the national program of family planning as a program of empowering couples to have their babies by choice and not by chance.

It is the developmentalists and economists who overlaid simple family planning services with others. The micro-level linkages between family size and economic development and the macro-level linkages through increased savings and investments were researched and published by a number of economists in the 1950s and 1960s, notably by Gary Becker, Ansley Coale and others, but at that time there was no objection from women's groups.

The rich demographic dividends reaped by the East Asian countries because of their rapid reduction in fertility in the 1970s and 1980s have been well documented and appreciated worldwide (see David Bloom 2000). China led this global rapid fertility transition. It declared a one-child policy in the early 1970s, implemented it ruthlessly and reduced their TFR levels by half in 10 years (from 5.2 to 2.6), overriding individual rights. Other countries such as Korea, the Philippines and Thailand were also under military dictatorship when they achieved rapid declines in fertility. Post facto analysis reveals that these rapid reductions in aggregate fertility in most of the East Asian countries, especially in China, were associated with curtailment of human rights and women's rights in particular. This gave rise to women's movements throughout the free world that gathered momentum in the late 1980s and came up with strong resolutions on individual rights, women's rights and free choice as the crucial factors for promoting family planning at the ICPD, held in Cairo in 1994. By this time, India was in the midst of her demographic transition and as a democratic country was caught in the crossfire of such global politics and signed the ICPD program of action. It is true that some mistakes have been committed in the past in the Indian program by overenthusiastic administrators, but those mistakes are in no way comparable to the one-child policy implemented in China.

The target-free approach and the embedding of family planning services and education in a plethora of other activities by India since 1995, because of her commitment to the ICPD program of action, have slowed down the pace of decline not only in fertility levels but also in many other reproductive and child health parameters, especially in the states of Bihar and Uttar Pradesh where rapid reductions in fertility will have rich demographic dividends. But as of now, there is a sizable number of unwanted births taking place in these states due to lack of proper family planning education and services. To correct this imbalance between couples' desires and inappropriate state policy and strategy, the following recommendations are made, specifically in the area of population policy and family planning programs.

The program placed almost total emphasis on sterilization as the major method of family planning from the very beginning—vasectomy until 1977 and tubectomy thereafter—and the quality of services offered in this regard was far from satisfactory and has not improved over time. With emphasis on sterilization, only high-parity, older women accepted the method, and younger, highly fertile and lower parity women were not covered by the program. While other developing countries such as China, South Korea, Malaysia and Indonesia started their family planning programs with spacing methods and later introduced sterilizations after the spacing concept was ingrained in the psyche of the population, India went the opposite way with limitation as the ultimate goal of family planning. Spacing methods such as IUD, oral pills, injectables and condoms are being used only by a small proportion of the eligible couples, even 50 years after the initiation of the program. Though there are wide interstate differentials in fertility levels, there are no large differentials in the pattern of use of the various methods. Sterilization is as dominant a method of family planning in Andhra Pradesh, Kerala and Tamil Nadu with below-replacement fertility levels as in Rajasthan and Bihar with a TFR above 3. This trend has to be reversed by specific policy and program measures.

The recent efforts to introduce the newer and safer form of IUDs in the FP 2020 program in the country are a welcome effort in the right direction. However, it has to be recognized that FP 2020 is largely funded by corporate agencies such as Bill and Melinda Gates Foundation, and they will be doing the planning and monitoring of these programs (Track 2020). It will be an acceptance of government's failure in this regard. It is ironical that the FP 2020 program, intended for the 70 poorest countries in the world, includes India!

1. One way to start the process of reverting to spacing methods and to wean couples away from sterilization is to stop forthwith any incentives offered for sterilizations to doctors, institutions and individuals. This can be achieved in two phases: first in those states that have already achieved low fertility, such as Kerala, Andhra Pradesh and Tamil Nadu, and then in a phased manner to

other states. The money saved from incentives should be used to improve the quality of services. This suggestion is worth serious consideration.

2. We should revert to the clinic-based approach with which we started the family planning program—the Margaret Sanger way—in the first two Five-Year Plans. Family planning clinics, providing good quality contraceptive services, including induced abortion on medical grounds, should be set up in every tehsil/block, and the services therein should be freely available to any couple below the poverty line asking for such services. Others above the poverty line should be asked to pay for the same at subsidized rates. The era of extension education for family planning motivation is over. There are examples of such excellent clinics run by NGOs, for example, the Surya Clinics run by the NGO Janani in Bihar and Rajasthan and Marie Stopes clinics run by Parivar Seva Sanstha (PSS) in Delhi and other places, where men and women line up to avail high-quality contraceptive services, paying for them. In the high-fertility states, there may be a need to continue with subsidies for all types of contraceptive services and in the setting up of these clinics by qualified NGOs, but there is no need for subsidy in states where the fertility levels are already low.

The next recommendation, sixth, in our view, is that the time and resources of the existing maternal and child health program personnel should not be wasted any more for the motivation of cases for family planning, and they should be asked to concentrate on their maternal and childcare duties. We seem to have come a full cycle in the delivery of contraceptive services, and it is time to delink the same from maternal and child health programs. Family planning clinics, as recommended earlier, should not be a part of the health system and, if agreed upon, can be considered a part of the Department of Women and Child Welfare. The design and construction of such clinics should be done by professionals and should carry the same insignia throughout the country. With our economy galloping in the top gear, it will be a wise investment to establish these clinics across the country. They should operate independently as clinics under a private agency or a governmental agency. The possibility of setting up a separate national corporation to establish and run these clinics can also be considered. Family planning should not erode into public health programs. In my view, integrating them with primary health care has slowed down the health care services, especially maternal and childcare services, and is beginning to harm both. While in some states such as Kerala, they can deal primarily with problems of sterility, in others, they can deal with facilitating women to space and limit their family size.

The next serious concern, seventh, that we should address is the problem of political representations in the context of differentials in population growth rates across the states in the country. During the Emergency, the Parliament enacted a constitutional amendment freezing the seats in the Parliament and state legislative bodies on the basis of the 1971 census until the year 2000, making it politically unattractive to the states to have a higher rate of population growth. This freeze has been extended again by the Parliament based on NPP 2000 recommendations until 2021. My recommendation in this regard is that the freeze should be made permanent so that in future states that gain or lose population because of differentials in growth rates or migration are not affected in their political representations in the state assemblies and in the Parliament. There are debates in the country whether such a freeze goes against the democratic principle of "one man one vote" and thereby goes against the fundamental rights and equality of citizens guaranteed in the Constitution. This has not been tested in a court of law. If the freeze has to be lifted some time or the other, there is bound to be large shifts in the regional political power equations in the country, which would have to be faced. Politically, the country has to be prepared for this. There should be a national debate on this topic (see Chapter 8).

The next major concern, eighth, is whether we should have a new population policy after the one in 2000 (i.e., NPP 2000). As mentioned earlier, different states are in different stages of demographic transition. There can be no uniform population policy at the national level. The center should encourage states to develop and implement their own state-level population policies and serve as a friend, philosopher and guide to the states. There is no need to have uniform demographic goals such as achieving replacement level of fertility by the year 2010 as mentioned in NPP 2000. Each state should be encouraged to have its own goal in terms of meeting the unmet need of contraception through the family planning clinics recommended earlier, whether in a private set up or in the government sector. There appears to be no need to have a new national population policy at this stage.

The next major concern, ninth, is to improve the organizational adequacy, effectiveness and efficiency of health systems in different states. In the states of Uttar Pradesh and Bihar, the system is practically non-existent in many areas, and even where few centers exist, they are totally inefficient. Under these circumstances, there is a need to take over 'health' in the central list of functions, and the central government should operate the health system in selected states for a specified time. I do not know whether this is possible under the existing constitutional allocation of responsibilities between the center and the states, but at least an effort should be made in this direction. Otherwise, a public health and medical corporation can be set up at the state level in which professional health officials from the state and the center can play a vital role in setting up family planning clinics and revamping the primary health centers. The best practices in the more successful states have to be adapted and implemented in the not-so-successful ones.

The next concern, the tenth, is that we feel family planning services should be delinked from any population policy. Contraceptive services of high quality, method choice and easy access, including treatment facilities for primary and secondary sterility, are the rights of every couple, and these should be treated with empathy. There is enough empirical evidence that increased spacing between births and limitation of family size not only contribute to improvements in the living standards, education of children and health of all the family members but also serve as a catalyst to accelerate economic growth and poverty reduction. However, the goals of any economic policy should not include any specific component of fertility reduction and targeted number of family planning acceptors. Fertility reduction will automatically take place as a by-product of meeting the unmet needs of couples for spacing and limitation, as discussed earlier. The fact that family planning provides an opportunity for couples to realize their developmental aspirations is a justification in itself for revamping the program on the lines suggested earlier.

The last recommendation is that the policymakers and administrators should realize that attending to population concerns as listed above may not be a panacea for all our developmental and health problems. In this regard, as *The Limits to Growth* studies reveal, humankind is facing the collective danger of mass extinction because of global warming attributable to emission of greenhouse gases, continued exploitation of nonrenewable resources, increasing disparities in income and wealth across the globe and within countries. In the context of human greed leading to conspicuous consumption of material goods and services by a small segment of the population and the control of many developed and powerful nations by the military–industrial complex, the beneficial effects of reducing population growth rates and avoiding unwanted births in developing countries is only a small part of redeeming this global scenario. But, it is a small but significant contributing factor and India as the second most populous country with the maximum number of unwanted births can show the way.

Finally, the question of toning up governance in the government systems at the central, state and local levels is of vital importance. In this matter, the introduction of modern technology at all levels of the government can be very useful in reducing corruption and cutting down on delays in the execution of projects.

The international arena or agencies or for that matter any donor agencies are the last places where we can seek solution to our internal problems. We can listen to them, observe them but we have to plan and decide our own strategies for action. The slogan should be "Observe globally, think nationally and act locally" rather than just "think globally and act nationally," as is usually drummed to us when it comes to sustainable development. In the latter case, we are bypassing the local national interests, thinking globally and acting nationally, which is valid when all the countries participate in such a thinking and action.

Appendices

Appendix A
National Population Policy:
A Statement of the Government of India (1976)

In New Delhi, on April 16, 1976, the Government of India issued a major policy declaration in the form of a statement entitled *National Population Policy by Dr Karan Singh, Minister of Health and Family Planning*. This was the first official population policy formulated by the government and passed by the Indian Parliament. The official text is reproduced below to highlight the urgency with which the curtailment of fertility was viewed as an important part of development. Reading it in retrospect, we can still feel that the passion for rapid reduction of population growth is essential for development.

1. With 2.4 percent of the world's land area, India has about 15 percent of the world's people. It is estimated that our population as of 1 January, 1976 has crossed the 600 million mark, and is now rising at the rate of well over one million per month. Since independence [in 1947] 250 million have been added, equivalent to the entire population of the Soviet Union with six times the land area of India. The increase every year is now equal to the entire population of Australia which is two and a half times the size of our country. If the present rate of increase continues unchecked our population at the turn of the century may welt reach the staggering figures of one billion. Indisputably we are facing a population explosion of crisis dimensions which has

largely diluted the fruits of the remarkable economic progress that we have made over the last two decades. If the future of the nation is to be secured, and the goal of removing poverty to be attained, the population problem will have to be treated as a top national priority and commitment.

2. Our real enemy is poverty, and it is as a frontal assault on the citadels of poverty that the Fifth Five-Year Plan (1974–79) has included the Minimum Needs Program me. One of its five items is an integrated package of health, family planning and nutrition. Far-reaching steps have been initiated to reorient the thrust of medical education so as to strengthen the community medicine and rural health aspects, and to restructure the health care delivery system on a three-tier basis going down to the most far-flung rural areas where the majority of our people reside and where child mortality and morbidity are the highest. Similarly, ignorance, illiteracy and superstition have got to be fought and eliminated. In the ultimate analysis it is only when the underlying causes of poverty and disease are eliminated that the nation will be able to move forward to its desired ideals.

3. Nonetheless it is clear that simply to wait for education and economic development to bring about a drop in fertility is not a practical solution. The very increase in population makes economic development slow and more difficult of achievement. The time factor is so pressing, and the population growth so formidable, that we have to get out of the vicious circle through a direct assault upon this problem as a national commitment. The President in his address to the Joint Session of Parliament this year reiterated the importance of stepping up family planning efforts, and the Prime Minister has on several occasions laid stress upon the crucial role that population control has to play in the movement towards economic independence and social transformation, especially in the light of the 20-Point Economic Program.

4. Considerable work has been done in our country in the field of family planning, but clearly only the fringe of the problem has so far been touched. In this context, after a thorough and careful consideration of all the factors involved as well as the expression of a wide spectrum of public opinion, the Government has decided on a series of fundamental measures detailed below which, it is hoped, will enable us to achieve the planned target of reducing the birth rate from an estimated 35 per thousand in the beginning of the Fifth Plan (1974) to 25 per thousand at the end

of the Sixth (1984). Allowing for the steady decline in the death rate that will continue due to the improvement in our medical and public health services and the living standards of our people, this is expected to bring down the growth rate of population in our country to 1.4 percent by 1984.

5. Raising the age of marriage will not only have a demonstrable demographic impact, but will also lead to more responsible parenthood and help to safeguard the health of the mother and the child. It is well known that very early pregnancy leads to higher maternal and infant mortality. Also, if the women of our country are to play their rightful role in its economic, social and intellectual life, the practice of early marriage will have to be severely discouraged. The present law has not been effectively or uniformly enforced. It has, therefore, been decided that the minimum age of marriage should be raised to 18 for girls and 21 for boys, and suitable legislation to this effect will be passed. Offences under this law will be cognizable by an officer not below the rank of a Sub-Divisional Magistrate.

6. It has been represented by some states that while on the one hand we are urging them to limit their population, those states which do well in this field face reduction of representation in Parliament while those with weak performance in family planning tend to get increasing representation. It is obviously necessary to remedy this situation. It has, therefore, been decided that the representation in the Lok Sabha (lower house of Parliament! and the State Legislatures will be frozen on the basis of the 1971 census until the year 2001. This means in effect that the census counts of 1981 and 1991 will not be considered for purposes of adjustment of Lok Sabha [Legislature] seats. Necessary constitutional amendment will be brought forward during the current year. Appropriate legislation for other elective bodies will also be undertaken.

7. In a federal system, the sharing of Central resources with the States is a matter of considerable importance. In all cases where population is a factor, as in the allocation of Central assistance to State Plans, devolution of taxes and duties and grants-in-aid, the population figures of 1971 will continue to be followed till the year 2001. In the matter of Central assistance to State Flans, eight percent will be specifically earmarked against performance in family planning. The detailed procedures in this regard will be worked out by the Planning Commission.

8. While there is a direct correlation between illiteracy and fertility, this is particularly marked in the case of girls' education. Wherever female literacy improves, it has been seen that fertility drops almost automatically. It is, therefore, necessary that special measures be taken to raise the levels of female education, particularly above the middle level for girls, as well as non-formal education plans for young women especially in certain backward States where the family planning performance so far has been unimpressive. The same is true with regard to child nutrition programs, as high infant mortality and morbidity have a direct impact on fertility. The Ministry of Education is urging upon the State Governments the necessity to give these matters higher priority than has been accorded so far and fully earmarking adequate outlays both for girls' education up to the middle level and child nutrition.

9. My Ministry is also in close touch with the Education Ministry with regard to the introduction of population values in the educational system, and the NCERT (National Council of Educational Research and Training) has already made a beginning in bringing out some text books on these lines. It is essential that the younger generations should grow up with an adequate awareness of the population problem and a realization of their national responsibility in this regard. Indeed, if I may venture to say so, exhortations to plan families are more important for the younger generations than for those who have already made their contribution to our demographic profile.

10. The adoption of a small family norm is too important a matter to be considered the responsibility of only one Ministry. It is essential that all Ministries and Departments of the Government of India as well as the States should take up as an integral part of their normal program and budgets the motivation of citizens to adopt responsible reproductive behavior both in their own as well as the national interest. A directive to this effect is being issued by the Prime Minister to all Ministries of the Government of India, and a letter will also be addressed by her [Indira Gandhi] to all Chief Ministers. The performance of family planning in the States will be more carefully and intensively monitored than in the past, and the Union Cabinet will review the situation in depth at least once a year.

11. Experience over the last 20 years has shown that monetary compensation does have a significant impact upon the acceptance of family planning, particularly among the poorer sections of society. In view of the desirability of limiting the family size

to two or three it has been decided that monetary compensation (both male and female) will be raised to ₹150 if performed with two living children or less, ₹100 if performed with three living children and ₹70 if performed with four or more children. These amounts will include the money payable to individual acceptors as well as other charges such as drugs and dressings, etc., and will take effect from 1st May, 1976. Facilities for sterilization and MTP (medical termination of pregnancy) are being increasingly extended to cover rural areas.

12. In addition to individual compensation, the Government is of the view that group incentives should now be introduced in a bold and imaginative manner so as to make family planning a mass movement with greater community involvement. It has, therefore, been decided that suitable group incentives will be introduced for the medical profession, for Zilla and Panchayat Samitis (district and block councils), for teachers at various levels, for cooperative societies and for labor in the organized sector through their respective representative national organizations. Details of these group incentives are being worked out in consultation with the concerned organizations.

13. Despite governmental efforts at Union, State and Municipal levels, family planning cannot succeed unless voluntary organizations are drawn into its promotion in an increasing measure, particularly youth and women's organizations. There is already a scheme for aiding voluntary organizations, and it has been decided that this will be expanded. Also, full rebate will be allowed in the income tax assessment for amounts given as donations for family planning purposes to Government, local bodies or any registered voluntary organization approved for this purpose by the Union Ministry of Health.

14. Research in reproductive biology and contraception is underway in several of our scientific institutions, and there are some very promising developments which, we hope, will lead to a major breakthrough before too long. This is a great challenge to our scientists, and efforts in this direction will receive special attention so that necessary research inputs are ensured on a long range and continuing basis.

15. The question of compulsory sterilization has been the subject of lively public debate over the last few months. It is clear that public opinion is now ready to accept much more stringent measures for family planning than before. However, the administrative and medical infrastructure in many parts of the country is still

not adequate to cope with the vast implications of nation-wide compulsory sterilization. We do not, therefore, intend to bring in Central legislation for this purpose, at least for the time being. Some States feel that the facilities available with them are adequate to meet the requirements of compulsory sterilization. We are of the view that where a State legislature, in the exercise of its own powers, decides that the time is ripe and it is necessary to pass legislation for compulsory sterilization, it may do so. Our advice to the States in such cases will be to bring in the limitation after three children, and to make it uniformly applicable to all Indian citizens resident in that State without distinction of caste, creed or community.

16. Some States have also introduced a series of measures directed towards their employees and other citizens in the matter of preferential allotment of houses, loans, etc. for those who have accepted family planning. In this sphere also we have decided to leave it to each individual State to introduce such measures as they consider necessary and desirable. Employees of the Union Government will be expected to adopt the small family norm and necessary changes will be made in their service/conduct rules to ensure this.

17. In order to spread the message of family planning throughout the nation, a new multi-media motivational strategy is being evolved which will utilize all the available media channels including the radio, television (specially programs aimed directly at rural audiences), the press, films, visual displays and also include traditional folk media such as the *jatra* (traveler's talk), puppet shows, folk songs and folk dances. The attempt is to move from the somewhat urban-elitist approaches of the past into a much more imaginative and vigorous rural-oriented approach. In this context my Ministry is working in close coordination with the Ministry of Information and Broadcasting, and is also trying to draw the best media talent available in the country into the structuring of the new program.

18. This package of measures will succeed in its objective only if it receives the full and active cooperation of its people at large. It is my sincere hope that the entire nation will strongly endorse the new population policy which, as part of a multi-faceted strategy for economic development and social emancipation, is directed towards building a strong and prosperous India in the years and decades to come.

Source: Government of India (1976).

Appendix B
Family Welfare Program: A Statement
of Policy (1977)

1. The President in his address to Parliament on March 28, 1977, stated, "Family planning will be pursued vigorously as a wholly voluntary programme and as an integral part of a comprehensive policy covering education, health, maternity and child care, family welfare, women's rights and nutrition." The Prime Minister has on a number of occasions underlined the vital importance of family planning as a means of individual and national development and well-being. This Government is totally committed to the Family Welfare Program and will spare no efforts to motivate the people to accept it voluntarily in their own interest and in the interest of their children as well as in the larger interest of the nation.

2. Family planning has, however, to be lifted from its old and narrow concept and given its proper place in the overall philosophy of welfare. It must embrace all aspects of family welfare, particularly those which are designed to protect and promote the health of mothers and children. It must become a part of the total concept of positive health. At the same time, it must find meaningful integration with other welfare program, viz., nutrition, food, clothing, shelter, availability of safe drinking water, education, employment and women's welfare. It will be our endeavor to bring about this integration in a greater degree. We expect the States to do the same.

3. The change in the name of the program from Family Planning to Family Welfare is a reflection of the Government's anxiety to promote, through it, the total welfare of the family and the community. It is our intention to take the program forward in the real sense as an investment in man. We wish to make it abundantly clear that in this task there is no room for compulsion, coercion or pressures of any sort. Compulsion in the area of family welfare must be ruled out for all rimes to come. Our approach is educational and wholly voluntary. There will, however, be no slackening of our efforts in this direction.

4. The Government attaches the highest importance to the dignity of the citizen and to his right to determine the size of his family. We have no doubt that by and large the people of India are conscious of the importance of responsible parenthood; given the necessary

information and adequate services, they will accept the small family norm. We will promote all methods with equal emphasis and it will be left to every family to decide what method of contraception it will like to adopt. Employees of the Union Government, State Governments, autonomous bodies, local bodies, etc., will be expected to set an example and to adopt the small family norm.

5. We are totally against any legislation for compulsory sterilization either at the Central level or by the States. Sterilization, both male and female, is a terminal method and suitable for those couples who have reached the optimum family size. Services for sterilization will be offered free of cost to those who voluntarily wish to adopt this method. Similarly, other services under the program will be available to the people free of charge. The acceptance of voluntary sterilization and IUD involves to and fro travel to a clinic, a brief stay in the hospital, resulting in possible loss of wages which the majority of our people cannot easily afford. In view of this, it has been decided to retain the provision for monetary compensation. Any medical complication resulting from a voluntary steriliza-tion operation will be attended to free of cost; and if in an un-fortunate case recanalization becomes necessary, this facility will also be offered to the individual concerned under the best possible professional care without any charge.

6. Nearly 80 percent of our population lives in villages. Medical services are not able to reach them in an effective way. An inte-grated rural health scheme is on the anvil and will be implemented shortly. It is of the utmost importance that adequate antenatal, natal and postnatal care is made available to pregnant mothers. To this end, a comprehensive scheme of training of indigenous midwives [*dais*] will be implemented. Under it, maternity ser-vices will be made available to all mothers who may need them. The program of immunizing children against common diseases such as whooping cough, diphtheria and tetanus will be expanded further. We expect that the State Governments will give neces-sary cooperation and assistance in this direction.

7. The direct correlation between illiteracy and fertility and between infant/maternal mortality and the age of marriage is well estab-lished by demographic studies. While on the one hand the Govern-ment will pursue its policy of according high priority to the improvement of women's educational level, both through formal and non-formal channels, it will also bring legislation for raising the minimum age of marriage for girls to 18 and for boys to 21.

8. In a federal system, the sharing of Central resources with the States is a matter of considerable importance. In all cases where population is a factor as in the allocation of Central assistance to State plans, devolution of taxes and duties and grants-in-aid, the population figures of 1971 will continue to be followed till the year 2001. Family Planning and Population Control is a subject in the Concurrent List yet the implementation of the Family Welfare Program is very much the responsibility of State Governments. Assistance for the implementation of the program is provided by the Central Government to the States on a cent-percent basis. In order to ensure a purposeful implementation of the Family Welfare Program, the principle of linking 8 percent of Central Assistance to the State Plans with their performance and success in Family Welfare Program will be continued.

9. Population education has so far not received the attention it deserves. The NCERT have developed some models for the introduction of population education in the school education system. These models have already been adopted by the Central Schools Organization. We would urge that the departments of education in the States should adopt these models, or their modified versions, in the syllabus in the schools. Forty-two percent of our population is below the age of 15 years. It is this population which will soon be entering in the area of matrimony. We must take steps without any further delay to see that the youth receive population education as part of their normal courses of study.

10. The population of India has been increasing at the rate of about one million every month. It has increased by nearly 270 million since 1947 and is today estimated to be 615 million. If the present rate of growth continues, we will be touching the one billion mark by the end of the century. This rate has to be arrested. The birth rate targets of 30 and 25 per thousand by the end of the Fifth and Sixth Plans respectively can be achieved only with die total and willing participation of the community in the Family Welfare Program. For this purpose, it is important that all media of publicity, including motivation through the extension approach, should be utilized fully by the Central and State Governments. We would very much expect that just as at the center, we have involved all media units of the Ministry of Information and Broadcasting in the motivational campaigns, in the State also the State Departments of Public Relations and other departments having their own publicity set-ups would be totally associated with the motivational effort.

11. It is of equal importance that trade unions, chambers of commerce, cooperative societies, organizations of women, federations of teachers, village panchayats and all other institutions which can influence public opinion should be associated intimately with the educational campaigns. The village panchayats can play a significant role in this task. Their potential as change agents needs to receive greater recognition and attention.

12. No program will succeed unless voluntary organizations particularly youth and women's organizations participate in its implementation fully and extensively. So far this participation has been very limited. The Government wishes to invite the suggestions of voluntary organizations and such public bodies as are engaged in the general task of Family Welfare for evolving suitable patterns of cooperation and assistance. Full rebate will be allowed in the income tax assessment for amounts given as donations for Family Welfare purposes to Government, local bodies or any registered voluntary organization approved for this purpose by the Union Ministry of Health.

13. While the existing methods of contraception will continue to be available to the people, it is important that the search for newer methods should be intensified. The Government will give special attention to the necessary research inputs in the field of reproductive biology and contraception.

14. The program and the approach for implementation of the Family Welfare Program as outlined in the above paragraphs will succeed only if there is willing cooperation from all in full measure. The Family Welfare Program embraces all the principal areas of human welfare. It will be wrong to leave it only to the Ministry of Health and Family Welfare in the center and their counterparts in the States. It is essential that all Ministries and Departments of the Government of India as well as of the States give due importance to this program and work for its furtherance. The performance of Family Welfare in the States will be intensively and carefully monitored and the Union Cabinet will review the situation in depth at least once a year. Suitable machinery for ensuring coordination with other connected programs of welfare may be set up in the States also.

Source: Government of India (1977).

Appendix C
Stated Objectives of the Recent Population (2000) and Health policies (2002 and 2005)

NPP 2000	NHP 2002	NRHM 2005
1. To address the unmet needs for contraception, health care infrastructure and health personnel, and to integrate service delivery for basic reproductive and child health care.	1. To achieve an acceptable standard of good health among the general population of the country.	1. To provide effective health care to rural population throughout the country with special focus on 18 backward states.
2. To bring TFR to the replacement levels of 2.1 by 2010.	2. To increase the aggregate public health investment through a substantially increased contribution by the central government.	2. To raise public spending on health from 0.9% to 2–3% of GDP in five years.
3. To achieve a stable population by 2045.	3. To ensure the increased access to tried and tested systems of traditional medicine.	3. To undertake architectural correction of the health system to enable it to effectively handle increased allocations.
		4. To revitalize local health traditions and mainstream AYUSH into public health system.
		5. Aim at effective integration of health concerns with determinants of health like sanitation and hygiene, nutrition and safe drinking water.
		6. To address the interstate and interdistrict disparities including unmet needs for public health infrastructure.

Appendix D
Stated Goals to be Achieved in Recent Population
(2000) and Health Policies (2002 and 2005)

NPP 2000 (to be achieved by 2010)	NHP 2002	NRHM 2005 (to be achieved by 2012)
1. Address the unmet needs for basic RCH services, supplies and infrastructures.	1. Eradicate Polio and Yaws by 2005.	1. Reduce IMR to 30 per 1,000 live births.
2. Make school education up to 14 free and compulsory and reduce dropouts at primary and secondary levels.	2. Eliminate Leprosy by 2005.	2. Reduce MMR to 100 per 100,000 live births.
3. Reduce IMR to 30 per 1,000 live births.	3. Eliminate Kala Azar by 2010.	3. Universal access to public health services such as women's health, child health, water, sanitation and hygiene, immunization and nutrition.
4. Reduce MMR to 100 per 100,000 live births.	4. Eliminate Lymphatic Filariasis by 2015.	4. Prevention and control of communicable and noncommunicable diseases, including locally endemic diseases.
5. Achieve universal immunization of children against all vaccine preventable diseases.	5. Achieve zero level growth of HIV/AIDS by 2007.	5. Access to integrate comprehensive primary health care.
6. Promote delayed marriage for girls, not earlier than age 18 and preferably after age 20.	6. Reduce mortality by 50% on account of TB, Malaria and other Vector and Water Borne diseases by 2010.	6. Population stabilization, gender and demographic balance.
7. Achieve 80% institutional deliveries and 100% deliveries by trained persons.	7. Reduce prevalence of blindness to 0.5% by 2010.	7. Revitalize local health traditions and mainstream AYUSH.

(Appendix D continued)

(Appendix D continued)

NPP 2000 *(to be achieved by 2010)*	NHP 2002	NRHM 2005 *(to be achieved by 2012)*
8. Achieve universal access to information/ counselling.	8. Reduce IMR to 30 per 1,000 and MMR to 100 per 100,000 live births by 2010.	8. Promotion of healthy lifestyle.
9. Achieve 100% registration of births, deaths, marriage and pregnancy.	9. Increase utilization of public health facilities from current level of < 20% to > 75% by 2010.	
10. Contain the spread of AIDS, and promote greater integration between the management of RTI, STI and NACO.	10. Establish an integrated system of surveillance, National Health Accounts and Health Statistics by 2005.	
11. Prevent and control communicable diseases.	11. Increase health expenditure by government as a percentage of GDP, from the existing 0.9% to 2.0% by 2010.	
12. Integrate Indian System of Medicine in the provision of RCH services and in reaching out to households.	12. Increase share of central grant to constitute at least 25% of total health spending by 2010.	
13. Promote vigorously the small family norm to achieve replacement levels of TFR.	13. Increasing state sector health spending from 5.5% to 7.0% of the budget by 2005 and further increase it to 8.0% by 2010.	
14. Bring about convergence in implementation of related social sector programs so that family welfare becomes a people centered program.		

Bibliography

AbouZahr, C., D. De Savigny, L. Mikkelsen, P. W. Setel, R. Lozano, and A. D. Lopez. 2015. "Towards Universal Civil Registration and Vital Statistics Systems: The Time is Now." *The Lancet 386* (10001): 1407–18. DOI: 10.1016/S0140-6736(15)60170-2.

Allen, J., T. Wolseley Haig and H. H. Dodwell. 1969, *The Cambridge Shorter History of India*. 3rd ed. reprint, 701–02. New Delhi: S. Chand and Co,

Ambirajan, S. 1976. "Malthusian Population Theory and Indian Famine Policy in the Nineteenth Century." *Population Studies* 30: 5–14. doi: 10.2307/2173660.

Antony, T. V., K. Srinivasan, and P. C. Saxena. 1989. "Case Studies of Population Policies and Programmes in India." In *Strategic Management of Population Programmes*, edited by Gayl Ness and Ellen Sattar, 219–56. Kuala Lumpur: International Council on Management of Population Programmes.

Arnold, David, and R. I. Moore. 1991. *Famine: Social Crisis and Historical Change* (New Perspectives on the Past), 164. Wiley-Blackwell.

Banerjee, Abhijit, Esther Duflo, Maitreesh Ghatak, and Jeanne Lafortune. 2013. "Marry for What? Caste and Mate Selection in Modern India," *American Economic Journal: Microeconomics* 5(2): 33–72.

Basham, Arthur Llewellyn. 1963. *The Wonder That Was India: A Study of the History and Culture of the Indian Sub-continent before the Coming of the Muslims*. Rev. ed. New York: Hawthorn Books.

Becker, Gary S. 1960. "An Economic Analysis of Fertility," in *Demographic and Economic Change in Developed Countries*, edited by National Bureau of Economic Research, 209–40. New York: Columbia University Press.

———. 1969. "An Economic Analysis of Fertility." in National Bureau of Economic Research, *Demographic and Economic Change in Developed Countries*, a Conference of the Universities, 209–40. New York: Columbia University Press.

———. *Accounting for Tastes*. Cambridge MA: Harvard University Press.

Bevir, M. 2012. *Governance: A Very Short Introduction*. Oxford: Oxford University Press.

Bhat, P. N. M. 1978. *Age Patterns of Marital Fertility in India.* Bangalore: Institute for Social and Economic Change (mimeographed).

————. 1989. "Mortality and Fertility in India, 1881–1961: A Reassessment," in *India's Historical Demography: Studies in Famine, Disease and Society*, edited by Tim P. Dyson. London: Curzon Press.

————. 1991. "ORG Surveys of Family Planning Practice in India: A Statistical Review." *Journal of Institute of Economic Research* 16(1 and 2): 71–88.

Bhatia, B. M. 1991. *Famines in India: A Study in Some Aspects of the Economic History of India with Special Reference to Food Problem, 1860–1990.* Stosius Inc/Advent Books Division.

Biswas, A., and S. P. Agarwal. 1985. *Development of Education in India: A Historical Survey of Educational Documents Before and After Independence.* New Delhi: Concept Publishing Company.

Bloom, David E., and J. Williamson. 1998. "Demographic Transitions and Economic Miracles in Emerging Asia." *World Bank Economic Review* 12(3): 419–55.

Bloom, David E., David Canning, and Jaypee Sevilla. 2003. "The Demographic Dividend: A New Perspective on the Economic Consequences of Population Change," RAND Research Paper, MR-1274, Santa Monica, California.

Bloom, David, David Canning, and Pia Malaney. 2000. "Demographic Change and Economic Growth in Asia." *Population and Development Review* 26: 257–90.

Bongaarts, John. 1978. "A Framework for Analyzing the Proximate Determinants of Fertility." *Population and Development Review* 4: 105–32.

Brass, William. 1975. *Methods for Estimating Fertility and Mortality from Limited and Defective Data Based on Seminars Held 16–24 September 1971 at the Centro Latinoamericano de Demografia (CELADE), San Jose, Costa Rica.* Chapel Hill: International Program of Laboratories for Population Statistics, Department of Biostatistics, The Carolina Population Center, University of North Carolina, Chapel Hill.

Caldwell, John C, P. H. Reddy, and Pat Caldwell. 1984. *Causes of Fertility Decline in South India.* New York: Population Council.

Carla AbouZahr, Don de Savigny, Lene Mikkelsen, Philip W. Setel, Rafael Lozano, Alan D. Lopez. 2015. "Towards Universal Civil Registration and Vital Statistics Systems: The Time is Now." *The Lancet* 386 (10001): 1407–18.

Cassen, Robert H. 1978. *India: Population, Economy, Society.* New York: Holmes & Meier.

Chandrasekaran, C., P. H. Reddy, V. S. Badari and K. N. M. Raju. 1985. "Has 'Modernization' Increased Fertility in Karnataka, India?" *Demography India* 14(2): 174–96.

Chandrasekaran. C. 1954. "Fertility Trends in India." In *Proceedings of World Population Conference, Rome, Italy, 31 August–10 September 1954,* 827–40. New York: United Nations.

Cleland, John, and Christopher Wilson. 1987. "Demand Theories of the Fertility Transition: An Iconoclastic View." *Population Studies* 41: 5–30.

Coale, Ansley J. 1965. "Factors Associated with the Development of Low Fertility: A Historic Summary." In *Collected Papers (Vol. 2),* 322–26. New York: United Nations.

Coale, Ansley J., and T. J. Trussell. 1974. "Model Fertility Schedules: Variations in the Age Structure of Childbearing in Human Population." *Population Index* 40: 185–258.

Coale, Ansley, and Edgar Hoover. 1958. *Population Growth and Economic Development in Low Income Countries.* Princeton, NJ: Princeton University Press.

Crimmins, Eileen M., Richard A. Easterlin, Shireen J. Jejeebhoy, and Krishnamurthy Srinivasan. 1984. "New Perspectives on the Demographic Transition: A Theoretical and Empirical Analysis of an Indian State, 1951–1975." *Economic Development and Cultural Change* 32: 227–53.

Dandekar, Vishnu Majadep, and Kumudini Dandekar. 1953. *Survey of Fertility and Mortality in Poona District,* p. 97. Poona: Gokhale Institute of Politics and Economics.

Daniel Kaufmann, Aart Kraay, and Massimo Mastruzzi. 2010. "The Worldwide Governance Indicators: A Summary of Methodology, Data and Analytical Issues." World Bank Policy Research Working Paper No. 5430. Available at: http://papers.ssrn.com/sol3/papers.cfm?abstract_id=1682130 (Accessed on 24 March 2017).

Das, Kumudini, Kailash Chandra Das, Tarun Kumar Roy, and Pradeep Kumar Tripathy. 2010. "Inter-caste Marriages in India: Has it Really Changed Over Time?" Paper presented at the "European Population Conference2010," Vienna, Austria. Available at: http://epc2010.princeton.edu/papers/100157 (Accessed on 24 March 2017).

Davis, Kingsley, and Judith Blake. 1956. "Social Structure and Fertility: An Analytic Framework." *Economic Development and Cultural Change* 4 (3): 211–35.

Davis, Kingsley. 1951. *The Population of India and Pakistan.* New York: Russell & Russell.

Davis, Mike. 2001. *Late Victorian Holocausts.* Verso Books.

Department of Family Welfare. 2012. *Family Welfare Year Book 2011.* New Delhi: Ministry of Health and Family Welfare.

Desai, Sonalde, and Amaresh Dubey. 2011. "Caste in 21st Century India: Competing Narratives." *Economic and Political Weekly* XLVI (11).

Diehl, Anita. 1977. *E. V. Ramaswamy Naicker-Periyar: A Study of the Influence of a Personality in Contemporary South India.* Stockholm: Esselte Studium.

Dutt, Romesh Chunder. 2005 (1900). *Open Letters to Lord Curzon on Famines and Land Assessments in India*. London: Kegan Paul, Trench, Trubner & Co. Ltd (reprinted by Adamant Media Corporation).

Dyson, Tim P., and Michael J. Murphy. 1985. "The Onset of Fertility Transition." *Population and Development Review* 11: 399–440.

————. 1986. "The Historical Demography of Berar, 1881–1980." Paper presented to the Department of Demography, Australian National University. Canberra, August 1986.

Dyson, Tim. 1991. "On the Demography of South Asian Famines: Part I." *Population Studies* 45: 5–25. doi: 10.1080/0032472031000145056.

————. 1991. "On the Demography of South Asian Famines: Part II." *Population Studies* 45: 279–97. doi: 10.1080/0032472031000145446.

Easterlin, Richard A. 1978. "The Economics and Sociology of Fertility: A Synthesis." In *Historical Studies of Changing Fertility*, edited by Charles Tilly, 57–133. Princeton, NJ: Princeton University Press.

Easterlin, Richard A., and Eileen M. Crimmins. 1985. *The Fertility Revolution: A Supply–Demand Analysis*. Chicago: University of Chicago Press.

Ehrlich, Paul R. 1968. *The Population Bomb*. New York: Ballantine Books.

Eurostat Data Base. 2011. "Marriage and Divorce Statistics." European Commission. Available at: http://epp.eurostat.ec.europa.eu/statistics_explained/index.php/ Marriage_and_divorce_statistics (Accessed on 24 March 2017).

Famine Commission. 1880. "Report of the Indian Famine Commission, Part I." Famine Commission, Calcutta.

Fieldhouse, David. 1996. "For Richer, for Poorer?" In *The Cambridge Illustrated History of the British Empire*, edited by P. J. Marshall, 108–46. Cambridge: Cambridge University Press.

Freedman, Ronald, and Bernard Berelson. 1976. "The Record of Family Planning Programs." *Studies in Family Planning* 7: 1–40.

Freedman, Ronald. 1975. *The Sociology of Human Fertility: An Annotated Bibliography*. New York: Irvington.

Ghose, Ajit Kumar. 1982. "Food Supply and Starvation: A Study of Famines with Reference to the Indian Subcontinent." *Oxford Economic Papers, New Series* 34 (2): 368–89.

Godbole, M. 2014. *Good Governance: Never on India's Radar*. New Delhi: Rupa Publications.

Goldstein, J. R., and C. T. Kenney. 2001. "Marriage Delayed or Marriage Forgone? New Cohort Forecasts of First Marriage for US Women," *American Sociological Review* 66(4): 506–19. doi: 10.2307/3088920.

Goode, W. J. 1993. *World Changes in Divorce Patterns*. New Haven and London: Yale University Press.

Government of India. 1867. "Report of the Commissioners Appointed to Enquire into the Famine in Bengal and Orissa in 1866." Vols. I and II. Famine Commission, Calcutta.

Government of India. 1945. "Bengal Famine Inquiry Commission (Woodhead Commission) Final Report," 96–184. Government of India, New Delhi.

———. 1946. "Report of the Health Survey and Development Committee (Bhore Committee); Vol. II: Recommendations," 485–87. Government of India, New Delhi.

———. 1977. *Family Welfare Program: A Statement of Policy.* New Delhi: Ministry of Health and Family Welfare.

———. 1989. "Report of the Standing Committee on Population Projections." Government of India, New Delhi.

———. 1992. *Eighth Five-Year Plan.* New Delhi: Planning Commission.

———. 2000. *National Population Policy (2000).* New Delhi: Ministry of Health and Family Welfare.

———. 2002. *National Health Policy (2002).* New Delhi: Ministry of Health and Family Welfare.

———. 2005. *National Rural Health Mission (2005).* New Delhi: Ministry of Health and Family Welfare.

———. 2014. *India's 'Vision FP 2020'.* New Delhi: Ministry of Health and Family Welfare.

Government of India. 1976. *National Population Policy: A Statement of the Government of India 16 April, New Delhi.* New Delhi: Ministry of Health and Family Welfare.

Gowen, Herbert. 1931. *A History of Indian Literature.* London: Appleton.

Grada, Oscar O. 1997. "Markets and Famines: A Simple Test with Indian Data." *Economic Letters* 57: 241–44. doi: 10.1016/S0165-1765(97)00228-0.

Grove, Richard H. 2007. "The Great El Nino of 1789–93 and Its Global Consequences: Reconstructing an Extreme Climate Even in World Environmental History." *The Medieval History Journal* 10: 75–98. doi: 10.1177/097194580701000203.

Gupta, M., C. Rao, P. V. Lakshmi, S. Prinja, and R. Kumar. 2016. "Estimating Mortality using Data from Civil Registration: A Cross-sectional Study in India." *Bulletin of WHO* 94: 10–21. DOI: http://dx.doi.org/10.2471/BLT.15.15358

Hardiman, David. 1996. "Usury, Death and Famine in Western India." *Past and Present* 152: 113–56. doi: 10.1093/past/152.1.113.

Henry, Louis. 1961. "Some Data on Natural Fertility." *Eugenics Quarterly* 8 (2): 81–91.

Hernandez, Donald J. 1984. *Success or Failure? Family Planning Programs in the Third World.* Westport, CT: Greenwood Press.

Hill, Christopher V. 1991. "Philosophy and Reality in Riparian South Asia: British Famine Policy and Migration in Colonial North India." *Modern Asian Studies* 25: 263–279. doi:10.1017/s0026749x00010672.

Himes, Norman. 1961. *Medical History of Contraception.* New York: Garmut Press.

Hufty, M. 2011. "Investigating Policy Processes: The Governance Analytical Framework (GAF)." in *Research for Sustainable Development: Foundations, Experiences, and Perspectives*, edited by U. Wiesmann and H. Hurni, 403–24. Switzerland: Geographica Bernensia. Available at SSRN http://ssrn.com/abstract=2019005

Hutton, John Henry. 1932. *Report of the Census of India 1931, Vol. 1*, 1–32. New Delhi: Government of India.

Iain, Anrudh K., and Arjun L. Adlakha. 1982. "Preliminary Estimates of Fertility Decline in India During the 1970s." *Population and Development Review* 8: 589–611.

IIPS and Macro International. 1993–2016. *National Family Health Survey (NFHS-1, 2 and 3), and Fact Sheets of NFHS-4*. Mumbai: International Institute for Population Sciences.

Imperial Gazetteer of India vol. III. 1907. "Chapter X: Famine." In *The Indian Empire, Economic*, 475–502 (Published under the authority of His Majesty's Secretary of State for India in Council). Oxford: Clarendon Press.

Indian Statistical Institute. 1963. *National Sample Survey (July 1958–June 1959), No. 76, Fertility and Mortality Rates in India*, 12. New Delhi: Government of India, Cabinet Secretariat.

Inglehart, R. 1970. *The Silent Revolution*. Princeton: Princeton University Press.

———. 1985. "Aggregate Stability and Individual-level Flux in Mass Belief Systems: The Level of Analysis Paradox." *American Political Science Review* 79: 97–116.

Inkeles, Alex, and David H. Smith. 1974. *Becoming Modem*. Cambridge, MA: Harvard University Press.

———. 1989. "Fertility Reduction and the Quality of Family Planning Services." *Studies in Family Planning* 20 (1): 1–16.

Isen, Adam and Betsey Stevenson. 2008. "Women's Education and Family Behavior: Trends in Marriage, Divorce and Fertility," *NBER Working Paper*, in "Topics in Demography and the Economy National Bureau of Economic Research, Inc."

Karve, R. D. 1931. *Birth Control Theory and Practice*, 123. Fourth ed. Bombay: Right Agency.

———. ed. 1927. "Samaj-Swasthya." *Qoumal* (Marathi) 1 (1).

Kaufmann, D., A. Kraay, and M. Mastruzzi. 2007. "Worldwide Governance Indicators Project: Answering the Critics (1 March)." World Bank Policy Research Working Paper No. 4149. Available at SSRN: http://ssrn.com/abstract=965077

King, Alexander, and Bertrand Schneider. 1991. *The First Global Revolution: A Report by the Council of the Club of Rome*. New York: Pantheon Books.

Kleiñ, Ira. 1973. "Death in India, 1871–1921." *The Journal of Asian Studies* 32: 639–59, doi: 10.2307/2052814.

Ranganathan, K. V., Krishnamurthy Srinivasan, and Betty Mathews. 1964. "Role of Community Leaders in Promoting Family Planning." Action Research Monograph, The Institute of Rural Health and Family Planning, Gandhigram.

Ratcliffe, J. W. 1978. "Social Justice and the Demographic Transition: Lessons From India's Kerala State." *International Journal of Health Services* 8 (l): 123–44.

Registrar General India. 1974, 1981, 1990, 1989a and 2014. *Sample Registration Bulletin*. New Delhi: Ministry of Home Affairs.

———. 1951–2014. *Census of India* (Paper 1, Paper 2 and Social Culture Table). New Delhi: Ministry of Home Affairs.

———. 1970–2014. *Sample Registration System*. New Delhi: Ministry of Home Affairs.

———. 1971–72, 1981 and 1989. "Survey of Causes of Death (Rural). Annual Reports." Ministry of Home Affairs, New Delhi.

———. 1979b. *Survey Report on Levels, Trends and Differentials in Fertility*. New Delhi: Ministry of Home Affairs.

———. 1989–2014. *Sample Registration System Statistical Reports*. New Delhi: Government of India.

———. 2009. "Compendium of India's Fertility and Mortality Indicators 1971–2007." Government of India, New Delhi.

———. 2013. "Sample Registration System Statistical Report 2011." Report No. 1 of 2013, New Delhi.

Rele, Jawahar Raghunath. 1962. "Some Aspects of Family and Fertility in India." *Population Studies* 15(3): 267–78.

Romaniuk, Anatole. 1978. "Evidence of Increase in Natural Fertility during the Early Stages of Modernization: Two Case Studies." Paper presented at the "Annual Meeting of the Population Association of America," Atlanta, 13–15 April.

Ross, John A., Manorie Rich, Janet P. Molzan, and Michael Pensak. 1988. *Family Planning and Child Survival: 100 Developing Countries*. New York: Columbia University.

Ross, John A., W. Parker Mauldin, Steven R. Green, and E. Romana Cooke. 1992. *Family Planning and Child Survival Programs: As Assessed in 1991*. New York: The Population Council.

Rouyer, Alwyn R. 1987. "Political Capacity and Decline of Fertility in India." *American Political Science Review* 81 (2): 453–70.

Samal, J. K. 1990. *Economic History of Orissa, 1866–1912*. New Delhi: Mittal Publications.

Satia, J. K., and Shireen J. Jejeebhoy. 1991. *The Demographic Challenge: A Study of Four Large Indian States*. Bombay: Oxford University Press.

Sen, A. K. 1977. "Starvation and Exchange Entitlements: A General Approach and its Application to the Great Bengal Famine." *Cambridge Journal of Economics* 1(1): 33–59.

Sen, A. K. 1982. *Poverty and Famines: An Essay on Entitlement and Deprivation,* ix, 257. Oxford: Clarendon Press.

Sen, Amartya. 1999. *Development and Freedom.* New York: Anchor Books.

Simon, Julian L. 1981. *The Ultimate Resource.* Princeton, NJ: Princeton University Press.

Srikantan, Kodaganallur Sivaswamy. 1977. *The Family Planning Program in the Socio-Economic Context.* New York: The Population Council.

Srinivasan, K. 1989. "Natural Fertility and Nuptiality Patterns in India: Historical Levels and Recent Changes." In *Population Transition in India,* Vol. 1, edited by S. N. Singh, M. K. Premi, P. S. Bhatia, and Ashish Bose, 173–92. Delhi: B. R. Publishing.

Srinivasan, K. 1995. *Regulating Reproduction in India's Population: Efforts, Results, and Recommendations.* New Delhi: SAGE.

Srinivasan, K., and K. S. James. 2015. "The Golden Cage: Stability of the Institution of Marriage in India." *Economic and Political Weekly* L (13).

Srinivasan, K., and K. S. James. 2015. "The Golden Cage: Stability of the Institution of Marriage in India." *Economic and Political Weekly* 50(13): 38–45.

Srinivasan, K., and M. S. Selvan. 2015. "Governance and Development in India: A Review of Studies and Suggestions for Further Research." *MIDS Working Paper No. 219,* September 2015.

Srinivasan, K., and Moye W. Freymann. 1990. "Need for a Reorientation of Family Planning Programme Strategies in Developing Countries: A Case for Birth-Based Approach." In *Dynamics of Population and Family Welfare 1989,* edited by Krishnamurthy Srinivasan and S. Mukerji, 3–22. Bombay: Himalaya Publishing House.

Srinivasan, K., and Shireen J. Jejeebhoy. 1981. "Changes in Natural Fertility in India, 1959–1972." In *Dynamics of Population and Family Welfare,* edited by Krishnamurthy Srinivasan and S. Mukerji, 91–117. Bombay: Himalaya Publishing House.

Srinivasan, K., Chander Shekhar, and P. Arokiasamy. 2007. "Reviewing Reproductive and Child Health Programmes in India." *Economic and Political Weekly* XLII (27 and 28).

Srinivasan, K., P. C. Saxena, Tarun K. Roy, and Ravi K. Verma. 1991. "Effect of Family Planning Program Components on Contraceptive Acceptance in Four Indian States." *International Family Planning Perspectives* 17(1): 14–24.

Srinivasan, K., P. H. Reddy, and K. N. Murthy Raju. 1978. "From One Generation to the Next: Changes in Fertility, Family Size Preferences, and Family Planning in an Indian State Between 1951 and 1975." *Studies in Family Planning* 9: 258–71.

Srinivasan, K., Shireen J. Jejeebhoy, Richard A. Easterlin, and Eileen M. Crimmins. 1984. "Factors Affecting Fertility Control in India: A Cross-Sectional Study." *Population and Development Review* 10: 273.

Srinivasan, K., T. K. Roy, and S. Gogale. 1980. *Family Planning Targets by States for India*. Vols I and II. Bombay: International Institute for Population Sciences.

Srinivasan, K. 2014. "India's Population Issues and Policies: Professionals' Perceptions." (Findings from a survey of professionals in the field), Report on a web-based survey submitted to the Indian Council for Social Science Research (ICSSR), New Delhi.

Srinivasan, Krishnamurthy. 1988. *Regional Variations and Associated Factors in Indian Fertility*. Bombay: International Institute for Population Sciences.

Srinivasan, Padmavathi, Nizamuddin Khan, Ravi Verma, Dora Giusti, Joachim Theis, and Supriti Chakraborty. 2015. *District-Level Study on Child Marriage in India: What do We Know about the Prevalence, Trends and Patterns?* New Delhi: International Center for Research on Women.

The Lancet. 2015. "Counting of Births and Deaths." *The Lancet* 386.

Turner, G. 2014. "Is Global Collapse Imminent?" MSSI Research Paper No. 4, Melbourne Sustainable Society Institute, the University of Melbourne.

UNDP. 2003 and 2012. "Human Development Report." United Nations Development Programme, Oxford University Press, New Delhi.

United Nations. 1961. "The Mysore Population Study." Report of a Field Survey Carried out in Selected Areas of Mysore State, India, Population Studies no. 34. ST/SOA/SER.A/34 Department of Economic and Social Affairs, New York, p. 84.

———. 1978. *Manual IX: The Methodology of Measuring the Impact of Family Planning Programmes on Fertility*. ST/ESA/SER.A/66. New York: United Nations.

———. 1994. *Programme of Action of the 1994 International Conference on Population and Development*. New York: United Nations.

———. 2012. "*World Marriage Prospects – 2012*." New York: United Nations. Available at: http://www.un.org/esa/population/publications/WMD2012/MainFrame.html (Accessed on 24 March 2017).

Unnithan, Thcttaman Kantan, and Kesavan Narayanan. 1956. *Gandhi and Free India: A Socioeconomic Study*, 75. Groningen, The Netherlands: JB. Walters.

UNSD. 1964–2014. *Demographic Yearbook* (various issues). New York: United Nations.

Varma, Ravi K., Asha A. Bhende, and Prakash Fulpagare. 1989. "Role of Incentives in the Decision-Making Process: A Study of Sterilization Acceptors in Madhya Pradesh." Dynamic of Population and Family Welfare, IIPS Bombay.

Virmani, A., S. Sahu, and S. Tanwar. 2006. "Governance in the Provision of Public Goods in South Asia." Prepared for SANEI, ICRIER, New Delhi, September 2006. saneinetwork.net/Files/07_04.pdf

Visaria, Pravinchandra Meghji. 1967. *Mortality and Fertility in India, 1951–1961*. Bombay: University of Bombay; Princeton, NJ: Office of Population Research, Princeton University.

Weiss, R. S. 1975. *Marital Separation*. New York: Basic Books.

———. 1979. *Going it Alone*. New York: Basic Books.

Wilcox, W. Bradford, et al. 2005. *Why Marriage Matters: Twenty-Six Conclusions from the Social Sciences, Institute for American Values*. Second Edition—A Report from Family Scholars. New York: Institute for American Values.

World Bank. 2015. *World Development Report 2014*. New York: Oxford University Press for the World Bank.

Yeats, M. W. 1931. *Census of India, 1931, xiv, Madras, Part I Report*, 46. Madras: Office of Superintendent of Census Operations.

Index

About the Author

Krishnamurthy Srinivasan has been making valuable contributions in the field of research in Population Studies for over four decades. He is an internationally acclaimed demographer who has served the country through various national and international committees and associations. He was a member of the National Commission on Population and of the National Statistics Commission. He was Senior Professor and Director of the International Institute for Population Sciences, Mumbai, from 1978 to 1992. As Executive Director of the Population Foundation of India during 1995 to 2002, he promoted and enhanced the role of non-governmental organizations in family planning, reproductive and child health programs. He was employed with the Population Division of the United Nations and his work was appreciated in other countries. As the chairman of a group set up by the WHO and the United Nations Populations Fund, he recommended policies for Population Research Centers in China.

Professor Srinivasan has authored or contributed to more than 15 books and has more than a hundred national and international peer reviewed academic publications to his credit. He obtained his MA in Mathematics from Madras University and subsequently graduated from the Indian Statistical Institute, Kolkata, with a Master's in Statistics. He went on to obtain a Master's degree in Public Health from Harvard University and PhD in Demography from Kerala University. He was a National Fellow on population at the Indian Council for Social Science Research (ICSSR) during 2013–15 and affiliated to MIDS, Chennai. At present, he is an Honorary Professor in the Institute for Social and Economic Change, Bengaluru.